REAL IMAGES

REAL IMAGES

Film & Television

BARRIE McMAHON & ROBYN QUIN

M

First published 1986 by
MACMILLAN EDUCATION AUSTRALIA PTY LTD
107 Moray Street, South Melbourne 3205
6 Clarke Street, Crows Nest 2065
Reprinted 1986, 1987 (twice), 1989, 1990 (twice), 1991,
1992 (twice), 1993

Associated companies and representatives
throughout the world

National Library of Australia
cataloguing in publication data

McMahon, Barrie.
  Real images.

  Bibliography.
  Includes index.
  ISBN 0 333 40139 5.

  1. Moving-pictures. 2. Moving-pictures plays –
  Technique. 3. Television programs. 4. Television.
  I. Quin, Robyn. II. Title.

791.4

Designed by Jan Schmoeger
Cover design by Tanya Bryant
Cartoons by Randy Glusac
Typeset in Garamond by
Setrite Typesetters, Hong Kong
Printed in Malaysia by
Chee Leong Press Sdn Bhd, Ipoh

Contents

Introduction

The purpose of this book is to provide senior school students with a framework for analysing film and television. The strategy adopted is to provide short segments of theoretical material, then some exercises based on this material. Ideally, teachers should have available support resources such as film making equipment, video tapes of appropriate materials and the opportunity for the class to frequently visit a hardtop cinema. However, it is realised that these ideal conditions rarely exist. The authors have therefore assumed that there will be occasional opportunities for video analysis and rare opportunities for cinema visits. It is recognised that in most cases teachers and students will be restricted to the traditional tools of text, pen and paper. The student exercises are structured accordingly.

The suggested approach is designed to develop in students a method of film analysis that will be valuable throughout life. As technical innovations occur or as content changes, they will thus be able to understand the developments. The authors believe that some of the historical, technical and classification approaches to film that have had currency have failed to do this. The best of the approaches have developed in students a love of the art, a limited understanding of the language, but little comprehension of the link between the 'language' of film/television and the relevance of these media to society. In this book, this link is seen as crucial. We seek to develop the understanding that film and television are systems of communication and that as such they interact with society — reinforcing values, developing new values, and helping to shape the society's understanding of itself and the larger world. That is, film and television are seen as carriers of ideology.

Ideology is a word that is loaded with meaning. In popular parlance it is often used to denigrate the belief system underlying a hostile political viewpoint. This book will use the more Mannheimian approach, which defines ideology as the dominant belief system of a culture (including one's own). It is also recognised that ideology is closely linked with the means of production in a society and, most importantly, the means of production of the society's images of itself. Who gets to produce the images is a matter of social significance, and for this reason it is not sufficient to study just the product. Questions of authorship and distribution are also of considerable importance. Just as it is important to identify variations that occur in the languages of film and television, it is also important to reveal differences in production, marketing and audience for the two media.

Approach

The material in this book is designed to be used sequentially. However, it is not essential for every student to complete all exercises. A more satisfactory approach is for the teacher to allocate exercises to class members and ensure that the experiences of all are shared through appropriate recapitulation and discussion sessions. That is, the book is designed as a student text, but the important part that the teacher has to play in determining such matters as the pace of student progress and the degree of teacher intervention is recognised.

As the book is designed for senior secondary students, it is assumed that their identification, comprehension and analytical skills are reasonably developed. Within each chapter there are some student exercises that emphasise identification and comprehension skills. At the end of each chapter there are more difficult tasks that demand more rigorous analysis by the student. These exercises are aimed at developing in students the ability to generalise from the specifics outlined in the text to a more universal framework that can be applied to any film or television programme.

This book is designed to give students the ability to analyse *any* feature film, but specific films are sometimes referred to in the first section of the book. It is certainly not necessary that students see all of these films, but it is desirable that they see at least a few. To aid the teacher in planning his or her programme around this text, the films referred to in the body of the work are listed below. Many are available on video tape. Those marked with an asterisk are discussed in some detail:

Star Wars
Raiders of the Lost Ark
*Indiana Jones and the Temple of Doom**
*Silkwood**
Chariots of Fire
The Man from Snowy River
*Phar Lap**
Elephant Man
Raging Bull

As a further attempt to stimulate intellectual dialogue between the student and this text, each of the major chapters begins by challenging the student with a task. The task is sometimes framed in production terms, assuming that the student will make a short film or television piece. Each chapter then resolves many of the problems posed in the task, but does not specifically comment upon the task. It is recognised that not all students will have the time or resources to enjoy the richer educational experience that results from purposeful practical work being done in conjunction with theory. They may have to be content with speculation rather than production, but even so, the problem that is posed should focus attention on some key issues. It is assumed that students who do embark upon production work will have, or can acquire, basic production skills. No attempt is made in this text to educate students in handling basic equipment.

The introductory problem exercises have been deliberately made difficult and often require a student (and teacher) to search for resources outside this text. Not all of the demands made will be able to be met, but it is hoped that at least an awareness will be created that there are larger issues that need to be addressed. No single book can provide all of the answers. It is hoped that this book succeeds in encouraging students to ask a lot more questions.

In summary, then, most chapters consist of:

A problem posed
Information-giving text
Identification and comprehension exercises
Information-giving text
Analytical and research exercises

References

Peter Berger and Thomas Luckmann, *The Social Construction of Reality: A Treatise on the Sociology of Knowledge* (New York: Anchor, 1967).

Raymond Williams, *Culture* (Glasgow: Fontana, 1981).

Part 1
Film

Chapter 1
Narrative

A problem posed

You plan to make the great film of all time, having been inspired by a very unusual event that you have just heard about. However, you do not really know where to start. Are films constructed like school essays? Are they like novels? Radio plays? Newspaper accounts?

You need a starting point, a skeleton upon which you can build your great tale.

Where can you start?

Narrative

A narrative is a chain of events in cause-effect relationship occurring in time. A narrative occurs when a story is told. The plot of the story that is being told is only part of the narrative, because the devices that are used in its telling are also part of the narrative. Feature films employ large crews, a fact which is quite apparent if you have ever watched the credits of a film. All of these people contribute to the narrative and their work on lighting, sets, costume and so on, forms part of the narrative. Later, further attention will be given to the codes and conventions associated with the development of narrative.

It seems that the development of narratives is a fairly fundamental human activity. In everyday life we are faced with a multitude of events and phenomena. We use narrative in order to make sense of the variables — to try to establish relationships between one event and another.

Exercise 1.A   Narrative

People try to make sense of their experience and establish relationships between events by using narrative skills. The narratives so created will reflect the creator's cultural background.

1 Refer to the six photographs. Write down a narrative surrounding these photographs.

- Compare your narrative with those of several other students. Compare also with the narrative created by the teacher.
- In what ways are they similar? How are they different?
- How do you account for these similarities and differences?

Do they occur because of the photographs or because of the people viewing them, or both? Do you think that people in Iran would construct similar narratives?

2 Using the discussion and experience that you have had as a basis, write down a summary statement about the narrative creating abilities of people; mention also the limitations of these abilities.

Exercise 1.B   Narrative

The development of narratives is a fundamental human activity. People use narrative in order to make sense of experiences.

1 Consider all of the things that you have seen and done in the past twenty-four hours.
  - Identify the incidents that are worth telling to a school friend.
  - How would the selection of incidents change if you were recounting them to a grandparent?
  - About how long would the account take in each of the above cases?

2 Write down one of the two accounts. Identify the devices that you have used to ensure that the incidents make sense to the listener/ reader.

3 Based upon understandings that you have gained from the above exercise, make a summary statement on the skills of narrative making.

Exercise 1.C   Narrative

The construction of a narrative involves attributing cause and effect relationships to elements within the story.

1 Often the agents of cause and effect in a narrative are characters but not always.

Look at the photographs of film posters and suggest the agents of motivation in each film.

From *King Kong*, the early version (1932)

2 David Bordwell in *Film Art* argues that even when natural causes (e.g. floods, fire etc.) set up the situation, human desires and goals usually enter the action to develop the narrative. Discuss this argument in the light of a 'disaster' film that you have seen.

Film is well disposed towards the creation of narrative because of its capacity to link scenes and shots together in a meaningful sequence. This has encouraged narrative to become a central focus in feature film whereas in some of the other visual arts it is less apparent. A painting hanging on the wall, or a single photograph may have a narrative, but other elements of these visual arts may seem more significant to the spectator (who may then indulge in a mental narrative, questioning the circumstances surrounding the captured image).

Even before the beginning of this century, film was being used in order to develop simple narratives. Early film makers, such as Méliès, created narrations by recording several scenes and stringing them together. Méliès mostly used illustrations so that a magical effect was created (he had a background as a magician), but still his narration drew from the experiences in real life. His rocket ships landing on the moon were as fantastic as any of the Star Wars series, but they still depended upon the audience being able to identify the screen events with real life events — his people appeared to be quite 'real' and even his moon was given human characteristics. In spite of its potential for creating some extraordinary effects, it was clear that the narratives in film would be similar to narratives created in other art forms in that they had to draw from life experiences.

In the process of creating narratives from these life experiences, film makers inevitably extracted the values that were linked with these experiences. These values were reshaped and reappeared in the narrative film. Thus a Western film is more than a story about pioneer America. It is also a story about the value system that operates in modern America. When we understand the ways in which the narrative is constructed the sorts of values that are being reworked become more apparent.

In the very early years of the twentieth century, film makers realised that there was a more effective way of developing a narrative than by stringing together several scenes in a manner that resembled a stage play. It became evident that the performance in front of a camera could be interrupted and the shot reconstructed. A technique of creating narratives through sequences of shots became the accepted means of developing film narrative. Since the pioneering days, the techniques of developing the visual narrative have been refined and added to. Refinements include the use of close-ups as important shots, use of 'cinematic' shots and sophisticated editing between shots. Other sub-narratives have been added to support the central visual narrative between series of shots and an accompanying musical sub-narrative. The written sub-narrative has now been replaced by character dialogue and the musical sub-narrative has been embellished by adding sound effects. The result of these developments over the years is that although feature films share many of the general laws of storytelling with other media, the narrative is developed in many ways that are peculiar to cinema. Further consideration needs to be given to these two dimensions of the film narrative.

Feature film making is a large scale industry that requires large scale funding. This money is put at risk in anticipation of large profits. The narratives that are constructed must attract millions of people who are prepared to pay for theatre tickets or video hire. Attracting such a large audience usually means international distribution, although there are examples of lower budget film industries operating within national boundaries. Transnational distribution means that the narratives that are devised must appeal to people of many cultures. The American feature film industry, based in Hollywood, has succeeded in doing this, partly by the use of narratives that cater for the dreams of audiences in various cultures and partly through financing and marketing techniques that have conditioned audiences around the world into accepting the 'Hollywood style' feature film as the norm. For this reason, attention in this book will be upon the 'Hollywood style' feature film. Many examples of Australian feature films will be used, but though these films have particular appeal to Australians, it should be remembered that the style and to some degree the content, is rather similar to the American model.

FEATURE FILM

| is |
| Narrative |
| dependent |

Exercise 1.D Narrative

Film narratives reflect the value systems of their creators.

The four stills from different Hollywood films all depict relationships between males and females. Although they were made in the recent past, each film is about events in earlier centuries.

1 If we assume that the films tend to reflect modern values and not necessarily those of bygone eras, what can you say about the ways in which our society perceives male/female relationships?

- Consider the photographs for evidence of who is expected to be

forceful	aggressive
daring	passive
protective	angelic
consoling	demure
dominant	rugged

2 Try mentally reversing the roles in each of the photographs. If the effect is ridiculous then it illustrates some expectations that we have about the way males and females should act. What are those expectations?

3 Based upon the evidence in the photographs, write briefly on male/female values in our society.

Gregory Peck and Jennifer Jones in *Duel in the Sun* (1946)

Laurence Olivier and Geraldine Fitzgerald in *Wuthering Heights* (1939)

Clark Gable and Vivien Leigh in *Gone with the Wind* (1939)

Rudolph Valentino and Agnes Ayres in *The Sheik* (1922)

Analysis and research

Library research

1 Many famous books have been made into films.

- Using the library resources and your own knowledge, compile a list of these book/films.

  Find a review of at least one of these films. *The New York Times at the Movies* (Keylin and Bent, editors, Arno, New York, 1979) is one very valuable resource book.

- To what extent do the reviewers depend upon their perceptions of the book for their opinions about the film? Alternatively, do the film reviewers treat the film as a product in its own right?

  Check the papers for a currently running film that is based upon a book. Find a review of this film.

- Similarly, analyse the review to determine the perceived relationship between the book and the film.

Note: If you have difficulty determining which current films are based upon books, check at your local newsagent. It is most probable that any such books will be displayed prominently.

While at the newsagent, inquire about the effect that a feature film has upon a book's sales.

- Record your findings.

2 Many films have developed their narratives around animals rather than human beings.

- Research in the library and make a list of famous animal films. Some of these have become sequels; some have been made into a series of films. Identify some of these.

- Select one of the films that you can see, have seen or have heard a lot about. Describe the human characteristics that the animal is given. What is it about this animal film that makes it such a profitable commodity?

- Compare your conclusions with those of others. To what degree are the 'lovable' animals extensions of those we find in comic strips? Do the 'evil' animals have any parallels in comics or other film styles?

Written response

'Oh, but I thought that the book was much better than the picture!'

This is a common comment when a famous book has been made into a film.

What do films and books have in common that allows such comparisons?

If you had to support an argument that 'The book was better', or 'The film was better', what common elements would you look at for comparison?

Chapter 2
Expectations

A problem posed

As a marketing expert, you have been commissioned to publicise the next James Bond film. Bond is to be played by an actor who appeared in earlier Bond films. The leading female role is to be filled by a screen unknown who is a former beauty contest winner. Many of the old villains will reappear in the new film.

The story centres upon a group of super-villains who have established a base in Antarctica. From there they plan to control the world's weather by using nuclear weapons to release the ice packs. With their stolen nuclear weapons they will control the temperature and water levels in the oceans. Thus they can flood cities or turn productive agricultural regions into deserts. They will make billions of dollars by holding governments to ransom. James Bond is commissioned to bring them to justice.

You have to create a narrative image for the film. This will include:
- *a movie billboard,*
- *audience expectation about the stars,*
- *audience anticipation of the stunts they will see.*

Millions of dollars have been invested, so you must explore all avenues to ensure maximum return on the investment.

How will you do it?

Marketing

Because feature film is a large scale industry with millions of dollars at risk, marketing is a very important part of the industry. Marketing involves selling the product to the potential customers so that as many of them as possible become paying customers. To do this, fragmentary elements of the narrative image that are most likely to appeal are selected and publicised. These fragments may be concerned with the film's plot, with the performers (or stars), occasionally with the director or even with circumstances surrounding production.

This advance publicity, both formal and informal, ensures that the potential customer is partially programmed into a set of expectations about the film. A *narrative image* has been created.

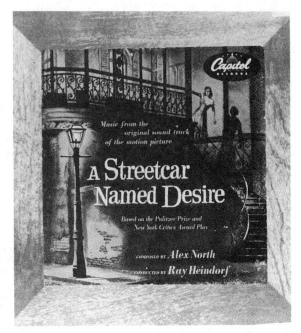

Publicity — formal and informal

Exercise 2.A   Narrative image

A narrative image may emphasise plot, performers, director, refer to past well known films, or to shared experiences.

1 Look at the film advertisements. Which elements are emphasised?

2 Choose three from the examples and write what your expectations are of the film. How do these expectations link with your prior knowledge of other films or your own life?

The *narrative image* is created in several ways. Even before the feature film is complete, publicists will be making press releases and planting stories with film journalists about the film, its stars or events surrounding its production. At the height of the 'Hollywood era' of films, the film gossip columns were important in maintaining audience interest in the marketable products: the Stars. The behind-the-screen stories provided titillation for the readers and also formed part of the motivation for the next cinema visit. Some countries, where a large percentage of the population still attend the indoor cinema regularly, retain this 1930/40 Western tradition. In western countries, the information still appears in the press, particularly the weekend press, but the format has changed. The information is often fragmented over several sections of the paper and even if it is concentrated into one section, the 'gossipy' element is not so pronounced because the star era of feature films has passed. Stories have to be hinged upon elements other than the 'gods at play'.

Exercise 2.B   Informal publicity

Publicists often generate 'news' about films, thereby gaining additional publicity.

1 Read the articles reproduced here on the actress Greta Scacchi. Make a note of the dates the articles were printed.

From your reading can you suggest any reasons why so many articles appeared over such a short space of time?

2 Underline or write out the 'advertisements' contained in the news articles. Why do you think these advertisements have been inserted in the text?

3 The actress herself is given a *context*. Describe this context.

Greta Scacchi in Perth yesterday.

Not all flattery for actress

By JILL CROMMELIN

GRETA Scacchi without make-up looks more beautiful than most women would after a tedious session at the beauty parlour.

But yesterday she explained that an actress doesn't always get the compliments she would like.

In Perth to promote the film "Heat and Dust" in which she stars, she recalled that the director James Ivory gave her no illusions about why she got the role.

"Well, it was three days before shooting started and we had no lead and well, Greta was there." That was what he told a press conference.

Nevertheless Miss Scacchi, a 24-year-old former Hollywood High School student, is now an international movie actress.

"I used to wag school to rehearse for parts with the University of WA dramatic society," Miss Scacchi recalled. "I was at Hollywood High from the age of 15 to 17."

Since then she has appeared in several films and after a holiday in Perth in a hotel near the beach, she will go to Melbourne for the making of a film called "The Cola Kid" produced by former Perth journalist David Roe.

Miss Scacchi's father, a sculptor, lives in Italy. She spends most of her time in London.

Asked whether she lives with anyone, she said firmly, "I don't talk about myself."

West Australian, 23 February 1984

Face on the bus finds stardom

Greta Scacchi. Her face has travelled from a poster on the back of a bus to international acclaim in the film *Heat and Dust*.

Independent, 26 February 1984

THE face that smiled on Perth from the back of an MTT bus is today wearing the smile of film stardom.

Greta Scacchi, 24, is home on a promotional trip for *Heat and Dust* , now showing at Perth cinemas. Four years ago her features first became widely publicised on a bus poster and on television. She was the model in the "Look of Love" advertisements for Mazzucchelli's the jewellers.

From here the former Hollywood High School student went to England to study at the Old Vic theatre. Since then she has appeared opposite such luminaries as Alan Bates and Lord Laurence Olivier.

With the release of *Heat and Dust* (see Frank Ashboth's review on page 40) she is on the threshold of superstardom. She plays the central character Olivia.

It's a far cry from the days when she admits to having wagged school to rehearse for parts with the University Dramatic Society.

Greta said she was a last resort for the part. "With just a few weeks to go before shooting was to begin in India, they still had no Olivia." Then James Ivory spotted her in a television play.

Greta has also completed a 2½ million Australian television series entitled *Waterfront*, opposite Jack Thompson.

Exercise 2.C Publicity

Reviews do more than simply offer an opinion about the film. They are a form of publicity.

1 The review 'A Brideshead set in India' appeared in the same newspaper as the article in the preceding exercise. Re-read the article and then read the review.
- Do the reviewer and the writer of the article share the same opinion regarding the actress? Is this to be expected? Why?
- From your reading of the review who do you think is the lead actress? Why?

2 Look at the advertisement below. Who does the advertisement suggest is the lead? Can you suggest a reason for this discrepancy?
- The review is ten paragraphs long. How many paragraphs are devoted to an assessment of the film? What does this suggest?
- To what previous knowledge/experience on the part of the audience is the reviewer appealing? Why is this appeal being made?

A Brideshead set in India

SUCH delicate splendour, such restrained visual beauty.

The viewer is lulled into a nice melancholy mood. That's *Heat and Dust* (Cinema City).

Style and tone bring to mind the excellent *Brideshead Revisited*. Like this television series, *Heat and Dust* will have its knockers and those who fall in love with it.

Indeed, the fact that *Heat and Dust* has even made it into the commercial circuit is a surprise. Its director, James Ivory, is best known for his ''arty'' films. The success of this, his latest, has surprised many.

Including the star, Greta Scacchi (in Perth last week promoting the film and visiting friends). She had accepted the part, her first major role, thinking that if she didn't look good, not too many people would see it. Luckily she is brilliant because the film has taken critics by storm. The accolades of her performance have been ecstatic.

She plays Olivia, a young English woman who, in the 1920s, goes to join her new husband, Douglas Rivers (Christopher Cazenove), at his post in India.

Olivia is in love with her husband, but soon becomes bored with the straight-laced lifestyle expected of her as a memsahib. The first hint of her subtle revolt is when she refuses to go to Simla during India's hot season with the other British ladies, simply to escape the awful heat and dust.

Olivia is drawn slowly away from her lifestyle and falls in love with the enchantment of India. She also falls under the spell of the local Prince, The Nawab (Shashi Kapoor), with whom the British Raj have an uneasy, distrusting peace.

When Olivia falls pregnant, her husband is overjoyed. ''He'll be blond,'' he says. ''The Rivers are always blond!''

The Nawab, of course, expects Olivia to have a dark-eyed, dark-haired child. ''Won't that give the English masters a shock!'' he exclaims with glee.

Exercise 2.D   Gossip column

Film gossip columns are important in maintaining audience interest in the products — the stars.

People

"It's a tough game, like shooting foul shots. You miss more than you make," says **Wilt Chamberlain**, 47, who after eleven years of retirement from pro basketball is putting on a full-court press for stardom in *Conan: King of Thieves*, due out this summer. In the sequel to 1982's barbaric hit, the 7-ft. 1-in. former N.B.A. champion dunks some nasty villains as the warrior Bombaata, who is on a perilous adventure with the shorter (6 ft. 2 in.) but broader Conan, portrayed again with brutish authority by Celebrity Iron Pumper **Arnold Schwarzenegger**, 36. Also along for the fun and grunts in the film, now shooting in Mexico, is the Amazonian Zula, played by Model–Disco Star **Grace Jones**, 30. How does Wilt the Stilt feel about trading his hoop spiking for a spiked club? "I figure if I'm going to be a baddie, I bet-

Gossett as Egypt's Sadat

ter have something serious to back me up," he says. "I designed it myself. I might take it with me the next time I'm out for a walk in New York."

■

It was intended by its U.S. producers to be a tribute to the late Egyptian President, but when the TV film *Sadat* was screened recently for a censorship committee that included Egyptian Minister of Culture Muhammed Radwan, something had obviously been lost in the translation. Charging that the 1983 film, which stars **Louis Gossett Jr.,** 47, contained "historical errors that distort the accomplishments of the Egyptian people," Radwan

Dressed to kill: Chamberlain and Schwarzenegger in *Conan II*

banned from his country not only *Sadat* but all films produced or distributed by Columbia Pictures. Egyptian objections to the four-hour movie are not so much that **Anwar Sadat** is played by a black actor, as some reports have suggested, but that accents are often Pakistani rather than Egyptian; some of the garb worn is found in Morocco, not Egypt; Nasser is shown kissing Sadat's wife, an abominated Westernism. Moreover, to the Egyptians the film seems to tilt inaccurately toward **Menachem Begin** in awarding credit for the Egyptian-Israeli accords. Nonsense, counters *Sadat* Producer Daniel Blatt. The real reason for the ban lies in the shifting sands of Egyptian politics, he says. "They no longer like Sadat and the peace he made."

■

His 30 seconds over Tokyo as an Air Force squadron commander during World War II earned now retired Lieut. General **James Doolittle** the Congressional Medal of Honor. Other highflying exploits earned him a Distinguished Flying Cross and a Silver Star. Of course, it still takes all those

medals and a token to get on the bus. But now Doolittle, 87, has an honor he could use while piloting his car along the lower altitudes of the California freeway system: personalized license plates. Following an act of the legislature, Doolittle and about two dozen other Congressional Medal of Honor winners living in the

Doolittle and Golden State plates

Golden State were paraded through the center of Sacramento and awarded the numbered plates on the steps of the capitol. (Doolittle, the fifth oldest, got plate 05.) Although "pleased and flattered," the general hasn't yet decided whether he will use the plates.

■

She had always wanted to write a memoir, but her dad did not favor the project. "You write it and I'll kill you," he said. **Antoinette Giancana** prudently decided to humor him, but in 1975 her dad **Sam** ("Momo") **Giancana** was shot down gangland-style. She waited a year—"You know, this Italian thing of letting the body get cold first"—and started to work with the help of a professional writer. Among the more titillating tidbits in *Mafia Princess*, to be published next month, is the implication

Giancana: Daddy dearest

that **Frank Sinatra** misspoke himself in 1981 when he told the Nevada state gaming control board that he had never been friendly with the Chicago-based mobster or shared interests with him in a Lake Tahoe casino. Giancana says that Sinatra and her father were good pals as far back as the mid-'50s and may have been quiet partners in the Cal-Neva Lodge; she quotes previously unreleased FBI documents as support. Giancana, 48, is upset, however, that news of the Sinatra snippet is "taking precedence over the humanistic part of the book. It was not done maliciously. I'm not a malicious person. Others may be, but I'm not." *—By Guy D. Garcia*

TIME, FEBRUARY 13, 1984

49

Gossip page: *Time*

NEW YORK
NEW YORK
with Frank Crook

A volley of adulation

It seems even idols have idols of their own. Tennis star Chris Evert Lloyd finally achieved one of her fondest wishes, to make contact with Tom Selleck, star of TV's *Magnum PI.* Chrissie hoped to meet the moustachioed hunk at last year's Wimbledon titles, when Selleck was in the stands for a few days. She even rushed out to the stadium one day when she wasn't scheduled to play, only to find that he had already left. Now she has his autographed picture, sent to her after some of her chums on the Virginia Slims circuit told big Tom of Chris' devotion.

Patsy's comes to the aid of Frank's 'privacy'

Patsy's Restaurant, an up-market Italian restaurant on Manhattan's west side, happens to be the favourite eatery of one Francis Albert Sinatra, late of Hoboken, New Jersey. Frank is, not surprisingly, an honoured customer. So author Kitty Kelley should not have been surprised when the waiters politely asked her to cease hanging around asking questions while researching her biography of the "chairman of the board". Frank is trying to get publication of Kelley's book stopped, and it doesn't hurt his cause if he gets a little help from his friends.

Beating around the bush

President Reagan will officially announce he will run for a second term sometime this month. So the Republican Party heavies are out and about beating the drum for him. Vice-president George Bush hit New York for a black-tie fundraiser at the Sheraton Hotel and Mrs Bush was asked if she was gearing up to go on the road for the '84 campaign. "Gearing up?" she expostulated. "Since we've been in this job I've never been off the road. Of 1,000 days in office, I've spent 511 travelling. And beginning right now I'm out of town five out of every seven days."

24 WOMAN'S DAY

Joan in a limited edition

Getting your body on a poster is the dream of most aspiring starlets. Just look what it did for Farrah Fawcett. But Joan Collins (above, with her son Sacha) the middle-aged sex symbol of TV's *Dynasty* wanted something special. Fans will have to pay $750 for a likeness of Joan. There are just 150 of them, all signed and numbered. One for every boyfriend?

Gore's recycled research

Waste not, want not: All the research author Gore Vidal did for his *Abraham Lincoln* TV mini-series, which was eventually rejected by the networks, is being put to use for Vidal's *Abraham Lincoln* book to be published by Random House.

Spinks splashes the cash

Michael Spinks, the light-heavyweight champion of the world, has never been known for being tight with his cash. The champ turned up at the Cafe Versailles with ex-dancer Sharon Shackelford for a cosy little meal that set Michael back $168. Spinks then left $400 in tips, $100 each to three waiters and the maitre d', before going upstairs to see the belly dancer.

What becomes a legend most? A little concrete!

It took 16 years of persuasion for adman Peter Rogers to talk Lucille Ball into posing for one of his "what becomes a legend most" Blackglama fur ads. Lucy sat for her shots with make-up artist Way Bundy. You will be pleased to know Lucy has lost none of her sense of humour. "I don't want a photographer," she told Bundy. "Just get me a plasterer and some concrete."

'We're still the best of friends . . .'

The happy couple at the premiere of *Never Say Never Again* are *Hart to Hart* actress Stefanie Powers and producer Tom Mankiewicz — but don't let looks deceive. Stefanie has called off their plans to marry, saying that "I just decided one day that I didn't want to be married, even though Tom is the most wonderful man I know." Both Stefanie and Tom are saying that they will remain the best of friends. That's nice.

Gossip page: *Woman's Day*, 9 January 1984

1 Read the two gossip pages, one from *Time*, an American magazine, and the other from the Australian *Woman's Day*. Read both pages carefully and then fill in the chart below.

Magazine	Number of articles on stars	Names	Photo
Time			
Woman's Day			

2 List as many associations as you can for each star, e.g. past films/TV series, personal events etc.
- What, if any, evidence do you have that the writers have met the stars?

3 List the possible sources of the photographs.
- How many of the gossip paragraphs mention 'soon to be seen' films? Can you find any blatant 'advertisement' in the gossip columns?

The creation of audience expectations even before the film has been completed has been taken a step further with the blockbuster series films such as *Superman* and *Star Wars*. Into the conclusion or classy credits of these is injected an enigma that will be resolved in the sequel. For example there is a suggestion in *Alien* that the Alien creature that has been terrorising the space ship in outer space may be returning to earth with that ship. In the sequel these audience expectations can be easily re-aroused in early publicity. Similarly, in the second Star Wars feature, *The Empire Strikes Back*, it is revealed in the final moments that arch villain Darth Vader is in fact hero Luke Sky Walker's father. This provides an expectation context for the next in the series, *The Return of the Jedi*.

Once the film is complete and ready for marketing the first concrete image that the potential customer is given is the display advertisement. The display advertisement for the film is such an important part of the marketing strategy that the attention it has received has allowed it to almost become an artform in its own right. Catch-phrases are carefully matched with images to create within the potential customer both recognition and curiosity. The potential customer will recognise something in the advertisement that is already familiar. It may be a familiar star or style (called 'genre'). There may be a catch-phrase that relates the film to a familiar occurrence in the potential customer's life. 'Just when you thought it was safe to go back in the water!', relates the familiar experience of swimming to the events that are promised in the film. There is also a suggestion in the statement that the experience provided in the film will take the viewer well beyond the familiar. The visuals that accompany the catch-phrase take the promise well beyond the realm of suggestion.

Exercise 2.E   Narrative image

Two elements at work in creating the narrative image are:
- **recognition**
- **curiosity.**

The display advertisement often incorporates both. [*Special equipment: newspapers*]

1 Examine the display advertisement for *The Right Stuff*. Read the text carefully. List the phrases that invoke recognition.

Recognition

- What do the three feature films mentioned have in common?
- How do these commonalities affect our expectations of this film?
- What does 'epic' mean? What do you expect from an epic film?
- What are the distributor's expectations of this film?

Curiosity

- How is our curiosity aroused? (This film is about pilots and astronauts.)
- What is the relationship between the image in the advertisement and the content of the film?

2 Choose a display advertisement from the morning paper.
- Identify the ways in which *recognition* and *curiosity* are aroused.

NOMINATED FOR
8 ACADEMY AWARDS
INCLUDING "BEST PICTURE"
PRESENTED IN **70 MM** & 6 TRACK DOLBY STEREO

In 1939 there was "GONE WITH THE WIND."
In 1965 there was "DR. ZHIVAGO."
In 1983 there was "GANDHI."

Now, 1984 ushers in a new motion picture epic ...

THE RIGHT STUFF [NRC]

ADVANCE BOOKINGS NOW OPEN!
COMMENCES FRIDAY MARCH 9
TOWN cinema
HAY ST. 321 2747

Exercise 2.F   Narrative image — enigma

Audience expectation is promoted by the development of an enigma. The pre-publicity often suggests an enigma, a puzzle, that the audience is stimulated to solve. It can only be solved by seeing the film. [*Special equipment: drawing materials*]

1 Examine the movie posters (on this and the next page) for *Love is a Many-Splendored Thing*, *Jaws*, *The Enforcer* and *Nine to Five*. Each poster poses an enigma for the audience. Identify the puzzle or problem posed in each poster.

2 For each advertisement, identify the way in which the enigma is posed — through the visuals or the accompanying text.

3 Create a poster for a film you have seen recently. Be sure to pose an enigma in the *visuals* not simply the text.

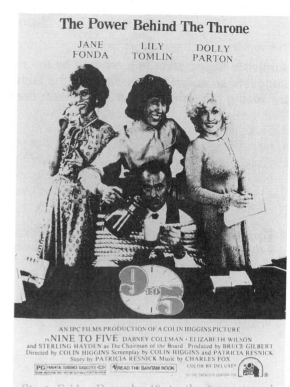

This combination of recognition and curiosity in the narrative image of the film that is being marketed creates an enigma, or riddle, that will be resolved when the spectator sees the film. Thus the enigma has great potential for turning the potential customer into a paying customer.

In addition to the formal marketing of the feature film, there are many semi-formal publicity structures that also arouse narrative expectations in the spectator. Film reviews appear in newspapers and film clips accompany television commentaries upon films. The degree of control that the marketers have over these forms of publicity varies so their influence upon the potential viewer is not as controllable. Both newspaper and television reviewers are dependent upon the co-operation of the film publicists for their preview tickets and film clips. Hence the degree of

hostility towards the product has to be tempered by the need to ensure continuity of supply.

There is also an informal publicity network that helps to generate audience anticipation for a feature film screened in a cinema. Publicists are well aware that word-of-mouth is very telling publicity. This can be of concern to someone responsible for marketing a multimillion dollar product because theoretically the publicists have no say in shaping word-of-mouth publicity. The dilemma for the marketer is that the potential to exploit word-of-mouth publicity cannot be ignored, but there is no guarantee that person to person comments will be favourable.

The situation can be partially overcome by generating initial word-of-mouth publicity through a film preview to select (but not élite) members of the public. Average Joe and

Jane citizens are selected to attend a preview of the film free of charge. They are given privileged status, first because they have not paid and secondly because they have been able to see the film before it is publicly released. Given this privileged position, they are more inclined to speak favourably about the film. To denigrate the film is to denigrate their own privileged position.

> 'We make sure that hairdressers are always given preview tickets. Each hairdresser talks to scores of customers about each preview film.'
> Max Reddin, Manager, Hoyts (WA).

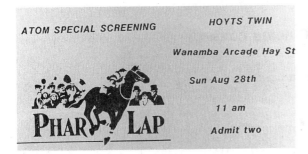

Preview tickets often include a photograph or sketch of the action of the film.

Publicity for a blockbuster feature effectively orchestrates the formal, semi-formal and informal types of publicity so that it becomes almost a cultural expectation that each member will want to, and mostly will, attend the super-film. In recent years a few Australian films have adopted this multi-million dollar marketing approach. *The Man from Snowy River* and *Phar Lap* are two examples. In addition to all of the strategies that have been outlined, peripheral paraphernalia such as toys and clothing help sell the feature as well as generate significant additional revenue.

In summary, because attending a cinema is a special event, the spectator is disposed towards finding out something about the film before attending. Because the feature film is a multi-million dollar product of a high risk industry, the film publicists wish to ensure that the publicity is favourable. A *narrative image* is established to encourage the potential customer to become a paying customer. If the paying customer's expectations are satisfied then the publicist further benefits through word-of-mouth publicity. This process reaches its height with the blockbuster films where formal, semi-formal and informal publicity are carefully orchestrated with large sums of money.

Context

With the very sophisticated marketing techniques that have been described, the film makers have created some foreknowledge about the film amongst the potential customers. This prior knowledge will, in part, shape the response of the paying customer to the film. A satisfied customer is crucial to the industry, partly because of word-of-mouth publicity and partly to ensure the successful marketing of future products.

The anticipation that has been created by an enticing narrative image is one of several factors that will influence the audience's reaction to a film. The narrative image has provided psychological context or a frame of mind. There are also physical contexts that will influence reactions.

Feature films are generally viewed within four different contexts:
- as a televised feature film
- as a hired video tape
- as a visit to a drive-in cinema
- as a visit to an indoor cinema

As one proceeds down this list of contexts, so the occasion becomes more 'special'. The televised feature film is an almost daily occurrence; the hired video tape is dependent upon family budget; the drive-in visit is more expensive and depends upon variables such as car availability and parental permission; the excursion to an indoor cinema requires transport, time and money.

The contexts concerning television and video feature film viewing will be considered later. Consider now the context of that very special event, a visit to an indoor, or 'hard top' cinema. There are two sets of expectations that context the film before viewing commences.

The pre-cinema context

The first is the *venue*. Sitting in a darkened cinema watching images on a large screen to the accompaniment of sophisticated sound is a different and pleasant experience. It provides a context for complete attention and for a great deal of spectator involvement —

but these occur in the course of the screening. The anticipation of this experience is in itself a context. Expectations are high and the cinema goer wants value for what is now a considerable entry fee. In pre-television days the *venue context* was probably even more important. The more prestigious cinemas were ornately decorated as 'picture palaces'. Just to be seated in these auditoriums gave a sense of occasion. Modern cinemas have some legacies from this era. The ornate curtaining across the screen is one example. Next time you visit an indoor cinema, take note of the number of 'extras' which primarily serve to enhance the sense of occasion rather than serve any functional purpose.

Exercise 2.G   Cinema context

An indoor cinema is for the viewing audience, a context.

1 Draw a rough sketch of the interior of a cinema you know well.
   Using labels and arrows identify those characteristics of the cinema that combine to form the viewing context.
   Consider
   • audience
   • decorations
   • furniture
   • sound
   • image

2 Compare your diagram with those made by others.

Once the feature film has commenced in the indoor cinema, the context in which the spectator receives the information becomes even more important.

The most distinctive features which context the film in an indoor cinema are:

- a darkened auditorium
- a great number of spectators
- audience silence (unless the person alongside is munching chips)
- image projection from behind you onto a screen that makes the characters larger than they would appear in real life
- a high quality sound system with speakers strategically placed so that on-screen sounds appear to come from the screen.

The first three factors combine to develop an unusual audience atmosphere that gives both a sense of community and a sense of isolation. The laughter in the audience will in turn encourage you to laugh. There are even some films that cause audiences to applaud the action, or sometimes the sobs of some audience members are quite audible. Any of these audience reactions will make you aware of them in spite of the darkened auditorium. It is also possible that some of the reactions will context your perception of the screen events. Laughter in particular, is very contagious.

Paradoxically, whilst you are sharing an experience with a large audience, the darkened auditorium allows a deep, quite personal involvement with the screen events. The darkness is an important factor in allowing you to quite willingly suspend the reality of being seated in a darkened room watching images being projected onto a screen. You quickly become involved in the story that is developing. The greater the skills of the film maker, the greater will be your willingness to do this. In relation to the screen events, you occupy a strange and privileged position. You are not part of the action on the screen.

The characters do not look at you and encourage a response from you, yet you are still there and able to witness the plot details as they unfold. The appeal of being an invisible witness has been described by film theorists as voyeuristic appeal. This sense of voyeurism is heightened by the fact that the images are projected from behind the audience. The beam of light onto the screen becomes 'invisible' and the magical effect of the screen images becoming the temporary reality is heightened.

High quality images and sound are characteristic of indoor cinemas. These factors, together with the size of the images, create a larger-than-life experience. You, the spectator, have been well prepared in order that you may suspend your disbelief in the mechanically constructed entertainment. You absorb and become involved to an extent that is described by some film theorists as dreamlike. The spectators who have been successfully contextualised to receive messages in this manner are certainly most vulnerable to the manipulations of the film maker. If they were not, then the film makers would have wasted their money.

Conclusion

The context in which a spectator views a film is most important. This contextualising of the spectator occurs both before and during viewing. In the case of contextualising the spectator for an indoor cinema visit, a great deal of money and effort is expended in favourably disposing the cinema goer towards the film and the special occasion of a visit to the cinema. This is necessary because each feature film is a multi-million dollar product within a multi-billion dollar industry. Publicists therefore do everything possible to ensure that the product realises a handsome profit.

Analysis and research

1 Select one blockbuster film that has been shown in the past year which you have seen.

From newspapers, magazines, film journals collect:
- a review
- a display advertisement
- a gossip column article about one of the stars.

Examine each for the narrative image and discuss the consistency of the image.

From your own experience describe the extent to which the publicity is accurate.

2 Here is a quote from *Australian Film, The Inside Story* by Ken Hall.

'*Jimmy Blacksmith* was splendidly made, convincingly produced and directed, and yet it failed disastrously. Why? Because the subject was wrong. If Fred (the director) had the foresight to check he would have found that no film dealing with Aborigines has ever succeeded commercially in Australia. Chauvel tried twice — in 1936 with *Uncivilized* and again in 1955 with *Jedda* — both met disaster. Others which failed were the excellent English film *Walkabout* made in Australia with Jenny Agutter, who is now a star; *Journey out of Darkness*, a poor film; and others less well known. The lessons must be learned *before* the cameras turn. In Fred Schepsi's case it cost 1.2 million dollars to discover this is still a racist country.'

Here is a list of Australian films that have made money for their investors. Find out as much as you can about these films and then suggest the themes that are marketable in Australia.

Phar Lap
Alvin Purple
The Adventures of Barry McKenzie
Breaker Morant
The Man from Snowy River
Mad Max
My Brilliant Career

To what extent do you think these themes are peculiar to Australian interests? Are similar themes present in some of the all-time commercial successes such as:

Jaws
The Godfather
The Exorcist
The Sound of Music
Gone with the Wind
The Sting
One Flew over the Cuckoo's Nest
Towering Inferno
Love Story

(Check the reference section on p. 234.)

Written response

- How does the context of a modern cinema provide a different experience from that of viewing a video at home?
- Respond to this quote from Kenneth Tynan taken from *American Film*, December– January 1979.

'*One thousand items have been deemed worthy of the Superman name, including a Superman bubble-bath decanter, Superman house slippers, even Superman underwear.*'

References

John Ellis, *Visible Fictions* (London: Routledge and Kegan Paul, 1982).

Christian Metz, *Film Language: A Semiotics of the Cinema* (New York: Oxford University Press, 1974).

James Monaco, *How to Read a Film: The Art, Technology, Language, History and Theory of Film and Media* (New York: Oxford University Press, 1977).

Chapter 3
Film's Narrative: Shared Elements

A problem posed

- *Create a humorous character for a 3 to 4 minute film segment. The character must contain a personality paradox that reflects in his/her costume. (For example Charlie Chaplin below the waist is a tramp, his costume above the waist is that of a gentleman. Chaplin's character is an extension of his costume. When he should be a gentleman he acts as a tramp, and vice versa.)*
- *Create a simple conflict for your character, and a humorous, but credible resolution.*
- *Plan a setting that is appropriate for the character, conflict and resolution.*
- *Script the film, ensuring that the elements of character, setting, conflict and resolution exploit the paradox suggested in the costume.*
- *Produce a film/video tape based on the script.*
- *Show the product to an audience not involved in the production. Assess their reactions during the film and question their reactions after the film.*
- *Conduct your own debriefing and address issues such as the following.*
  - *What things amuse audiences?*
  - *Do audiences laugh with a clown or at a clown?*
  - *Are the paradoxes in modern TV clowns as visible as in the Chaplin figure? If not, where does the paradox lie?*
  - *How important are stereotypes to the development of comic situations?*
  - *What could you have done to improve the impact of your mini-comedy? Consider props, mannerisms, settings, dialogue, delivery style.*
  - *To what extent are comic characters related to real life characters? Would your characters be as interesting or as funny to an Ethiopian?*

The following information could help to solve this problem.

It has been mentioned that narrative making is a very common human experience. Therefore it is not surprising that feature film narrative shares many characteristics with other media, particularly with the novel.

Important elements that feature film narrative has in common with novels are the development of:

- setting
- characters
- conflict
- resolution

Setting (or arena)

Entering a cinema and sitting before a large screen is a little like entering a time machine. The images before you can make you an invisible spectator in a New York street, in a medieval village or in a distant galaxy. If the film maker has manipulated the various resources effectively, each experience will seem quite 'real'. This illusion of reality is heavily dependent upon the visual setting. Whether the film is shot on location or in a studio, a great deal of trouble is taken to create a setting that looks real. At a later stage, more attention will be given to the conventions and codes associated with setting, but it is important to recognise now that setting is more than a visual backdrop. The setting should give the spectator some indication of time as well as place. It does not do this in isolation from other elements in the film, such as costume, but there should be sufficient cues for the audience to be able to identify an era. For example an early shot of suburbia that shows houses without television antennas on the roofs implies a time before the mid-1950s.

Just as important, a setting should provide some psychological boundaries for the performers. Given a Western setting, we have expectations about the way that the heroes, villains, men and women will behave. A setting of a police station produces another set of audience expectations.

When a setting style becomes highly con-ventionalised, as the Western has done, the format is known as a *genre*. Within a genre, there will be some variety in setting. For example in the musical genre, the hills can be alive with the *Sound of Music* or the streets a-go with the sight of flash dancing, but there is a consistency in that both are supra-real. They bear more resemblance to a live stage backdrop than do other genre settings. These supra-real settings also allow the performers to supra-emote. The psychological portrayals can be exaggerated to a greater extent than a more 'realistic' setting would allow.

The setting therefore provides an important arena, the boundaries of which are shared by both spectator and performer. Because they are shared, the spectator is able to predict, anticipate and then enjoy the realisation or non-realisation of these predictions. The skilled film maker will be able to inject novelty into the pattern that has been partly created by the setting. The less skilled will produce a genre film that is quite formulaic and therefore quite forgettable.

Exercise 3.A   Setting

Setting should establish time and place. In addition, setting may also establish the psychological boundaries for the plot and audience expectations about the sort of actions that they will witness.

1 Describe the time and place in each of the settings shown here.

2 Describe the different expectations that the audience would have in each of the films.

3 Consider how the settings set limits on plot and performers. Give particular attention to the attitudes and moods that can be generated by the settings. What sorts of dilemmas are possible? Which are not?

From *Cannery Row*

From *Rio Grande* (1950)

From *The Cabinet of Dr Caligari* (1919)

Characters

At a later stage, greater attention will be given to the performance codes that enable the characters in feature films to develop. At this stage, it is important to draw a distinction between the characters that we meet in everyday life and those we see on the screen. Although screen characters appear to resemble people we meet in the street, they are far more regulated than real people. The film maker only has time to develop a limited number of character traits. These must be quickly recognisable by the millions of viewers; therefore, they will largely conform to a recognisable pattern. The preferred types, heroes, villains and fools, will have traits that we have seen in countless other films. The hero will be poor but honest; perhaps rich but still humane; or perhaps the battler against all odds yet integrity remains intact. The pattern has to be familiar, but each character must be given sufficient idiosyncrasies to make her/him recognisable, but interesting.

The characters have psychological boundaries placed upon them by the setting that has been established. For example, a western hero is more likely to be the strong silent type, a man of action rather than words, for this is a trait most appropriate in a pioneer setting. Conversely a law court setting invites words in preference to deeds.

Feature film narrative is heavily dependent on character. Once the type of character has been established, there is a strong tendency to build the conflicts around that character. For example, the poor but honest character will survive many traumas so that the honesty is demonstrated. Often the resolution to the conflicts that the character has been forced to face comes in the form of a reward. Our society decrees that the reward is frequently love or money — not that such a reward is realistic in our own lives, but because both are highly valued in the culture.

Character and conflict

Screen characters are loosely based upon real life characters and this aids audience identification. However screen characters tend to be larger than life. The conflicts that they face are more apparent, rather larger than life. The conflict may be internal. The audience is aware through dialogue and action that the character is suffering an internal dilemma. For example in *Phar Lap* one of the internal conflicts is the prospect of wealth through the horse's success juxtaposed against the likelihood of injury to the horse through over-racing. A lot of the film's interest centres around the way that several of the characters react to the dilemma.

The external conflicts of the characters are more evident and in most cases, larger than life. The external conflict allows the central character to demonstrate his/her attractive, or sometimes heroic, qualities.

Conformity

The compassion, the wit or other positive character traits, are just as important to the narrative as are the physical attributes that allow the hero to succeed. It is because of these culturally deemed 'acceptable' qualities that the hero is allowed to triumph over enemies, who embody qualities that are frowned upon by the culture. It follows that an examination of the values that the central characters embody will give some insight into the values contained in the culture that created the film. However some caution needs to be exercised because simplistic interpretations can be misleading. The triumph of an 'honest' hero over a dishonest villain could result in a simplistic interpretation of honesty being a value held in high cultural esteem. This may be so, but it is more likely that other elements in the film's narrative will give a fuller perception of the culture's values. For example, the means by which the hero is triumphant may provide further clues. Does he win because he is stronger, better looking, smarter, wealthier or lucky? The reasons are likely to be those that are culturally acceptable.

Central characters

Characters in films are not real people, they are constructions. This means that the audience does not immediately know a character in the film but must learn about the character during the course of the narrative. Richard Dyer in *Stars* says that there are signs the audience 'latches on to' in order to understand a character. Dyer lists these signs as:

- audience foreknowledge
- name
- appearance
- object correlatives (symbolic objects)
- speech of character
- speech of others
- gesture
- action
- structure

It is through these things that we, the audience, come to understand a character. The exercises on the following pages explore each of these elements.

Exercise 3.B Audience foreknowledge

Often people know quite a lot about a film before they enter the cinema door. There are many ways they might have gained this knowledge: perhaps they read a review or saw an advertisement; perhaps they already know the story. [*Special equipment: drawing materials*]

1 Look at the old advertising poster for *Pride and Prejudice*. List the ways in which the audience might have known about the major characters before they saw the film.

2 Suggest a reason why the advertisers tell the audience about the stars' previous films. What clues does this information give us about their roles in *Pride and Prejudice*?

3 Consider a book you have read recently that has not yet been made into a film. Design an advertising poster for a film based on this book that will offer the audience some foreknowledge about the characters. Make sure you mention whom you would choose as your stars.

4 Discuss:
- Your choice of star. What made him/her particularly suitable?
- Has this star been in other films of the same genre or played a similar role?

Exercise 3.C   Character appearance

We learn about characters partly from the way they look. A character may be old/young; handsome/ugly; white/black; nice/nasty. The character's costume will tell us about his/her social class, personality, time period and so on.

1 Look at the photograph of the two central characters from *Romancing the Stone* (Jack Colton played by Michael Douglas and Joan Rivers played by Kathleen Turner.) For both characters circle the word that you think best describes the way they look.

Jack Colton	*Joan Rivers*
young/old	young/old
soft/rugged	pretty/ugly
handsome/ugly	feminine/masculine
nice/nasty	sexual/asexual
clean/dirty	clean/dirty
crude/sophisticated	nice/nasty
	romantic/unromantic
	attractive/unattractive

Add any more suitable words that you can think of.

2 Look back over the words you have circled and use them to build up a one- or two-line profile of the characters.

3 Take two of the oppositions above and reverse them for the character. For example how would it change one interpretation of the character if Jack Colton was a very old man or Joan Rivers a very ugly lady. List the aspects of appearance that you consider to be the most important indicators of character.

From *Romancing the Stone* (1984)

Exercise 3.D   Dialogue and gesture

What a character says (and how he/she says it) indicates personality. Similarly, what other characters say about a character can tell us something about both.

1 Read the script below. Try to get some idea of the personalities of the characters and then write in the directions for the delivery of the lines. That is, indicate for the actors *how* they should say the lines so as to add to the characterisation.

The scene is a confrontation between the hero Harry and the villain Suleman. Suleman has Harry's girlfriend captive.

Suleman: Good evening Harry my dear friend. I am sure you recognise this young lady. After questioning her closely, a procedure which alas caused her a little discomfort, I am at last convinced that she does not know the whereabouts of the property in which my friends and I are interested. She is no longer of any use to me, except perhaps as a medium of exchange.

Harry:	I want the girl. I will trade.
Suleman:	I'm interested Harry. I'm interested.
Harry:	Give me the girl, boat, fuel and water to get off this island.
Suleman:	Reasonable Harry. Very reasonable of you.
Harry:	And I want the jewelled tiger head.
Suleman:	Harry, Harry. Greedy.
Harry:	You can have the diamond. In comparison the head is nothing.
Suleman:	You are a hard man Harry. Too hard.
Harry:	What will I get out of it then?
Suleman:	Your life and be grateful for it.

2 After you have decided how the lines should be delivered ask other members of your group to act out the scene. Direct the action, remembering to tell the actors how to stand, what facial expressions to use, how to deliver the lines and what gestures to use. If you have access to a portapak record the scene.

3 Discuss:
- How could the characterisation be changed by the delivery of the lines?
- Describe the actors you would choose for these roles.
- What extra dialogue could be inserted that would enhance the characterisation?

Minor characters

The more interesting characters are often the minor characters — those who support or obstruct the central character in the journey through the narrative. Like the central characters, the supporting characters are dependent upon audience sympathy, therefore they have to be developed in fairly conventional ways. Because they are not central, they are often allowed to display some idiosyncrasies that may not be praiseworthy, but are at least forgivable. The human weaknesses that the supporting characters display will often complicate the problems of the central character. Cadet reporter Jimmy Olsen (who has now been a cadet for over forty years) is very curious and often over-enthusiastic. Superman's task of capturing the super-criminals is frequently complicated by Jimmy's actions. He will often have to rescue Jimmy from his own mis-adventures which have caused the young reporter's path to cross with that of the super-crim.

The robots in the Star Wars series perform a similar function. Their curiosity causes them to wander into trouble. Though they are presumably highly sophisticated computers, they do not seem to have the ability

Jimmy Olsen makes life a little more complicated for Superman.

R2D2 and C3PO in *Star Wars* (1977)

to reason their way out of trouble. Instead they have to rely upon the superhuman deeds of the central human characters for their rescue from the clutches of the enemy.

Perhaps the implication that people have the power to control the technology that they have developed, rather than the reverse, has audience appeal. Perhaps the explanation for their appeal is rather simpler. The robots behave in the same manner as our favourite young cousin, nephew or niece. They have a childlike innocence that allows the human weaknesses of a little lie, over-curiosity or a lot of fear. It is even more likely that their appeal is the result of a combination of the more obvious child identification and the more deeply rooted cultural fear of technology being allayed.

Not all supporting characters have to be as cute as those in the super-adventures. In *Phar Lap* for example, there are several supporting characters who display character flaws. Jockey, Jim Pike, is boastful, but the audience can forgive him this because he is able to make good his boasts. The trainer, Harry Telford, has difficulty in relating to others, is not totally honest and is quite avaricious. Again, the audience is able to forgive because his overriding ambition is to succeed in his job and establish a comfortable home for himself and his wife. These are esteemed values in our culture and so gain a great deal of audience sympathy.

Having established the type of character that the supporting actor will portray, the director has to ensure that all of the symbolic codes develop and reinforce the character traits. Actor Martin Vaughan is admirably suited for the part of head trainer in *Phar Lap* because he is stocky and has facial characteristics that can suggest working class, struggle, austerity and a history of disappointment. Costume, make-up and hair styling further develop the potential that is present in body and face. Again, there is evidence of many codes interacting to develop the desired meaning. The result of the various interacting elements is a character that is more 'rounded' than the central character of the *Phar Lap* feature, Tommy Woodcock. Whereas Woodcock must exhibit almost heroic qualities and total devotion to his horse, the trainer, Harry Telford, is permitted some of the more interesting dimensions of real life characters.

The blocking characters, those who block the path of the central character in the journey towards the story's resolution, are similarly interesting. In films such as the Star Wars series, Superman or the James Bond series, all films which are heavily dependent for their appeal upon the adventure rather than rounded characters, the blocking characters tend to be totally evil.

Those with incredible arrogance or with a lust for unlimited power must be shown to get their deserts. Such characteristics pose a threat to the stability of the culture, therefore those who embody them cannot succeed. Towards the end there may be some explanation for the dastardly deeds, as in the case of Darth Vader, the great blocking character of the Star Wars series. In the final episode, Vader partly redeems himself with a rare act of benevolence towards the young space hero, but the sustaining interest in the series of films is his consistently evil nature.

In films that are further removed from the comic strip style, the blocking characters do not need to be totally evil. For example, in *Phar Lap* Dave Davis, part-owner of the horse, is developed as a blocking character. His greed creates a threat to the well-being of the horse and his preparedness to accept the glory that rightfully belongs to others does

From *Phar Lap* (1983)

not endear him to the audience. However, he is a more rounded character because he can be quite charming and his greed is not totally consuming. He also gains some audience

The comic-strip-type baddies in *Flash Gordon* embody character traits that are culturally scorned.

talker (with an American accent — what does this say about our cultural values?) and his make-up de-emphasises any facial flaws. As with the supporting characters, this greater complexity has made the blocking character more lifelike than the central character Tommy Woodcock and consequently, more interesting. The audience accepts that there is something of a paradox being presented in the part-owner.

In summary, although narratives are no longer as closely locked into the characters as they were when the star system was a more significant marketing component of the film industry, the characters are still quite central. The conflicts and resolutions are dependent upon them, but they in turn are governed by the setting that is created for them. The characters resemble people in real life but are more narrowly and specifically structured. They are designed for a mass audience, therefore must embody a value system that has mass acceptability.

affection because he represents a challenge to the Establishment. A champion racehorse is his entry ticket into the upper strata of society, which finds it very difficult to accept him into its ranks. Comments that have already been made about the interaction of many codes that develop performance, also apply here. Davis is a smart dresser, a smooth

Exercise 3.E   Character traits

Characters are constructed in a narrative, they are collections of character traits. In general a character will have the number and kind of traits needed to function adequately in the narrative. [*Special equipment: magazines, scissors, glue*]

Character traits can involve attitudes, skills, preferences, psychological drives, details of dress and appearance, and any other specific quality the film creates for a character.

1 Build up a profile of character traits you would consider necessary for the hero in the narrative outlined below. Cut out an appropriate face from a magazine, cut out or sketch details of costume and list the attitudes, skills etc. the hero would possess.
'The central character, a rich upper class fop, is despised by his wife for being a dandy. Secretly, however, this character rescues hundreds of innocent people during the French Revolution.'

2 List as many of the character traits as you can think of for each of these well known screen characters.

James Bond	John Wayne	Superman
drinks dry martinis	sharp shooter	able to fly

Conflict/resolution

The forms of conflict and resolution in feature films are similar to those seen in other media, particularly the novel. The traditional forms of conflict are person versus person, person versus nature and person versus self. As with setting, the film's genre will determine to some degree the various combinations of these that are presented. For example a space genre film will strongly emphasise person versus person, with a few complications thrown in because of hostile surroundings (person versus nature). The potential conflict contained in a person struggling against self is not exploited to any great degree. When this conflict does emerge, an additional dimension is added. In the third of the Star Wars sequence, *The Return of the Jedi*, the young hero is confronted with the realisation that the arch villain is in fact his own father. Does he continue to fight this embodiment of evil or does he have a greater loyalty to his father? The resolution to this internal dilemma sustains interest in the second part of the film.

The patterned or *genre* expectation is one of several factors which govern the way in which the conflict can be resolved. A feature film is made in order to make a profit, so the audience must be satisfied at the conclusion. If not, they will tell their friends not to see it and 'negative' word-of-mouth publicity is almost certain to create a box office flop. The *genre* expectation that the American cavalry will ride to the rescue is an acceptable 'resolution' for an audience even though it has been seen many times before. If enough novelty has been injected into the plot there will be sufficient interest in *how* the resolution was achieved, thus avoiding disappointment with a predetermined resolution.

In addition to being conventionally satisfying, the resolution provided by the American cavalry is also culturally satisfying. Subconsciously, it reassures the spectators that law and order will not let them down. Even when we venture into the unknown and are confronted with uncivilised forces and people, we are able to be rescued by the watchdogs of civilisation who so efficiently eliminate the threat.

Father versus son in a *Star Wars* sequel. From *Return of the Jedi* (1983)

These cultural predeterminations help define the audience's predictions and anticipations as they watch the film. The audience knows that Superman will devote a lot of his attention to rescuing Lois Lane rather than saving the children of a Third World country from starvation. This is known because protecting the meddling but ultimately helpless female is a common stereotype in our culture.

As the characters have interacted with their settings to create conflict and plot, a 'reality' peculiar to that film has been created. The audience will accept that Superman is real, even though he has various supernatural powers. The resolution and the conflict must conform to the reality that has been established. *Superman* I was generally received with less acclaim than *Superman* II, perhaps because the resolution in *Superman* I lay outside the reality that had been created. The resolution had *Superman* I changing the course of history by going back in time, re-creating history so that Lois Lane would no longer be dead. The audience also saw him single-handedly prevent a major earthquake by pushing a fault line apart. Even for Superman, these acts lacked credibility and left the audience with a sense of disappointment. *Superman* II had a more credible resolution. Certainly the world

The narrative image established by the publicists must be related to the resolution of the conflict. If a film's central character has been established in the narrative image as a great man-eating shark, the resolution must be in keeping with this. It would be a preposterous anti-climax for the thrill-seeking audience if the resolution had the shark being kept in a backyard swimming pool as a pet! From *Jaws*, (1975)

was saved by the man of steel, but the conflict that had been established and its resolution were more consistent with the dilemmas that our super-hero is expected to face — superman against himself.

The characters in the film interact with each other and with their settings and a plot develops. Within the plot (characterised by conflict and resolution) there are smaller dilemmas, which must be resolved in ways that are in keeping with the genre of the film. An adventure story such as *Raiders of the Lost Ark* will present the hero with many physical and human obstructions that must be overcome before the hero can complete his journey. He must encounter pits full of snakes, treacherous women and evil Nazis before the heroic resolution is achieved. The audience knows that the hero will resolve these dilemmas but is interested to find out how he does it.

To some extent, therefore, resolutions are culturally predetermined. Those who transgress the norms (and usually the laws) of our society must be punished, whilst valour must be rewarded.

From *Superman* (1978)

Exercise 3.F Conflict and resolution

Conflicts in films have a resemblance to those in novels. The struggles are person against person; person against nature; person against self. As with novels, the resolutions must be consistent with the 'reality' that has been created in the film.

1 The conflict is both stated in words and implied in visuals in the film poster for *The Front Page*. What is the conflict? Do the visuals suggest the type of film it will be? Suggest a genre for the film.
2 Taking into account the film style and the narrative image that has been presented to the public, outline a 'realistic' resolution to the film. Check your resolution. To what extent does it satisfy existing values in our society?
3 Suggest a resolution that would not meet with audience approval because it is outside the norms of our society.

Conclusion

Film narratives share many characteristics with narratives in other media. They have a setting, characters, conflict and resolution.

The settings are important in establishing time and place and also for creating boundaries within which the performers must physically and psychologically perform.

The characters, whether central, supporting or blocking characters, gain an illusion of reality because they share common cultural traits with the audience. However although they suggest reality, they are not real because they are not as multi-faceted as real people. Narrative feature films are very heavily character dependent and the conflicts tend to be constructed around the possible fates awaiting the central characters. In the extreme, some film narratives have been constructed purely as vehicles for particular central characters (stars).

The conflict and resolution in each film must be clear, and the two must be clearly related. This is because the film is viewed as a complete entity, not as a series (as with television). Clear identification provides greater audience satisfaction, which in turn will result in greater profits. Within each narrative, there will be lesser conflicts (or dilemmas). The sorts of conflicts that are created tend to be a mixture of the traditional, person versus person, person versus nature or person versus self. The resolutions to these conflicts are governed by the form of 'reality' that has been created, by convention (of film style and of previous resolutions) and most importantly, by cultural expectations.

Finally, a little more should be said about the fact that the spectator experiences the film narrative in a discrete and complete session (usually about two hours). Several ploys are used in order to heighten a sense of completeness for the audience. The resolution is the traditional 'closing', but other devices are also used. Music that has introduced the film may be repeated in the finale. There may be a return to a well established early scene or there may be a segment of dialogue that is mentioned early, but gains significance during the resolution. Such closing devices encourage audience satisfaction in the completeness of their film experience.

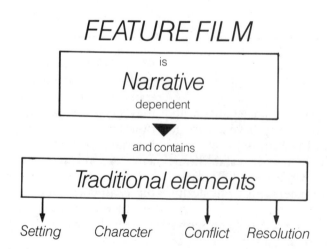

The Boat (1982) used as its closing device an image which was visually close to the opening image. The start of the film has the boat sailing out of the harbour, the closure is the boat sailing in.

FEATURE FILM

is
Narrative
dependent

▼

and contains

Traditional elements

Setting   Character   Conflict   Resolution

Analysis and research

Select a film for analysis. (It is preferable if a few people can choose the same film so that comparisons can be made.)

- Analyse the film in terms of setting, character, conflict and resolution.
- What devices are used to close the narrative?
- To what extent do the narrative devices of setting, character, conflict and resolution conform with expectations that have been created in earlier films of a similar genre?
- To what extent do the four elements reflect the reality of everyday experience — both physically and in terms of our values?
- How appropriate is the movie's poster in establishing an appropriate narrative image?

Library research

Select from film books images that relate to one genre (e.g. Western, musical, crime, horror).

- Examine the images for evidence of setting, character, conflict and resolution.
- On the evidence that you have gained, describe the common characteristics of each of the four elements within the genre.
- Create a movie poster for an imaginary film of that genre. The advertisement must give an indication of the ways in which the expectations of the public are standardised in a genre.
- Repeat the poster, but add an element that is quite out of keeping for the genre.
- Test your products on others and assess their responses.

Written response

1 Some people have a definite preference for films of a particular genre — science fiction, horror, musicals, Westerns, etc. Choose a genre that interests you and describe the major characteristics of this genre in terms of setting, characters, conflict and resolution. Refer specifically to films you have seen.

2 'In their establishment of patterned activity, film genres, because of their wide appeal, serve the purpose of creating modern mythic structures.' (Stanley J. Solomon, *The Film Idea*) For example in the private-eye genre representatives of the dark world of hypocrisy and greed (the baddies) impinge upon the moral order until the hero is alerted and single-handedly sets about restoring the proper moral balance.

Solomon is saying that genre resolutions are essentially culturally generated and approved. Comment upon this view with reference to the genre resolutions offered on westerns or romances or gangster films.

3 You have been to a film that is about a very famous person or event in history. You enjoyed the film and felt that it gave you a far better understanding of that historical event.

Shortly after seeing the film, you used it as a basis for an answer to a school history assignment. In spite of your excellent presentation, you scored poorly. What went wrong? What are some of the differences between modern cinema's view of history and the views found in history books?

Practical exercise

Script a scene for a genre film. Your script does not have to encompass the whole film, it can simply be a crucial scene. You may choose to write out your script or storyboard it.

As a group choose a script, appoint crew positions and decide such things as setting, costume, dialogue, props etc. Remember this is to be a genre piece so you may have to check your research notes for appropriate genre material.

Shoot your script on film or video.
Replay and discuss:

- How true is your scene to its genre type?
- What changes would you make if you did it again?

- Can audiences recognise the genre?
- What are the major characteristics of the genre you have chosen?

References

Richard Dyer, *Stars* (London: British Film Institute, 1979).

John Ellis, *Visible Fictions* (London: Routledge, 1982).

Jurij Lotman, *Semiotics of Cinema* (Michigan: Ann Arbor, 1976).

Stanley J. Soloman, *The Film Idea* (New York: Harcourt Brace Jovanovich, 1972).

Chapter 4

Film's Distinctive Storytelling Forms

A problem posed

Create a 4 to 5 minute video drama that establishes two different characters in two different locations. The resolutions to your drama must involve a meeting between the two characters and this meeting must culminate in an emotional moment. Use Eisenstein's technique of montage to develop the emotional moment. Your film must indicate that before the meeting, each of the characters (preferably typed) is carrying out her/his actions simultaneously with the other. Use techniques associated with montage and the manipulation of time to achieve this.
   The following information could help to solve the problem.

If film's narrative consisted only of the traditional elements of setting, character, conflict and resolution, there would be little point in studying the medium. It would be sufficient to examine novels and apply these understandings to films. However, narrative is the sum of all of the elements in its construction. What is being said is affected by the way in which it is said. All elements affect the way in which the 'reality' behind the narrative is interpreted. Indeed there is a strong case for any claim that construction of the 'reality' is more significant than the simple story that is being constructed.

Over the past one hundred years, film has developed a very distinctive form of expression. Certainly it drew elements from other forms, particularly the stage play and the novel, but quite early, techniques evolved that were more in keeping with the new medium.

The earliest films were shot in real time, that is the action was staged in front of a camera and the recorded action equalled the time the performance took. The effect was very similar to sitting in a live theatre watching the performers, except that the resulting films were recordings of short action pieces, rather than complete narratives as we know them today.

Very soon, film makers realised that shooting in real time was quite unnecessary. Redundant information could be eliminated by stopping the camera and beginning again when the action was significant. The next step was to stage the shots so that the camera (and therefore the spectator) was afforded the best view of the action. A technique of film construction based upon a series of shots (a montage) began to emerge.

Montage

Early film makers staged some scenes so that distant action moved towards the camera into relative close-up. Some of the pioneers realised that the close-up afforded their audiences a larger-than-life look at part of the broader scene. They realised that their power to choose what was to be shown in close-up gave them greater control over audience reaction to their creations. Pioneers such as D.W. Griffiths did not continue with the procedure of keeping the camera moving as performers moved from a distance towards the camera. Instead they filmed the long shot; cut; then moved the camera to the action to film the important detail in close-up. A new convention had been created in film language — close-ups were used to emphasise what was significant.

The effect of early close-ups upon unsophisticated film audiences is reported to have been quite startling, but the technique is now taken for granted by audiences, even though they may not be conscious that the transitions from one type of shot to another are occurring.

Some film theorists and film makers have argued that the technique of cutting to close-up is inappropriate because it does not conform with our everyday perception of the world. Whether this is so or not is not significant in this analysis. It is significant that the technique of cutting from long shots, to medium shots, to close-ups, became a convention that was peculiar to film, particularly the films made in Hollywood. As the Hollywood feature film quickly became accepted by cinema goers around the world as the 'norm', the quite artificial technique of story construction became 'naturalised'. Any film not using this technique could be unsettling to the audience, consequently its chances of obtaining an economic return were jeopardised.

This method of cutting from one shot to another is known as *montage*. In modern cinema, it is common when cutting from one shot to another, to ensure that there are visual cues in each shot that justify the cut and justify the information in the shot. For example, if a medium shot shows a woman drinking coffee, a close-up of the cup at the lips would be justified because we would have seen in medium shot, the hand moving the cup in that direction.

The development of narrative through related shots is the simplest use of montage. Through the use of montage it is also possible to control the development of the narrative in many other ways.

In the pioneering days of film making, considerable debate raged about the way in which montage should be used. The majority of film makers argued that it was a language of related shots that aided the development of the narrative. The Soviet film maker, Eisenstein, believed that montage could be put to more powerful use. Although 'montage' is merely the French word for editing, Eisenstein ap-

Close-up

Medium shot. Below: Long shot. From *Phar Lap* (1983)

Above and right: Justified cut. From *Phar Lap* (1983)

The faces of the Soviet people: typage in *October* (1928)

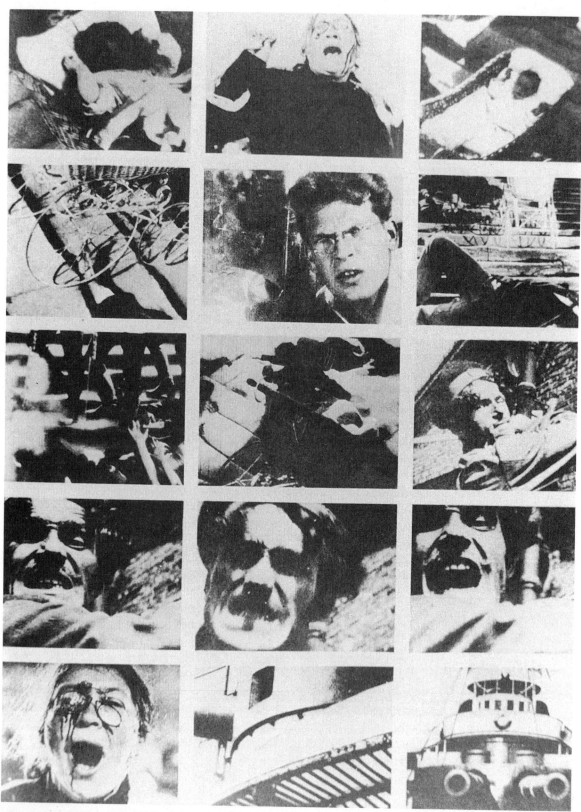

From Eisenstein's *Battleship Potemkin* (1925)

plied the term to explain the way in which the filmic units of expression were combined into one whole. He had a broad view of what comprised a filmic unit, having in mind something akin to the various codes that are discussed later in this text. However most of the early discussion centred around the combination of the individual visual units — the shots.

Eisenstein opposed the assembly line view, that the shots should be strung together to develop the story. He saw montage as a collision of ideas presented in the shots. Out of this collision would emerge a new understanding that was not inherent in either shot. That is, there was not necessarily a 'linkage' from one shot to the next. For example, a shot of a soldier with bayonet followed by one of a terrified child, then another of blood trickling down steps, become related through their juxtaposition. They create an audience reaction that is not inherent in any of the shots. The juxtaposition created by the film maker has directed the spectator's emotional response.

Eisenstein controlled audience response to his images by using typed characters in his shots. Heroes, villains, cowards and the helpless were all immediately recognisable by their appearance (see p. 45). He believed that there should be conflict between the shots at all possible levels, for example in scale, depth and even direction of action.

The Eisenstein technique is not as popular today as the montage technique that is more heavily dependent upon linkages, but it does have more than historical interest. The technique is still widely used where the creators want to carefully control the sort of emotional experience of the audience. This makes it significant in advertising. The typed characters are combined with fast, almost flashing images, that create a positive emotional response in the audience. Eisenstein was quite open about the fact that his technique would be used by him to further his and his country's Marxist viewpoint. It is therefore somewhat ironic that this potent propaganda weapon is now being used by those at the other extreme of the political spectrum.

Although Eisenstein's technique has limited application today, the use of the close-up is still significant. The close-up still makes an important contribution towards the film's narrative, but it has a clear relationship to images that have preceded it and with those that are to follow. In fact, its meaning is largely parasitic upon those images that surround it. Of the several possible meanings in the above medium or long shots, the close-up narrows down, or anchors the meaning (see the 'justified cut' on p. 45).

Audiences are now attuned to accepting the close-up as the means by which meaning is anchored. Although they are not consciously aware of it they are prepared for the establishing medium or long shot, then the cut to close-up. The audience will also respond appropriately when in moments of high drama, the close-up is replaced by the big close-up. This is another convention that has developed in the language of film that works even without the spectator being conscious of its employment.

Exercise 4.A   Montage

The Eisenstein technique of montage depends upon conflict between the successive images. The viewer has an emotional response that is a result of the juxtaposition of images, but by themselves the images do not support the emotion. For example knife and horrified eyes = terror. [*Special equipment: magazines, scissors, glue*]

1 From magazine pictures or with your own drawings create a montage of ten shots. Your montage must develop *one* of the following emotional responses:

- fear
- pride
- aggression
- joy of living
- apprehension

2 Show your montage to someone else, and discuss with that person the effect of your montage. What shots would make it more effective?

3 Conduct a detailed examination of a high budget television commercial (e.g. Coca-Cola). What emotion is the montage trying to develop? How many shots does the commercial contain? Are the characters typed? If so, are they consistent in their typage? For what age range do you think the advertisement is intended?

4 Write briefly about your conclusions.

Time and space

Time

Sophisticated use of montage techniques has allowed film makers to manipulate time and space.

Time is a strange phenomenon that we tend to think of only in terms of a ticking clock. It is true that when we enter a cinema, we see a film that lasts about two hours in real or clock time, but other 'times' are also occurring. The narrative may be constructed so that the story occurs in a day or a decade. Because the spectator becomes involved in the story, it will be accepted that in the two hours of clock time, ten years or even several lifetimes may be seen to pass. Perhaps film is the closest that we will ever get to travelling in a time machine. The film maker has the capacity to take us forwards or backwards in time and also to adjust the speed at which we travel!

Within the narrative's time span, montage is used to show other sorts of time. A film segment can be constructed to show simultaneous time. For example, once the dastardly villain has tied the helpless man to the railway tracks, the next series of shots will show the train roaring down the tracks and the heroine hastening to the rescue. Although the shots are strung together in sequence, they will be interpreted by the audience as being simultaneous events. The excitement lies in anticipation of the two separate pieces of action coming together. Will it be a dead heat, in which case both helpless male and heroine get mangled by the locomotive? Will the train win or will convention prevail and good win in the nick of time? Montage that

Simultaneous time. From *Phar Lap* (1983)

Wonder horse Phar Lap is late for the race.

The crowds are assembling at the race course.

creates simultaneous time has created the excitement.

Lengthy, boring passages in films can be shortened by the use of montage. A three-hour car journey can be condensed to ten seconds by using three shots. Shot one shows the driver entering the car. Shot two shows the car speeding along the highway and the final shot shows the driver leaving the car at the destination. Appropriate cut-aways are other ways of showing, through montage, that time has passed. The most used cliché is the cut to the clock face; slightly more sophisticated is a cut to an extinguished cigarette, an abandoned meal or an empty glass. Audiences will now subconsciously accept that many cut-aways may be interpreted as time passing.

Cut-aways can also be used to lengthen time. The drama in a momentary action can be increased if additional cut-aways are used. For example, a one-hundred-metres running race lasts about ten seconds. If it is shown in real time, a great deal of the drama will be lost. Instead the film maker may choose to use shots of the start, close-ups of the feet, several cut-aways to excited spectators, more close-ups of the runners' facial expressions, more spectators, then the climactic finishing line shot. The ten-second race could well be extended more than one minute by such techniques. *Chariots of Fire* is one film that effectively used this technique in order to heighten the dramatic impact.

Montage is not the only way in which time is manipulated in a film's narrative. Montage is often used in conjunction with fades, wipes and dissolves to suggest the passing of time. These quite artificial conventions are now universally accepted, though subconsciously, by the cinema-going public. Through the various devices that manipulate film time, the film maker is able to control the *pace* of the film. Tense moments may seem an eternity, or pass so quickly that they have a shock effect. If the appropriate pace and variation of pace is achieved, audience satisfaction will be maximised, and so will profits.

Simultaneous time. From *Phar Lap* (1983)

Running late

Meanwhile, back on the course

Time running out

At the course

Dramatic arrival

We want Phar Lap — the two sequences come together.

Film's Distinctive Storytelling Forms   49

Shortening time.

The race finishes.

Cut-away

Horse and jockey return to the saddling yard.

Cut-away

After the ceremony

The proud trainer

The sequence is complete.

Lengthened time

The action in slow motion

Insert

Little development in the action. (Action in slow motion.)

Insert

A moment in time is drawn out. (Action in slow motion.)

We have considered the real or running time of the film; the flexibility the film maker has to set a film in the past, present or future and to make the narrative time hours, days or years; the power of montage to create simultaneous time, lengthened or shortened time, or to suggest time has passed. Time also has a fourth dimension because whether the film is set in the past, present or future, the spectator, that invisible voyeur in the film, experiences that time as *now*. This allows the spectator to identify quite strongly with the characters and the events. Though Gandhi may have died decades ago, while we are in the cinema watching an actor perform as the Indian leader, he is alive. History tells us he is dead, but the film's narrative makes him live. His assassination is so disturbing because we perceive it as happening before our eyes *now*. It is not some distant historical event.

Montage and time — summary

Through montage (and other devices) the film maker can suggest:
- simultaneous time
- shortened time
- lengthened time

No matter when the events of the film are set — past, present or future, the time for the viewer is *now*. This increases the impact upon the viewer.

Exercise 4.B Simultaneous time

Simultaneous time is created by parallel cutting. Re-read the example of the dastardly villain tying the helpless man to the railway tracks and the heroine speeding to his aid. [*Special equipment: drawing materials; it would be desirable to have video equipment and video of a chase scene*]

1 Draw the shots that would be needed to create simultaneous time.

2 Check your storyboard for close-ups. If you have not included them, reconsider and mark the approximate length of each shot.

3 Nominate where close-ups should be inserted.

4 Show your storyboard to someone else in the class to check whether it can be 'read' as simultaneous time. If not, make the necessary corrections.

5 What sound would assist in giving the impression of simultaneous time?

6 Compare your effort with those of others in your group. If possible, watch an example of simultaneous time in a film. (Chases provide useful examples.) Compare your effort (timing, shot choice) with the professional product.

7 As a result of this comparison, make a summary about conventions associated with the construction of simultaneous time in film.

Exercise 4.C Time manipulation

A film maker has a number of techniques available to him/her to allow time to be shown as simultaneous or lengthened or shortened. Some of these techniques are wipes, fades, dissolves, cutting, slow motion.

1 Read each of the script outlines below. Your task as a film maker is to storyboard the script excerpts indicating the ways in which you will manipulate time to create the maximum impact whilst sitll making your film comprehensible to the audience.

  a A young couple pull out of the driveway in their new car. They drive down the road and turn the corner. On the next block a little boy is throwing his ball for his dog. The child is playing near the road but not on it. The young couple turn into the street at the same time as the boy's dog runs across the road. The little boy calls his dog but it does not respond. The car approaches. The child runs out on to the road to retrieve his dog.

  b The scene is a railway station. A young woman laden with luggage climbs aboard the train. She manages to find a seat as the train pulls out. She settles down to read a book for the duration of the journey. Two hours later the train arrives at a Paris railway station. The young lady collects her cases and alights on to the crowded platform. She looks anxiously around for the young man she is to meet.

  c A safe is seen in medium close-up. Attached to the door of the safe is a short thread. The thread leads to a large bomb that sits on the floor. The thread is alight and burns its way in less than two seconds to the bomb. Some distance away the thieves sit waiting for the bomb to detonate.

2 After you have completed your storyboard compare it to the efforts of others in the class. Have you all used the same techniques to manipulate time? Were there alternative techniques available?

3 Make a group summary of the techniques that were used.

Space

The images in a cinema are projected on to a flat screen. This flat screen, with its frame as an artificial boundary, is a severe limitation for the film maker's attempts to recreate reality for the audience. Techniques have been developed to create an illusion of a world that has an existence outside the screen's frame. Additionally, the film maker attempts to overcome the flatness of the screen and suggests in the images that the created world has depth. It is as if the film maker is given a flat surface and through many techniques, has reshaped the flat screen into a cube. The techniques allow the spectator to forget she/he is staring at a flat screen, but is viewing a world that does stretch sideways, upwards, downwards, away and towards her/him. It is an illusion of the world we see in our own lives. Montage is an important technique in creating this cube of space, then in expanding the size of the cube so that its edges are no longer clear.

Many techniques may be used to suggest that a world exists beyond the frame. Sounds may be heard that supposedly originate from a world outside, though in reality they are derived from a sound effects record or tape. Animals, cars or people may be seen entering and leaving the frame, apparently going about business that is unrelated to the main screen events. How often do we see, in a period film, an old car entering and leaving the frame while the characters continue their performance. From *Taxi Driver* (1976)

The way in which space is used inside the frame can generate different atmospheres. For example a crowded scene with performers directing their attention inward can be quite claustrophobic. Such scenes almost deny a space beyond the frame. (From *Once Upon a Time in America*, 1984)

The frame around the image is an artificial boundary that does not have an equivalent in life. In our everyday experience, if our view is blocked we can swivel our head or move to get a better view. Conversely, the film spectator is immobile in front of a fixed screen with clearly defined boundaries.

Montage can be used to suggest a world that exists outside the screen. Interior shots will be preceded by shots that establish the location of the interiors. In reality, there may be no connection between the interior shots and the location shots. Indeed the interiors may not even be genuine, but may be sets in a film studio, but in the film's 'reality', a space or an implied world has been created outside the frame.

Because it is implied that a whole world exists outside the frame, conventions have emerged that allow performers to conform to the 'reality' of the make believe world. For example, entry and exit points must be consistent. If an actor is walking in one direction and is seen to exit on the right of the screen, the next shot must show him entering from the left.

Exercise 4.D   Space

A film maker needs to create the illusion of space outside the limitations of the frame. A film maker will try to give the impression of space existing upwards, sideways, forwards and backwards. This can be done through associated shots and use of sound effects. [*Special equipment: drawing materials*]

1 Look at this still from *Cross Creek* (1984).

2 Sketch in storyboard form two preceding shots and two following shots that will create a sense of the immenseness of the country through which the people are moving.

3 Although the woods are immense, your actors feel enclosed by the wall of trees. Sketch a medium shot that will convey a sense of claustrophobia. What sort of lighting would heighten this feeling? Bright or dark and gloomy? Indicate on your sketch, the lighting variations.

4 Compare your results with others in your group.

5 Compile a group summary of the ways in which a sense of immenseness was created. Also summarise the ways in which claustrophobia was suggested.

Exercise 4.E Time and space manipulation

[Special equipment: video playback facilities; any Western movie]

1 View the first 10 minutes of any Western film (perhaps one featuring John Wayne).

2 In preparation for discussion make brief notes about the following:
- the geographic location of the set (be specific, for example, 'desert')
- the period when the events occurred
- the relationship of any buildings to the broader scene (where are they located?)
- the location and relationship of the characters in the film to the scene (for example, 'the bartender works in Nell's saloon', 'The cowboy has ridden out of the desert')
- properties and people who seem to be there as 'window dressing'.

3 Replay the same 10 minutes of video tape in order to detect the ways in which the film maker has constructed the world you have just seen and noted. Observe particularly the sequence of shots that create the space. How do you know the time period? Is it indicated in any way or do you know merely because you have seen other Westerns?

4 Discuss your theories with others in your group.

5 Make a group summary list of the ways in which time and space are created in the 10 minute segment.

'Cinematic' film

Montage is a crucial element in film language, and we have seen that it is used to form a narrative sequence, to evoke an emotive response from the audience and to control the presentation of time and space in a film. But not all shots in feature films conform with the static montage style. In its least imaginative form, a montage could be comprised of a series of still photographs and a narrative could still be developed. Such a static film style would not exploit any of the potential of the movie camera. It is possible to move the camera whilst filming. It is possible to swivel the camera on its horizontal or vertical axis. It is possible to stage action so that a series of events is drawn into the frame. A filming style that exploits some of these more fluid techniques, thus enabling several montage-type shots to be merged into one shot, is called cinematic film style. In modern feature films, these cinematic shots will be interspersed with traditional montage shots. They may be used to suggest space beyond the frame, to change the pace of the film or to keep the audience's attention upon a subject, without the distraction of a series of cuts.

Early film making styles were not cinematic. Film makers were psychologically bound by the association that their craft had with live theatre. The movie camera was locked into a fixed position as if it were a spectator in a live theatre. The hand driven cameras also presented difficulties when they were moved. The first effort to expand beyond the frame and move away from the proscenium stage mentality of early film makers was to stage action in such a manner that additional action could be fed into a static frame. The French called this modification mise-en-scène or 'putting it in the scene'. However, these attempts were still very theatrical because the camera was still stationary, the focal distance of the lens was fixed and the camera angle was frontal and at eye level. By the early 1920s (the end of the silent film era) the occasional tilt or pan was accepted as part of Hollywood film language. The meaning of the term mise-en-scène was broadened to incorporate these camera movements.

Since the mental breakthrough of the pan and tilt image, a great deal of attention has been given by film makers to technology that will allow them to develop their images beyond the static frame. These developments have allowed the images to flow from one occurrence in the narrative to the next, without the interruptions associated with montage. Track laying was an early method of ensuring that the camera could move while retaining some control over camera speed and image jerkiness. Dollies and cranes contributed further in the quest for 'cinematic' film.

The events in Europe, particularly in Italy, did have some effect upon Hollywood film making, although the innovations occurred slowly. 'Real' locations were gradually sought out, artificial light filters or gels over windows were no longer considered necessary, because light flares were deemed to be part of reality. Working in these confined 'real' spaces such as rooms in houses, created a need for even more flexible cameras.

Mobility was further aided by lighter cameras that could be hand held. In both Germany and Italy, innovation had occurred during the Second World War that allowed lighter cameras to record propaganda footage on site. After the war, Italian film makers were unable to use the damaged studios and were forced into more 'real' locations. This move was aided by the development of lighter cameras.

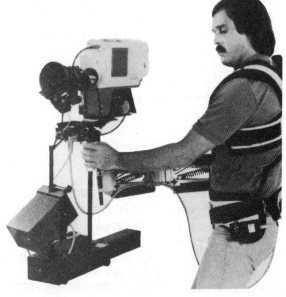

The potential for greater use of point of view shots was enhanced when steadi-cams were developed for the film *Rocky* in 1976. The steadi-cam has a gyroscope mechanism that allows the camera to remain steady, no matter how rapidly the operator moves.

Schoolteacher John Grant (Gary Bond) in *Wake in Fright* (1971). Film makers will often use a cinematic technique to establish or conclude a sequence of action, or when an even rhythm in the film is particularly important. The 'cinematic' shots at the beginning of *Catch 22, Wake in Fright* or *Diva* are excellent examples of the technique.

Explicit attention to these camera movement techniques will be given in the section on the technical code.

All of the techniques that have been mentioned have allowed the film maker to merge what would previously have been several shots of comparatively static action into a single flowing or 'cinematic' shot.

Conclusion

A most significant component of any narrative is the way in which it is constructed. At the heart of film narrative's construction is the technique of montage.

Montage allows a film maker to develop segments of action into an understandable story. It allows the flexibility of shooting the segments out of sequence, then editing them into a narrative sequence at a later date.

Montage allows a film maker to heighten the emotional response of an audience through the careful juxtapositioning of images. The approach may not be as heavy-handed now as it was when Eisenstein was developing the technique, but the potential is still exploited.

Montage allows a film maker to manipulate time and space in ways which contribute to a sense of reality for the spectator.

The static montage style of early films has now been modified and more cinematic approaches are blended with the traditional forms. This does not mean that montage has been replaced. The conventions associated with montage are now too deeply embedded to be abandoned. Although the conventions such as use of the close-up are artificial, they seem quite natural to the spectator. Major departures would be too jarring.

There are many other conventions and codes that contribute towards the construction of the film narrative, but all are to some degree governed by the fundamental component of language.

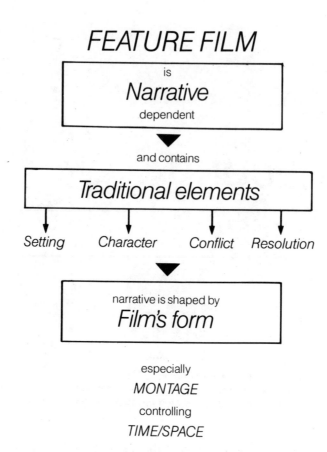

FEATURE FILM

is
Narrative
dependent

▼

and contains

Traditional elements

Setting   Character   Conflict   Resolution

▼

narrative is shaped by
Film's form

especially
MONTAGE
controlling
TIME/SPACE

Analysis and research

1 Examine in detail, 10 minutes of a feature film. Give particular attention to the use of close-ups and to the development of time and space.
   - To what extent do the close-ups depend upon the preceding and following shots?
   - Are there any big close-ups used? If so, why? If not, why not?
   - What space is suggested outside the frame? How is it suggested?
   - In what time period is the film set? Past, present, future? How much time do the 10 minutes of viewing time represent in film time?

2 Montage affects the way that space is shown. Other techniques and developments also affect the development of screen space. Consider the following:

   - *The split screen* — the technique of showing geographically separate events (for example, two people in telephone conversation) simultaneously on the screen.
   - Is split screen a common technique in modern cinema?
   - What effect does the split screen have upon the illusion of reality that the film maker is trying to create?
   - *Widescreen or cinemascope* — how has widescreen affected the traditional rules of photographic composition?
   - Does widescreen give the spectator a

greater choice regarding where to focus attention?

- Does widescreen create more space, therefore a greater illusion of reality?
- How is the widescreen illusion of reality affected when the cinemascope image is 'squeezed' and shown on television?

Written response

Film theorist Jurij Lotman regards the close-up as the fundamental method of attaching the screen's perimeter, that is, the most important means of suggesting a greater space than that which is shown. Hence the close-up adds to the illusion of reality. Film theorist Andre Bazin believes that the close-up helps destroy the illusion of reality that is being created. Both cannot be correct.

- What is the effect when a big close-up is used instead of a close-up?
- Expert film makers are able to largely control the thoughts and emotions of the cinema audience. Do close-ups assist or hinder this degree of control?

Library research

1 D. W. Griffiths and Sergei Eisenstein were two directors who made significant contributions to the language of film.
  - Research the contribution of one of these directors.
  - How important was that contribution to modern cinema?

2 The neo-realist period in Italian cinema (1945–49) was a short, but significant era.
  - Research the neo-realist film movement and find out what were the peculiar features of the movement. What factors caused the movement to develop?
  - What effect has the movement had upon modern cinema?

Practical exercise

Activity 1 [*Special equipment: portapak*]
Experiment with the potential of the mobile frame by trying the following activities. All of the exercises depend on a moving camera so it is worth using a child's pusher, a wheel-chair, a barrow or something that will make you steady and mobile.

- Moving camera and space. Use the camera to create this effect:

long shot

to

close-up

to

introduction of another character

to

attention to significant detail.

- Moving camera and time. Use the camera to slow time with a tracking shot from a single figure to the background.

Activity 2
Reconsider the problem posed at the beginning of this chapter.

Use the knowledge that you now possess to construct a film or video tape along the lines suggested.

References

Andre Bazin, *What is Cinema?* Volume 1 (Berkeley: University of California, 1967).

Andre Bazin, *What is Cinema?* Volume 2 (Berkeley: University of California 1971).

David Bordwell and Kristin Thompson, *Film Art: An Introduction* (Massachusetts: Addison-Wesley, 1980).

David Cook, *A History of Film Narrative* (New York: Norton and Co., 1981).

Sergei Eisenstein, *The Film Sense* (London: Faber and Faber, 1968).

Jurij Lotman, *Semiotics of Cinema* (Michigan: Ann Arbor, 1976).

Chapter 5
Film's Conventions and Codes

A problem posed

You are a script consultant for an important film producer. Your producer has given you a script that has some potential because it has quite a dramatic ending. However, as it stands, there is not much chance that there will be many people left in the cinema by the end of the film, because the script lacks smaller dramatic moments within the earlier part of the narrative.

Your task is to generate some of these dramatic moments. How will you do it?

This chapter will provide some of the ground rules so that you can solve the problem.

Conventions and codes

A convention is the accepted method of doing something. It is a convention to shake hands when people meet, to say 'please' or 'thank you', to begin a news programme with identifiable music. Some conventions have a very functional purpose. For example, it has become a convention in films to shoot a card game from a high camera angle so that the cards and players can more easily be seen. The functional purpose of other conventions has been lost or has become obscure. The handshake was once an indication that no weapon was being concealed. When we shake hands today, we no longer check for daggers but take the gesture as a symbol for friendliness.

To a greater or lesser degree, conventions will generate a coded meaning. As the term implies, a coded meaning is meaning that is not immediately apparent. The meaning may be thinly disguised, or quite obscure. The hidden meaning may be so insignificant that the search for it may hardly be worthwhile. Conversely some codes may be so important that they contain the real meaning. For example, if a news presenter reads a statement saying that the government promises to cut taxes, then at the end of the statement he/she looks at the audience and cynically raises one eyebrow, the verbal message is totally negated by the coded meaning in the facial expression.

When the newsreader raises an eyebrow after quoting a government statement, it is likely that almost all of the viewers will also react cynically to the statement, even though they may not be sure of the reason for their cynicism. Some have made a conscious interpretation of the code while others have received the communication subconsciously. In each case there is a common 'reading' of the code. That is, codes are dependent for their meanings upon a common cultural interpretation.

Over the past eighty years, hundreds of film conventions and codes have been developed. The conventions and codes interact with and support the fundamental conventions and codes associated with montage, to form the language of film. The language is most complex and like other complex languages, capable of subtlety, innuendo, varieties of interpretation and also great moments of satisfaction. Film language is different from the written language because it does not take years of conscious learning. Years of exposure, yes, but not daily study in the way that we learned to read and write.

If the language has been subconsciously learned over the years, why bother to make it

Though the audience may be primarily influenced by the newsreader's raised eyebrow, this code does not operate alone. There are many other coded messages being delivered as the presenter reads the news. The jacket and tie suggest respectability (and therefore credibility?), the hairstyle probably supports this image and the smooth reading style implies control and intelligence.

media. In order to do this, the complex language will be simplified. However, it is important that the simplified language is not used in a simplistic manner. The purpose of understanding the language of film is so that the 'reality' created in the film can be compared with the 'reality' of everyday experience. There is little value in detective games such as 'spot the symbol'.

Figure/ground

The codes of cinema can only work if the film goer knows of them in advance even though she/he may not be conscious of them. For example, a fade in a film denotes the passing of time. The cinema spectator may not have consciously learned this, but has been subjected to it so many times that it has

visible now? A conscious comprehension of the largely invisible language of film and television is crucial to your understanding of yourself and your relationship to society. Most of the information you receive about your society is second-hand, and most of this second-hand information is delivered by film and television.

Whether you are watching a news programme, a soap opera or an entertaining film, you are receiving a coded version of the real world. All programmes will indirectly affect you and your society. Obviously when you see yet another killing on television, you will not go out and shoot somebody, but the myths that are enacted will inform or reassure you about your behaviour patterns. If the medium's patterns are consistently racist or sexist, then the medium is not just reflecting existing values. It is reworking and reshaping the values, thereby giving them new life. These values affect you, the viewer, because you react to them and interact with them.

Consequently it is necessary to understand how the values are constructed in the two

From *The Man from Snowy River* (1982)

become a subconsciously shared language with the film maker.

Spectators do become consciously affected by other codes. For example, the utensils around a kitchen may depict a time or place or particular life style that is consciously recognised by the viewer. The adept film maker is able to manipulate the audience perception of the codes so that different elements of the narrative are emphasised.

For example, the articles in the background in the still from *The Man from Snowy River* (on the previous page) are suggesting that the action is occurring in a room that lacks some sophistication. The furnishings are not consciously analysed in detail by the spectator even though the film makers were quite meticulous about their placement. The spectators are probably more concerned with the dialogue between the man and the young girl. The dialogue is figured prominently, so is said to be *figure*. The items on the mantelpiece are in the background, or *ground*. In any sequence, some codes are *figure* and some are *ground*.

If in the course of the dialogue, the man said that something terrible was going to happen at five o'clock, audience attention would immediately switch to the clock on the mantelpiece. That is, for a short time, the clock becomes *figure* and the actors, *ground*. It is through manipulation of the codes such as this, that some of the meaning of the film is created. This is not much different from our own lives, when we are conscious of some things in our own environment, whilst other things go unnoticed until something draws our attention to them. The difference is that in film, the choice is not up to the individual spectator, but is made by the film maker. Consequently film makers are very powerful people because they have the ability to *create* a meaning, a reality that is shared by millions of people.

Exercise 5.A   Figure/ground

Combinations of codes are interplayed to develop meaning. It is useful to observe the codes that are ground and those that are figure, so there can be some understanding of the ways in which film meaning can be constructed. [*Special equipment: video deck and television or projector, feature film*]

1 Watch 10 minutes of the early part of a period drama, for example *Elephant Man, Chariots of Fire, Gandhi, Phar Lap*.

2 Take your attention away from the main characters, and concentrate upon the *ground* that is developed to create the scene and the atmosphere. Try to become aware of verbal and audio cues.

3 Individually, make a list of all of the ground components that you have identified.

4 Compare your list with others. Make a composite list. Discuss in particular, the *atmosphere* that has been created.

5 It is most likely that in the first 10 minutes of the film, there is a dramatic moment. Discuss as a group, what this dramatic moment is.

6 It is very likely that this dramatic moment is at least in part dependent upon a figure/ground reversal. Replay the section and discuss whether or not there has been a figure/ground reversal.

7 How effective do you think the film maker has been in grabbing the attention of the audience?

8 At this stage of the film, have any forces of good and evil been identified, that is, has the film maker established a point of view for you? How was the point of view established?

Exercise 5.B   Figure/ground

The interplay of figure and ground can create meaning and also heighten the drama in a scene.

1 Divide into groups, each group taking as a basic film set, the classroom in which you are working.

2 Select one of these plot outlines for your group.
  Note: It is not necessary to act out the sequence, just plan it.
  - It is late at night. The school is empty, except for two people alone in the classroom. They look scared. There have been rumours of strange occurrences late at night.
  - The classroom is a nuclear fallout shelter. The bomb exploded a day ago. Four people are alive in the shelter but there has been no contact with the outside world. Two people are checking the food supplies, two are playing cards in the background.
  - It is five minutes before the end of the day on the last day of the school year. Everyone is bored. The teacher's attention is upon two students in the front row. They are whispering about something.
  - The classroom is an unemployment office, with people queued waiting for an interview. An interviewer is talking to an interviewee.

3 Discuss the ways in which you will decorate the set for a scene in your film. Detail the props that you will use.

4 In each plot outline, the figure has been nominated and you have supplied some of the ground. Music and sound effects can also be ground. Detail the music and sound effects that are part of your scene.

5 Create something in your scene that turns ground into figure, thus heightening the drama, that is, make something happen. Detail this 'happening' outlining what elements of ground become important for the audience.

6 Compare your outlines with those of other groups, giving specific attention to the items and sounds that carried coded messages. Give extra attention to the figure/ground transitions.

The preceding exercises should have encouraged you by indicating that you already know something about the codes and conventions of film. However, greater awareness can be achieved if you have the ability to draw upon a detailed knowledge of the film codes. For this reason, a very structured, methodical approach follows.

However a final word before proceeding with an analysis of the codes as part of the language of film. Such an analysis will not spoil the enjoyment of film for you. You will not become so involved in code detection that you cease to be immersed in the film. In fact your enjoyment will be heightened because you will still become totally involved in the film's 'reality', but after it is over, will be in a position to appreciate the great skills that have been used to create the illusion for you. Nor will you necessarily become a cynic, detecting detrimental hidden values in all that you see. Instead you will be an enlightened cinema goer, equipped to condemn, appreciate or acclaim, as you see fit. You will not have to depend upon others for opinions.

The approach

Because, to a greater or lesser degree, all film conventions contain a coded message, from here on the term 'conventions and codes' will be abbreviated to 'codes'.

For convenience, the film codes have been divided into four sections:

- technical
- symbolic
- audio
- written

Technical codes

The technical codes are the codes of construction; that is, the devices that are used by the film maker to create the image. Camera angle and choice of lens for the camera are two examples. These choices affect the way in which the image is perceived.

Symbolic codes

The symbolic codes are the codes that draw meaning from the visual content on the screen. Each of the images photographed contains a literal and a symbolic meaning. For example, a slouch hat is an instrument for keeping the sun off one's head, but also has a coded message of 'Australiana'.

Audio codes

The audio codes refer to the interpretation of music, speech and sound effects in the film.

Written codes

The written codes embrace titles, captions and any written material used in the course of the film.

It is emphasised that this is a division of convenience, particularly between the technical and symbolic codes. For example, lighting on a film set could be treated as either technical or symbolic. The distinction is quite arbitrary. Again it is emphasised that the codes do not work in isolation. It is the interaction and intertwining of various combinations of film codes that creates the meaning or 'reality' of the feature film. In this way, the codes are rather like everyday speech. Words by themselves have limited meaning, but when organised into structures they become very powerful communication.

However, providing the limitations of commencing a study of the codes in isolation are recognised, it is still a very useful strategy in order to make some of the invisible elements of film language visible.

Conclusion

Film language, like other languages, has its conventions and codes that are shared by both the creators and receivers of the narrative. At worst, these codes are used in an extremely predictable manner that will provide very little audience satisfaction, therefore minimal box-office returns.

More imaginative film makers have the ability to manipulate the codes in a manner that will evoke positive responses from spectators. The spectator may emotively respond with laughter, anger, tears or horror. As long as some satisfaction is given, the film has a chance of making a profit. One important manipulation is to develop combinations of codes into an interplay of ground and figure.

The more successful a film maker is in manipulating the codes, the greater will be the illusion of reality that has been created. This effect provides greater spectator satisfaction, but also makes her/him particularly vulnerable to the point of view that is being presented as a supposed reality.

In order to engage in a deeper study of the language of film, it is appropriate to divide the codes into technical, symbolic, written and audio categories.

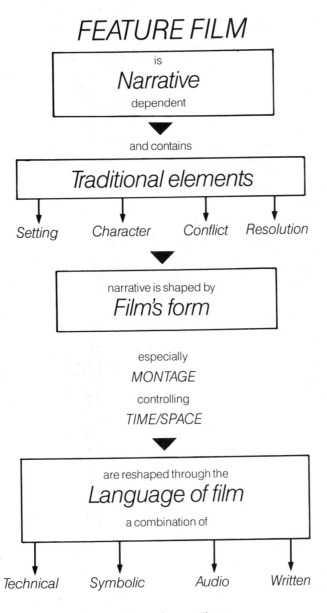

FEATURE FILM

is
Narrative
dependent

and contains

Traditional elements

Setting   Character   Conflict   Resolution

narrative is shaped by
Film's form

especially
MONTAGE
controlling
TIME/SPACE

are reshaped through the
Language of film
a combination of

Technical   Symbolic   Audio   Written

codes and conventions

Analysis and research

Library research

- Select from the library a film book that contains many photographs from many different films.

  Choose from the book a film that you have seen. Describe very briefly, your recollections of the film. (These recollections remain the *figure* in your memory.)

  Refer to the photographs in the book that are from the film that you selected. List the things that they highlight about the film (that is, the figure in the photographs). How do the two 'figures' compare?

  What, if anything, happens to figure/ground relationships when a feature film is frozen into a few still shots? Is the drama captured? What receives greater or less emphasis? Are stills an effective means of creating a narrative image?

- Refer back to the question that was asked at the end of chapter 1 — the question that required a comparison between a book and a film with the same title.

  After the introductory work that you have done on codes and figure/ground, what can

you add to the book/film debate that was not previously apparent?

Written response

- 'Films very quickly identify the conflict and establish a point of view about the conflict.' Discuss the validity of this statement by referring to the early minutes of a film that you have seen recently.

References

Umberto Eco, *A Theory of Semiotics* (Bloomington: Indiana Press, 1979).

John Fiske, *Introduction to Communication Studies* (London: Methuen, 1982).

Jurij Lotman, *Semiotics of Cinema* (Michigan: Ann Arbor, 1976).

Marshall McLuhan, *City as Classroom: Understanding Language and Media* (Ontario: Book Society of Canada, 1977).

Christian Metz, *Film Language: A Semiotics of the Cinema* (New York: Oxford University Press, 1974).

Chapter 6
Technical Codes

A problem posed

You have been commissioned to make a feature film that is to be set in the 1930s. It is a grim script, about alienation, about people's inability to draw close to each other, about poverty and general hard times. Such a sorry saga does not sound as if it is going to have customers racing for cinema seats, but your backer says that you have to make a profit, otherwise you will not get the chance to make another film. She/he makes your job even more difficult by saying that the film must seem to be 'real' — so a musical is out!

You have some important decisions to make at the pre-production stage.
- *What film stock will you use?*
- *What special skills will you require of your Director of Photography?*
- *What sort of lenses and shots will you use? Zooms? Wide angle shots?*
- *What special effects will you use to create a 1930s feeling?*

As a film comprises a series of still photographs, it is not surprising that many of the technical codes are derived from photography. The principal technical codes are:

> Framing
> — camera distance
> — lens choice
> — camera angle/movement
> Shot duration
> Film choice
> Lighting
> Special effects

Framing

Crucial to an understanding of the effect of the technical codes is an appreciation of the importance of framing. The framing of the image decides what the audience will see because the frame:
- decides the size and shape of the image
- delineates on- and off-screen space
- controls our vantage point by means of camera distance, lens choice, height and angle
- is mobile because the modern camera can move and so continually change its frame.

When we view the world, it is through a cone of vision that does not have clearly defined edges. In contrast, the screen frame is a defined, artificial boundary. One of the most important decisions for a film maker is not only a consideration of what appears within the frame, but also the positioning and relationship of objects in the frame. This will determine what is and what is not important.

Early film makers had to frame their subjects on a screen that had a very similar aspect ratio (length : breadth) to the still photographic frame of that time. It is not surprising therefore that the basic rules of photography (and before that, western European painting) were adopted for cinema.

In the beginning, film makers drew upon the traditions of live theatre and framing was dictated by live theatre conventions. For example, performers on a stage tend to enter from the wings of the stage because the area has little depth. Film makers quickly realised that variety could be added if the action began as a long shot then moved towards the camera into medium shot. The technique was particularly appropriate in Westerns where the subjects, such as stage coaches or horse riders, had an inherent mobility.

Stagecoach in the distance heads towards the camera.

Stagecoach now in mid-shot goes right of camera.

The effect upon the audience of staging the action in this manner was to suggest that the vista was larger than the physical screen size. The technique is still in common usage.

Split screen technique was another development that allowed the film maker to suggest a broader vista of action. The split screen could simultaneously show several different locations on the screen. The technique did not become very popular with feature film makers, perhaps because it quite clearly did not equate with the 'reality' that the spectator was used to seeing in everyday life. Television has rekindled interest in split screen technique and the reasons for this will be discussed later.

Split screen shows simultaneous and related actions on the screen, even though the events are separated geographically.

Bergman achieves a split screen *effect* (though it is not a split screen) by positioning the camera so that action can be viewed in two rooms at the same time. Still from *Face to Face* (1976)

A significant breakthrough in overcoming the limitations of screen size occurred with the development of cinemascope in the 1950s. The broader screen has allowed several elements of action to be incorporated into one shot so that the viewer, as in real life, appears to have a choice of focus points. Naturally the film maker will ensure that attention will be focused precisely as the film maker desires, but the broad screen does allow action supported by supplementary information. When used for maximum effect the cinemascope screen has allowed a greater sense of 'reality' to be experienced by the spectator because the panoramic view appears to give the spectator an approximation of a real life cone of vision.

When films that have been shot with a cinemascope lens appear on television, the framing becomes grossly distorted from the original because of the differences in aspect ratios of cinema screens and television screens. Cinemascope films that have been cropped for television can often be detected when the introductory titles are shown, if they have been superimposed over dramatic action. In order to fit the titles on to the screen, the image is projected without the cinemascope lens. The effect is that the titles will appear on the screen but the characters and sets will be elongated.

Once the titles are complete, the cinemascope lens is replaced, the sets and characters return to normal dimensions, but the image is severely cropped on each side. The image has been drastically 're-framed' for television and the result is aesthetically unpleasant for lovers of film. Heads that should be dominant on the screen appear in part on the television set, or may not appear at all. The picture composition balance that has been part of our culture for centuries has been upset. It is also likely that the coded messages associated with cinemascope screen size will change. Cinemascope allows a screen area of peripheral vision for the spectator, a life related effect that increases the illusion of reality. With this space, the film maker is able to

'Normal' and wide screen

allow the spectator to personally select the significant detail. That is, it is not as necessary to cut to close-up. Even the close-up when used can be more meaningful because it can be shown in relation to the

Cinemascope image from *The Parallax View* (1974). How would the meaning change if the image was cropped for television?

larger environment, rather than appear in isolation. When the image has been cropped for television consumption, none of these advantages remain. In the transfer, the sub-codes operating have undergone change, therefore it is likely that the effect upon the audience, and the meaning to the audience will also change.

Camera distance

Framing can give the audience the sense of being a long way from or close to the action.

Lens choice

The type of lens that is mounted on the front of the camera significantly affects the type of image seen on the screen. A wide angle lens (which allows for a wide angle of viewing) will distort size and shape.

The telephoto has much less breadth of vision. It is useful for street scenes because the camera can be placed some distance from the performer, thereby making other street users unaware of the camera (and consequently act in a more natural manner). Surprisingly, the telephoto may also be used to imply great distance, even though it does enlarge distant objects rather like a pair of binoculars.

A significant film innovation was the development of the zoom lens. The zoom allows the cameraman to vary the shot anywhere in the range from wide to telephoto without stopping the camera. The zoom may also be used to direct audience attention to detail within a general shot. The general shot is established, then there is a zoom in on the detail. Before the invention of the zoom, the cameraman would have established with a medium shot then cut to a close-up. However, this use of the zoom has become a cliché and many film directors prefer to use a crane, a dolly or tracks if they wish for this type of flowing or cinematic image. The zoom has greater use in television, particularly live television.

Some film directors have refused to use the zoom lens because it is not a natural eye

Medium shot (from *Splash*, 1984). The medium shot allows the audience to see people in the image more clearly. Gestures and body language are easily seen, and this helps character development.

Long shot (from *Breaker Morant*, 1980). In the extreme long shot the environment takes precedence. People will be barely visible but this shot offers the audience the opportunity to see the total environment — the landscape, the city etc. The characters' position in a setting is quite clear.

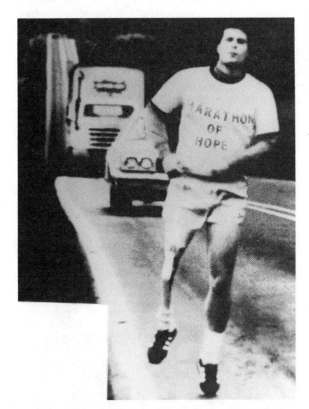

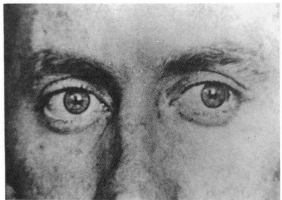

Big close-up (from *Face to Face*, 1976) — heightened drama

A telephoto shot looking directly down a road at a very distant oncoming vehicle creates the impression that although the vehicle is moving at regular speed, it is not getting any closer. (From *The Terry Fox Story*, 1983)

Close up (from *The Bounty*, 1984). The close-up is usually an emphasis shot in film — it can emphasise facial expression or drama such as a close-up of a hand reaching for a hidden gun.

In *Chinatown* (1974) director Polanski shot almost entirely with a wide angle lens so that the performers' elongated features looked more sinister in close-up.

movement — we cannot zoom in on an object with our eyes.

It is questionable whether directors can argue against the zoom on the basis that it is not a natural eye movement. Even at this early stage of analysis, it is probably becoming apparent that there is very little that is 'natural' about the images that appear on the screen. It is more important to consider what is appropriate, what works, rather than what is natural.

The zoom lens is probably the most spectacular development in lenses in recent years, but perhaps as significant is the progress that has been made in designing lenses for shooting low light situations. Stanley Kubrick's feature, *Barry Lyndon*, saw the combination of the newly developed lens and very light-sensitive film to shoot candle lit scenes without additional, artificial light sources. The effect was to heighten the sense of realism in the scenes. That is, highly sophisticated computer technology has been used in order to create this feeling of 'natural'. Yet another sophisticated sub-code of meaning has emerged.

Director Peter Bogdanovich, in the film version of *Paper Moon* (1973), refused to use a zoom lens on the set because the film was set in the 1930s and he wanted to give the audience a feeling of that era. He argued that black/white and static cameras were a feature of film making at that time, so the audience's sense of the 1930s would be enhanced if he reverted to those styles. Bogdanovich used the *absence* of the zoom as a coded meaning.

Grainy film — John Voigt in *Coming Home*. (See 'Film Choice', p. 81.)

- Why was a zoom used? What effect did it have?
- Why was a zoom used instead of a cut to a new camera distance?

Exercise 6.A   Lens choice

A *wide angle lens* generally distorts perspective. Close objects appear larger than life while distant objects appear smaller. They have extreme depth-of-field and are good for hand held work because they minimise shake.

A *telephoto lens* has extremely small depth-of-field so is useful for isolating objects from their background. These lenses amplify camera shake.

A *zoom lens* is a wide angle, normal and telephoto lens in one. It will bring the action closer but not change perspective. [*Special equipment: TV monitor, video recorder*]

1 Look at the photo of a class of students. If you were filming a sequence in this room suggest how you would choose a lens to create the following effects.
- isolate one boy from the others so as to focus audience attention on him.
- suggest that one student is about to do something dramatic — grab a knife?

- show the whole class as in the opening shot of a documentary.

2 What lens would you use for a hand held shot walking up the aisle as you focus on each student in turn? What affected your choice?

3 Watch 5 minutes of a television drama. Take careful note of the use of the zoom.

Camera movement

The most significant difference between still and moving images relates to the film maker's options regarding camera use. The still camera captures one image — a moment in time. The movie camera records a series of images and while this process is occurring, the film maker may choose to rotate the camera to change the information within the frame, or to have the camera physically moved while the action is being shot. Trade terms have been developed to describe these possibilities.

Camera movement affects on-screen and off-screen space by revealing new areas for the audience. The mobile camera has the ability to fasten the audience's attention on persons or objects by keeping them in the frame even when they are moving. The moving camera can redirect the audience's attention by moving away from a person or object on to a new image. Sometimes the mobile camera can create drama simply by moving through empty spaces. Consider how our expectations are raised when a camera pans around an empty room or tracks down a deserted street.

Camera movement also affects the audience's sense of time. A slow, drawn out tracking shot reflects real time and has the effect of slowing down the pace of the narrative. A fast track in to an object will increase its significance in the eyes of the audience simply because of the dramatic effect of the camera movement.

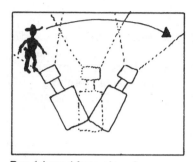

Pan (viewed from above) —
camera moves through a
horizontal plane.

Tilt — camera moves through a
vertical plane.

Track — camera (often on tracks)
moves with the action.

Camera mobility

Attempts to make cameras more
mobile are not new, though this
scene is re-created in *Phar Lap*.

A camera is mounted on the outside
of a car. This creates a greater
illusion of reality than a back
projection.

Tracks allow the camera to move
smoothly with the performer.

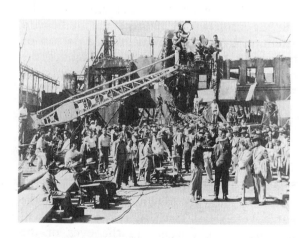

Large camera crane that can move horizontally,
vertically and dolly along its tracks

A dolly moves with the action.

Exercise 6.B   Camera movement

All camera movement will powerfully affect the image. It will affect the size and shape of the frame; the way the frame defines on-screen and off-screen space; the vantage point of the audience; the amount of information available in the frame. Also the moving camera will act as a surrogate for our eye and direct our attention. [*Special equipment: drawing materials*]

1 Look at the example of a scripted moving camera shot. This is a single shot.
   This mixture of pan and track is common in films. It is useful to show the relationship of the character to his/her surroundings and direct audience attention.

2 Draw a floor plan of your backyard or your bedroom or any other area you know well.

3 Consider the various positions you could place a camera that would through a combination of panning, tilting and tracking be able to cover a person entering the area, moving through it, stopping at a significant point and then exiting. Use arrows on your floor plan as a guide for camera movement.

4 Now translate this floor plan into a short storyboard that will show the changing dimensions of the frame. See example earlier.

5 Make notes on what you consider to be the effect upon an audience of slow pans and tracks, compared with a more static montage style of shooting.

6 Discuss your opinions with your group. On the basis of this discussion, make a group summary of why film makers may choose to include cinematic type shots early in their films.

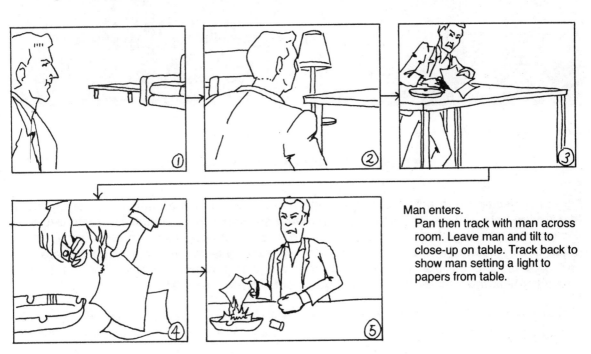

Man enters.
   Pan then track with man across room. Leave man and tilt to close-up on table. Track back to show man setting a light to papers from table.

Exercise 6.C   Closed and open frames

If the image in a frame seems to be complete, and the viewer is not encouraged to imagine a world beyond the frame, then the frame is said to be 'closed'. If the shot has been composed and within it there are strong reminders to the viewer that there is a world outside the frame, it is said to be 'open'. Open frames are created in many ways. Incidental animals, characters, vehicles that enter and leave the scene; sound effects coming from afar; incomplete images that show part of a car or part of a room, all 'open' the frame.

1 Examine the pictures from *Voyage of the Damned* and *The Devil's Playground* and suggest which are closed and which are open frames.

2 Identify the components that 'open' the frame.

3 Suggest some sounds that could be added to the film to open the frames even further.

4 Why would a film maker choose to close the frame? What is the coded message?

From *Voyage of the Damned* (1976)

From *The Devil's Playground* (1976)

Exercise 6.D   Depth within the frame

Film is projected on to a flat screen, but the film maker creates an illusion of depth within that frame. Sets and the performers' movements are carefully designed to create depth. In the process, the significant elements of the scene are emphasised. Three ways in which depth is suggested are through the use of foreground objects, with overlapping characters and objects, and through convergences that suggest perspective. The photograph from *Notorious* illustrates all three. [*Special equipment: film magazines*]

1 Find an example of a still from a film magazine that suggests a shot with great depth.

2 Identify the factors that create the depth.

3 To what extent do you think the scene has been constructed, or is the illusion accidental?

4 Using the picture that you have selected, suggest ways in which greater depth could be created through camera movement.

Ingrid Bergman and Cary Grant in *Notorious* (1946)

Camera angle

Camera angle refers to the position of the camera in relation to the subject. The 'standard' camera angle is eye-level or a fraction below eye-level to the performer. This allows the cinema spectator to view the performer from a 'human' level but still remain invisible to the performer. This invisibility is retained because the performers do not look at the camera. In the few feature films where the performer directly addresses the camera, the effect is unsettling to the audience. *Annie Hall* used this technique which is more akin to television convention.

Camera angles other than eye-level are the exception, but not rare. Because they are unusual, they need a clear purpose. High and low angles may be used to indicate a height differential between two performers or the different angles may allow for better framing of the subject. These are functional uses.

The camera angle can also contain coded meaning. A high camera angle can suggest that the subject is inferior or helpless.

Conversely, a low camera angle implies dominance, power or even cruelty. Extremely high camera angles, such as those used in helicopter, aeroplane or crane shots may also suggest a degree of remoteness from the subject. They inhibit close audience involvement with the action. These extremely high camera angles may also suggest surveillance of the subject — the god-like spectator who can observe from above.

Cameras mounted directly above the action were once a well used convention. For example, all of the action in a card game is best observed from directly above. The convention has lost popularity because the aim in 'Hollywood type' feature films is to disguise the cuts from one shot to another so that the audience attention is not distracted from the flow of action. The shot from directly above is so different that it can attract audience attention and affect the film's flow. That is, although all camera angles are artificial, this shot is not as 'natural' for the spectator eyewitness.

High camera angle (from *The Big Chill*, 1983). Right:
Low camera angle (from *Indiana Jones and the
Temple of Doom,* 1984)

Eye-level (from *Indiana Jones and the Temple of Doom,* 1984)

Exercise 6.E Camera angle

Camera angles can be used simply to give the best view of what is happening, to deceive, or to convey coded meaning.

Examine the pictures from *Voyage of the Damned* and *Safety Last,* then answer the questions.

1 The picture of the man hanging from the clock face is part of a very famous stunt in a silent film. The actor was never in any danger. There was no net and no special effects were used. How was it done?

2 What camera angle has been used for the shot of Orson Welles? What is the effect of this camera angle?

3 What camera angle has been used for the shot of the crowd? Why has this angle been used? What effect would have been created if a low angle shot had been used?

Harold Lloyd in *Safety Last* (1923)

Orson Welles in *Voyage of the Damned* (1976)

From *Voyage of the Damned*

Exercise 6.F Camera angle

Vladimar Nelsen in *Cinema as a Graphic Art* describes an interesting experiment. A film maker wanted to tell the story of a statue of a horse in the park suddenly rearing up and charging a passer-by. The entire film focuses first on the statue, then the eyes, then its bulk and finally the charge. The statue never moves — the whole effect is done with dramatic angles. [*Special equipment: drawing materials*]

1 Use your knowledge of the dramatic power of camera angles to storyboard this script outline.

2 Discuss your storyboard with others. Have you used similar angles to create the effect? What governed your choice of angles?

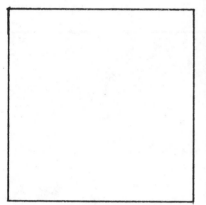

Two small, frightened boys slink through a graveyard at night.

The tombstones seem to loom up at them like mountains.

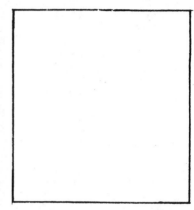

The trees in the twilight seem sinister and brooding.

A bird screeches and dives at the boys.

The boys' faces show their fear.

Shot duration

The duration of a shot affects the audience's sense of time in a film. The duration of the shot (how long it lasts) does not usually correspond with real time (how long the event lasts).

First, technical manipulations such as slow motion or fast motion will 'cheat' real time and prevent any simple equivalents between real and screen time. Secondly, a narrative film may span years in terms of its plot but can still only last a couple of hours on the screen. Earlier in the discussion of montage we examined how the joining of shot to shot affected screen time but the length of the actual shot is important too.

The long take

Early cinema tended to rely on shots of longer duration and as editing became more sophisticated, shorter takes replaced the long ones. However, there are many directors who favour the long take (some have takes lasting several minutes). A director may choose to present a scene in one long take or a series of short ones edited together. It is usual that a long take will incorporate camera movement to ensure the audience vantage points change and provide the shifts in viewpoint that editing might otherwise offer. The long take usually has a strong internal structure and logic, that is, it has a clearly definable beginning, middle and end.

Film choice

Film can be manufactured with various sensitivities to light. A film that is not very light sensitive is low speed or 'slow' film. It generally has the advantage of high quality image with very little grain (those sand-like specks that seem to 'swim' on the moving image.) Its disadvantage is that it cannot be used in low light conditions.

High speed or 'fast' film is more suitable for low light but is usually grainier (see p. 72). The technical limitation of grain has now come to be interpreted by the audience as suggesting seamy dingy scenes. Grain can be a nuisance if this effect is not required. Recent developments in film stock have allowed the high speed qualities to be retained while reducing the amount of visible grain. The 1983 film *Blue Thunder* took advantage of these developments to feature quite clear night shots of Los Angeles that did not 'swim' with grain.

Available light (from *Sixteen Candles*, 1984). Right: Outdoor shots are often lit with giant 'brute' lights and reflectors — as is this scene in *Phar Lap*.

The film maker also has a choice of colour or black/white monochrome film. Before the 1960s the cost of making a colour feature was considerably higher than black/white film costs. Costs could be reduced by sacrificing some colour 'realism' and this method was used frequently in Westerns that tended to be larger than 'real' life anyway. Musicals, which were also 'larger than life', were also suitable subjects for the cheaper colour techniques. Only the biggest budgeted films such as *Gone with the Wind* were able to afford the best quality colour technology. In the 1960s there were technological advances in film stock manufacture that allowed colour film to be competitive with monochrome. Since that time, most feature films have been shot in colour. The reasons are economic rather than artistic preference. Monochrome films do not get the box-office returns that are enjoyed by colour films. For that reason, very few modern films are shot in monochrome. In recent years *Elephant Man* and *Raging Bull* have been the exceptions. In the case of *Elephant Man*, this was an artistic choice. The film maker wanted to give the impression of the starkness of the nineteenth century industrial landscape. Monochrome film was a technical device that allowed this impression to be coded for spectator consumption. The use of monochrome film in *Raging Bull* was in part the outcome of an artistic choice (much of the action was set in the 1950s when monochrome film was more common). It was also in part a protest by the director, Scorcese, against the poor archival quality of modern colour film stock. By the 1980s directors were becoming aware that films only ten years old were almost unviewable because of colour loss from both prints and negatives. Since the protests, some improvements have been made.

Monochrome film also suffers economically when cinema returns have been exhausted and the film is due for television release. Colour programmes have far greater appeal to the television viewer therefore the programmers are reluctant to pay top prices for mono-

chrome films. In fact there is a reluctance to purchase them at any price!

The market popularity of colour film has placed some restrictions upon film makers who wish to create sombre or nostalgic atmospheres. Alternatives to monochrome film are sepia, brown or yellow filters. Fast, grainy film used in conjunction with low light levels could also suggest gloom.

From *Butch Cassidy and the Sundance Kid* (1969). How would sepia tone add to the symbolic effect?

Lighting

Lighting is one of the most significant technical sub-codes of the cinema and one that illustrates the often arbitrary division between the technical and the symbolic codes.

It is the Director of Photography's (D.O.P.) principal task in any feature film to attend to the lighting detail. This task goes well beyond the functional requirements of ensuring that the available or generated light matches the requirements of the film stock being used.

The D.O.P. makes decisions about the intensity of light to be used in a scene. A brightly lit scene will allow camera operators to shoot with a large depth-of-field. The effect of this could be to create a stark scene, a scene reminiscent of pre-World War time films or a scene that does not focus attention through the use of selective focus. The context of the rest of the film will determine which

possibility the large depth-of-field lighting technique serves.

Shallow depth-of-field (that is, only a small segment of information is in focus) will tend to isolate information. If the depth-of-field is shallow, the choice of which information is sharply focused will determine where the spectator will focus attention. Audience attention can be changed if focus is changed or 'pulled' within the one shot. A film maker who pulls focus frequently risks making the audience conscious of the technique. Once a technique consciously intrudes, there is the danger that the spellbinding or *diegetic* effect of the film is lessened. People go to cinemas in order to become immersed in the drama before them, not to be dazzled by camera trickery. All of the techniques must be used

Shallow depth-of-field adds emphasis to the facial expressions (from *Indiana Jones and the Temple of Doom*, 1984)

Large depth-of-field emphasises the spectacle provided by the setting (from *Indiana Jones and the Temple of Doom*)

Pulling focus — what is the coded meaning in this shot?

Interpretation of the film is affected by the placement and quality of lights as well as by the volume of light. The Director of Photography has available a wide array of gels, reflectors, soft and harsh lights to achieve the required effects. These illustrations give some indication of the importance of the lighting code.

to weave a great spell, not merely as a boast of the film maker's prowess.

It is important to remember that none of the codes act in isolation. No scene will be totally dependent upon lighting for its effect. Some striking effects can be obtained when lighting codes interact with the framing codes. For example, an image photographed away from the horizontal and vertical norms of everyday life will be sufficiently disorienting to symbolise a highly dramatic moment. If 'flat' lighting is also used a sense of coldness or starkness will be added to the dramatic impact.

The tilted camera adds drama to the image (from *The Wild Ones*, 1954).

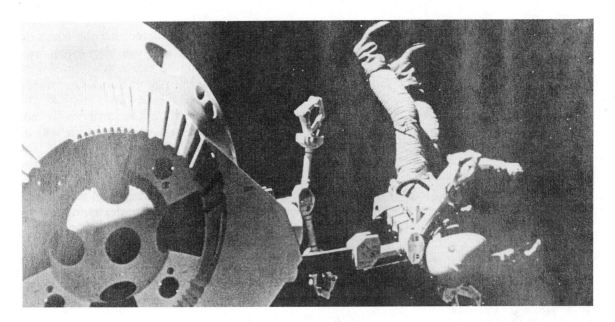

Special effects

The use of special effects is so common in modern film making that it no longer is very 'special'.

There are many techniques that are used in order to create an illusion of reality. Some work simply because the audience accepts a convention. For example, a split screen showing more than one action (two distant people conversing on the telephone) is a highly artificial convention that is acceptable to the audience.

Some techniques work because the limitations of the film medium have been exploited so that the restrictions become advantages. Film models are used to take advantage of the two-dimensional nature of the screen, of the rigid frame line that constrains the spectators' insight into the events, and the fact that people can only determine size if they are given other objects as reference points. Shots of models can therefore be cut into live action and enhance rather that reduce the illusion of reality. Other techniques, such as animation, fast and slow motion, front and back projections all exploit the peculiarities of film as a medium of expression.

Models used in *2001. A Space Odyssey*. Below: Special effects in *Alice in Wonderland* (1972)

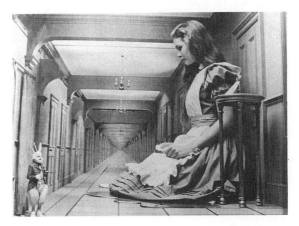

Conclusion

Film has a language all of its own. This language allows the meaning to be created for the spectator. A significant part of the language is derived from the ways in which the film is constructed, that is, the technical aspects of film making. Even though the audience may not be aware of the technical processes that the film maker is using, the effect of their use will be to advance the sense of 'reality' that the film goer experiences when sitting in a cinema watching the images upon the screen. Because the language is affecting the viewer in a largely subconscious manner, the term 'code' is used to describe the components of this language. The film's technical codes are:

Framing
— camera distance
— lens choice
— camera angle/movement
Shot duration
Film choice
Lighting
Special effects

It should be remembered that the codes do not operate in isolation from each other, nor in isolation from the other components of the film language. An examination of the technical sub-codes is a first step in the interpretation of film. The analysis is not carried out so that the magic of film will be destroyed. Even with understanding, the magic of film will remain while you, the spectator, sit in a darkened cinema. Once the experience is complete, there is more satisfaction to be gained from understanding how the magic spell was cast.

In diagrammatic form, the steps that have been taken towards film interpretation to this stage are:

FEATURE FILM

is
Narrative
dependent

▼

and contains

Traditional elements

Setting   Character   Conflict   Resolution

▼

narrative is shaped by
Film's form

especially
MONTAGE
controlling
TIME/SPACE

▼

are reshaped through the
Language of film
a combination of

Technical

codes and conventions

Analysis and research

Library research

There has not been time in this chapter to mention many of the special effects that create the illusion of cinema reality.

Research in your library and find out the meaning and purpose of these special effects:

- matte
- wipes
- dissolves
- front and back projections
- miniaturisation
- animation

Give examples of films and scenes within these films where some of the above have been used with very good effect.

From *Easy Rider* (1969)

Written response

View either a 20-minute educational documentary or a feature film. During your viewing concentrate on *one* of these technical codes: framing or camera movement. After you have completed your viewing write a short discussion paper on the film maker's manipulation of this code. Consider the effects created, the degree of novelty of its use, problems in its use and your opinion of the film maker's skill. Comment upon the way in which the technical codes create meaning in each of the stills from *Easy Rider* and *Once Upon a Time in America*.

What is the effect of a long take? What are the dangers a director must guard against if a decision is made to include several long takes in a sequence? Describe a scene from a film (real or imaginary) that would be most appropriate for long takes.

Practical exercise

[*Special equipment: Portapak*] Comic strips are very cinematic in their construction.

1 Look at the comic strip on the next page and treat it as a film storyboard. Using the comic

From *Once Upon a Time in America* (1984)

frames as a guide to the type of shot you need prepare a shot list. Remember the strip is a guide only and you may add or change frames as necessary.

2 This is an activity to increase your understanding of the technical codes so consider carefully your use of zooms, camera movement, pans, tilts etc.

3 Shoot the exercise on video.

4 Replay and discuss:
- effectiveness of your use of the codes
- changes necessary
- pace of your film.

References

Charles Barr, 'Cinemascope: Before and After' in Gerald Mast and Keith Cohen (eds) *Film Theory and Criticism*: *Introductory Readings*, 2nd edn (New York: Oxford University Press, 1979).

Sergei Eisenstein, *The Film Sense* (London: Faber and Faber, 1968).

Christian Metz, 'Current Problems in Film Theory', in *Screen*, vol. 14., no 2, Spring/Summer 1973, (London: Society of Education in Film and Television, 1973).

Chapter 7
Symbolic Codes

A problem posed

You are the producer/director of a feature film. You have read the script and like it. Your next task is to hire actors, costume designers, set designers, lighting technicians and so on. To each of these people you will need to be able to offer some conceptualisation of the film, that is, how you think it should look.

The script you have chosen is an adventure/romance set in the present. There is a lot of action in which your lead actor must figure as the hero. Your female lead provides the romantic interest.

Whom will you choose as your lead actors? How do you decide who will best fit the part? Are there any advantages in known stars? What might be the disadvantages? What suggestions will you make to your designers about sets, lighting props and costume?

The symbolic codes refer to the parts of film language that are contained within the image as opposed to the codes associated with the construction of the image. In the still photograph, the important symbolic sub-codes are objects, setting, body language, clothing and colour. As moving film is comprised of sequences of still images, it is not surprising that each of these sub-codes has relevance to moving images.

In fictional film construction, the symbolic codes of objects, setting and clothing are sufficiently important to warrant specialised personnel. The professions of set and costume design are highly regarded in the film industry. Under the supervision of the director, they manipulate the sets, clothes or artifacts to generate the desired meaning. They may choose 'real' locations, real properties or street usable clothes, but they structure the 'reality' to suit the director's needs.

The film specialists who operate at this aspect of film making are able to achieve their effects because the objects, clothes and settings have symbolic associations for the spectator as well as functional purposes. The properties person knows that both the cigarette and cigar give the user similar oral gratification. The properties person, however, is not concerned with the actor's gratification. The choice of whether the actor should have a cigarette or a cigar (or neither) is determined by the symbolic associations that are desired. The cigar will be preferred if power or authority or maturity is to be suggested. The cigarette has a different range of coded meanings, including nervousness, manliness, female liberation (although changes in society are making the latter associations less likely). It is the spectator's culture that injects the symbolic associations into the film set. The same codes are used outside the cinema, so it is a common language system that the film makers and spectators are sharing. It is this common language that allows communication to occur.

> Symbolic code
> — performance
> — setting
> — costume/appearance
> — lighting

Exercise 7.A Objects and costumes

Object and costume are used symbolically to inform the audience about a character's personality, motivations and life style. They also indicate time and place (setting) of the action.
[*Special equipment: drawing materials*]

1 Look at the still from the Australian film *My Brilliant Career* (1979). It shows the central character, Sybylla Melvyn, sitting alone in her bedroom. Carefully analyse the objects, costume and elements of set design that inform you about the character.

Objects and clothing indicating:

character's personality	character's social class	time period

2 Summarise your findings; that is, write one or two lines about the character's personality, social class and the setting of the action.

3 Use your knowledge of the way objects, clothing and set can be used symbolically to design the set above for the modern day. You must transform Sybylla Melvyn into a modern young lady by choosing appropriate symbolic clothing and objects whilst *still keeping your information about her personality the same.*

4 Swap your set design with another person and ask them to describe the sort of person they think Sybylla Melvyn is now. Have you achieved your aim? Can your character be read in terms of its symbols?

Performance

When people are photographed with a still camera the body language symbolic codes become important. Body language includes stance, facial expression, gesture, hair styling and clothing (because clothing is an artificial expressive skin). Each of these elements contains meaning for the viewer of the still photograph. In some cases it is possible to subscribe a common, universal meaning to the component of body language. A grin is one example of universally shared meaning, although readers will be aware that the surrounding context within a photograph can affect the interpretation of the grin. A photograph of a grinning villain about to pounce upon an unsuspecting victim is subject to different interpretation to an image of a grinning child with a dog.

Interpretation of most body language will be subject to cultural variation. An image of someone giving a 'thumbs up' signal will be variously interpreted as greeting, victory or aggression, depending upon the culture. These cultural variations in interpretation would appear to pose a problem for the screen actor who is performing for an international audience. No doubt there are some cultural variations in audience interpretation, however the penetration of 'Hollywood style' feature films into all cultures has been so deep that it has had its own 'universalising' effect.

Body language is an inadequate term to describe this set of symbolic codes once movement is injected and actors are employed to create the film's fiction. The term 'performance' is more appropriate to describe the use of the multiple codes associated with people.

Analysis of performance is further complicated because an actor's performance cannot be isolated from the meaningful sequence of events that is being created by the performance. That is, the meaningful sequence of events, or narrative is inextricably intertwined with performance. Even the cliché of a car chase in a film is dependent upon the actors' performances in developing credible characters. For a chase to succeed in producing an audience response, the spectator needs to understand and identify with some of the characters taking part.

Stars

A star is a performer who is so well known to the mass audience that she/he attracts a large following outside of the context of a particular performance. When film was the most significant of all of the mass media, the film star was so central to the industry that a profit could be guaranteed merely by the appearance of the star in the film, irrespective of the quality of the film or of the performance. This meant that stories were created to suit particular stars. The spectator came to the cinema with preconceptions about both the screen and private life of the star. It was expected that the new vehicle for the star's performance was in harmony with the established image. It would be unthinkable for a gentleman star to be seen slapping a woman, but it may be within the parameters of action for a 'tough guy' star.

Today, only a few of the sex symbol stars carry on this old tradition. Clint Eastwood,

Steve McQueen and Ali MacGraw in *The Getaway* (1972)

Burt Reynolds or Bo Derek films are patterned to suit the image. Other stars, such as Meryl Streep or Dustin Hoffman, are far less typecast.

Charisma — stars

An important component of the Hollywood feature film industry has been the elevation of performers into 'stars'. These stars embody a great deal more than an ability to perform in front of a movie camera. In fact, many of the great name stars have begun as rather indifferent actors, although most improve as a result of repeated opportunities. Stars are well known to the potential audience before they see the film. People are aware of their screen image, some aspects of their private lives and of the type or role that the star will consistently play. That is, the star is 'typed' in a similar manner to the characters used in an Eisenstein film. From the spectator's point of view, this typage permits an informed choice to be made about which film to attend. As far as the producer is concerned star typage allows a more predictable commercial package to be delivered, thereby providing a greater likelihood of profit in a high risk industry.

There is another parallel between the typage of the Hollywood star system and the Eisenstein creations in the ways in which

Doris Day — the girl next door

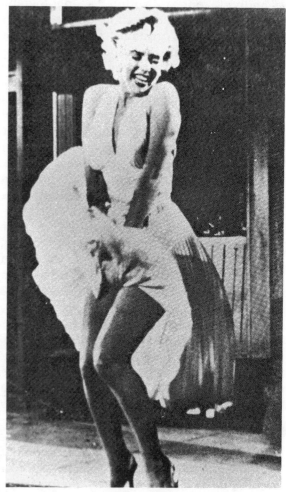

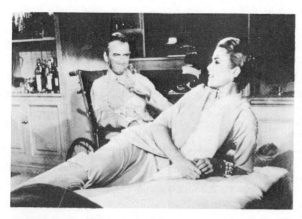

Grace Kelly — the aristocratic type

Marilyn Monroe — the temptress

92   *Real Images*

each anchor meaning. Eisenstein's characters were instantly recognisable as poor but honest, evil etc. Modern Hollywood stars may not be quite so transparent (though often they are) but they do personify specific cultural norms. Past audiences knew that Ingrid Bergman would always play 'the lady', that Marilyn Monroe would be 'the temptress', that Grace Kelly would be the 'aristocratic type' and Doris Day would be the working girl next door. Even if the performers wished to shift from these stereotypical roles, the studios that created, managed and marketed the films insisted that they conform to the profit making package. The familiarity of the film goer with the stereotypical role seemed to create a bond between performer and spectator that became a small part of the spectator's life. Fostering this allegiance of spectator to particular stars reduced the risk associated with film production. A film that featured a top star would guarantee high box-office returns. Under this system, films were developed as vehicles for a particular star. Instead of the performance contributing towards the development and resolution of the narrative, the narrative existed only to provide novelty in a well known and much anticipated performance.

Marketing has always been an important part of the star image. In fact Hollywood's first accredited 'star', Florence Lawrence, achieved her stature largely through a marketing exercise. In 1910 the film producer Carl Laemmle circulated a rumour that Miss Lawrence was dead, then publicly denounced his own rumour. He then staged a grand entry of his leading lady at a train station and thousands of fans attended in order to witness the fact that Miss Lawrence was still alive. The marketing exercise proved so successful that the other studios soon developed their own publicity ploys. However, although the creation of Hollywood's first star was a manufactured event, there had to be general public interest in the people behind the screen images if the ploy was to succeed. It is likely therefore that the

John Wayne — Has he been replaced by Sylvester Stallone?

performers who became stars had elements within their performance (and probably within themselves) that had broad cultural appeal. They were successful because their marketers were giving the audience some of its own cultural aspirations. If the performer could not do this, then it was better to discard him/her and find a performer who did strike a note of close audience identification. Again, some caution should be exercised about drawing direct links between the performer and the cultural values. For example, John Wayne was a star whose stature continued to grow over several decades. Most of his performances were as cowboys or war heroes, but this does not mean that his audiences in the 1930s or 1970s wanted to be either. What is more likely, is that they came from a culture that approved of the values that were consistent in a Wayne performance. For example, he was a man of action rather than words; he overcame great obstacles to save the town or family or to punish those who went outside the community's norms; he frequently demonstrated that the individual was more powerful than the 'system'; he invariably established the superiority of his culture over alien cultures.

Wayne was the visual evidence for the audience that their culture was not only effective, but also victorious. All of the elements within the performance code reinforced this cultural message — the face that looked as if it was chipped from rock; the casual way he wore costume; the roll of his walk; the raw, almost flat delivery of lines. He was the tough, no-nonsense American. The scripts that he was given had to be consistent with this image or the charisma would have been in jeopardy. Wayne could not have played the role of a pacifist, a homosexual or a college professor. He could not because the studios would not have allowed it, the audiences would not have wanted it and he would have objected because the roles would have been contrary to his own personality — for there had to be a lot of the 'real' Wayne in the performances for them to be so consistent. John Wayne's screen performances therefore were a form of explanation of the values that his society esteemed. These performances that were repeated throughout the many films that he made were part of the modern mythology, for a myth is an explanation of a society's values. They were societal myths just as surely as the ancient myths of King Arthur or Robin Hood were explanations of the esteemed values of bygone cultures.

For a star system to survive there has to be a mass audience that frequently looks towards entertainment for satisfaction. Before television became a popular mass medium a film would depend to a large degree upon the stars who performed. In those days a visit to the cinema was at least a weekly occurrence for most people in western countries. Significant subsidiary industries developed around the star system. Columns about the stars sold newspapers, public appearances by the stars were major events and film fan magazines were a part of everyday life.

These industries both assisted in the marketing of the stars and in satisfying the curiosity of the audiences. When television became commonplace in western homes, the cinemas lost their regular mass audience. Films could no longer be effective vehicles for the cultural explanations because the people only visited the cinema as a special occasion. There was a greater inclination to attend a cinema in order to see something different rather than to enjoy the comforting familiarity of a well known star giving his/her well known performance. The latter need was now satisfied in the lounge room in front of the television set. Some stars survived because they had been created in the pre-television days (John Wayne was the elder statesman of this ageing group). Attempts were also made to create new stars, but the old marketing techniques did not work because the star image had transferred to the more current mass media, namely television and the popular-music industry. Stars would still be named when a narrative image for a film was established, but the inclusion of any star could no longer guarantee a box-office success. It is true that some stars are paid amounts in excess of one million dollars for a single performance but they remain a risky investment for the film makers. There are many modern examples of million dollar performers acting in box-office flops.

Charisma therefore is no longer such an important element in determining film performance as it once was. The result has been that there is a reduced tendency towards typage. It has been possible for actors to emerge who pride themselves on their ability to play a variety of roles. Dustin Hoffman, for example, has performed as lover, prison escapee, female impersonator, journalist and comedian.

He is recognisable as Hoffman in all of the roles, but does not as readily embody an established set of cultural values. Instead he, and the other film actors who have emerged in the post-television era, have been able to refine the performance codes that are particularly suited to the large screen. Perhaps they

Hoffman in *Tootsie* (1983)

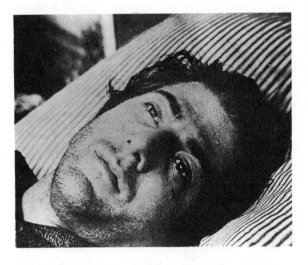

Hoffman in *Midnight Cowboy* (1969)

can best be summarised as the codes with economy; that is, economy of gesture, of language, of expression. The spectator in front of a large screen will easily recognise a slightly raised eyebrow, the gradual clasping

of a hand or the undertones in a quietly delivered line. An actor who performs with the exaggeration that is often necessary in a large live theatre will create a comic effect, which is fine so long as the film is a slapstick comedy.

The performer is able to suggest rather than emphasise because the film maker is able to use other codes in order to draw attention to the significant elements of the performance. Control over what appears in the frame and how it appears are the principal weapons. The use of close-up and selective depth-of-field are two examples. This interaction of performance with the various technical codes provides further illustration of the interaction of the various codes that is necessary to create an entertaining film. The film is a constructed message with many interacting components.

Central characters

Even though the central characters of films are no longer charismatic stars who bring to the film a well known set of behaviours, there is still an element of predictability about the central characters once the plot unfolds. The spectator may not be able to name the actor or actress, but once the narrative is under way, a set of expectations is generally met. In an adventure film, the hero or super-hero will conquer the wrongdoers; in a romance, the lovers will share some bliss (either as a finale or in preparation for a tearjerking conclusion). This predictability suggests that we do have some shared values about what is appropriate or desirable behaviour. It seems, therefore, that although there is no consistent value system attached to a particular star (because there is no 'star' in the traditional sense of the term), there are certainly values associated with the interaction of character with narrative. (This interaction of performance/character/narrative will be discussed in greater detail in the chapters about television.)

Some degree of central character predictability is essential if the film is to be marketable because the predictability implies that there is conformity to what is regarded as 'correct' behaviour in the society. We expect transgression to be punished and conformity to be rewarded. A film that is quite out of step with the society's expectations would not satisfy a large audience and would therefore lose a lot of money. Hence novelty in a central character has to be limited to the superficial, for example, the novel costume or occupation. Central characters may be very likeable (because they are explanations of what we applaud in our own society) but it is difficult for them to be highly interesting.

Performance: conclusion

Performance is perhaps the most significant of the symbolic codes, for it is largely through performance that characters are built in order to drive the film narrative forward.

Characters are not the same as real people, but the performers must make them as convincing as real people. They are different from the people whom we meet in everyday life because the conflicts that they face (both internal and external) are more sharply defined. So too are the resolutions to these conflicts. They are also different because they comprise a selection of character traits rather than a complete series of combinations.

Performers are able to relate to the audience because they draw from the same pool of cultural experiences as the audience. Their features, mannerisms, gestures, costume, stance, style of line delivery all contain cultural suggestions and therefore assist the spectators in identifying and empathising. In the heyday of the Hollywood feature film industry, this phenomenon was commercially exploited by the large studios, through the development of the star system. The star system was a method of marketing some particularly appealing cultural traits in order to ensure the success of a highly valuable commodity — the feature film.

Performers who play support roles, either as supporting or blocking characters, are often able to develop more interesting characters than those who play lead or central roles. This is because they do not have to develop the same degree of positive audience response. Both supporting and blocking characters may contain positive and negative cultural elements in their performance.

However, whether performers are developing lead or supporting characters, they use a common set of symbols in order to communicate meaning to their audience. These symbols comprise a common language system between performer and audience.

Setting

One important difference between feature films made for the cinema and dramas that have been made for television, is the size of the screen upon which the dramas will be viewed. Feature films have traditionally been shot with a large viewing screen in mind (though some modern feature films are designed specifically for a television audience and this has meant some changes in the techniques that are used). The large screen allows the performers to be placed in a setting that provides a considerable amount of detail. These detailed settings provide a context for the performers and therefore affect the interpretation of the performance. For example, a male actor, performing in an effeminate manner in the setting of a city bar, could foreshadow a serious drama. The same performance in a Western setting would evoke mirth from the audience. This is an extreme illustration, used to establish that the symbolically coded meaning of the setting interacts with and further defines the coded meaning of the performance.

Feature films may have location or studio settings, or a combination of both. Sets that have been created in a studio are more controllable than location sets. Vagaries of weather do not have to be considered, lighting is more easily structured, bulky cameras are more easily positioned, sound recording is not ruined by extraneous noise and transport/accommodation costs are minimised. Because of the greater possibility for control, the Hollywood studios of the pre-and early post-Second World War era tended to shoot on constructed studio sets. The method ensured that a high output of films could be delivered on schedule. The disadvantage of the constructed studio set is that it may not look as 'real' as a location setting, and it may not be as spectacular. Westerns of the pre- and post-war era were able to combine the spectacular scenery of middle-west America with the artificially constructed Western towns, whilst interior shots were still created in indoor studios. This combination helped make the Western one of the distinctive Hollywood film genres.

Since television has become a part of everyday life, film has been forced to specialise in what it can do best. People now go to the cinema as a special occasion rather than as part of a weekly ritual, as it was in the pre-television days. A special occasion demands special entertainment and the spectacular settings that are shown on the large screen can help provide this. Many film makers will accept the hazards of location film shooting in order to achieve more spectacular or more 'realistic' films. Others will work on sound stages and with a variety of special effects create a spectacular, often surreal world. The science fiction and comic strip film such as the Superman and Star Wars series are examples of these spectacular creations.

It may appear to be a contradiction of earlier statements to suggest that audiences are interested in exotic settings; those that they are not able to experience in the course of their everyday lives. It is an apparent contradiction because it has been stated that the audience must be able to readily identify with what is being viewed on the screen. The contradiction is more apparent than real because the exotic settings provide an

Spectacular sets were developed for Hollywood musicals without much concern about their 'reality', but in other genres, reality was an important concern. (From *The Gay Divorcee*, 1934)

Models create 'reality'. (From *Fire over England*, 1937)

important means of injecting novelty into the familiar. The spectators have not visited outer space or stepped through the seamy corridors that house inner city crime, but they can be excited by the opportunity to make these film journeys. The second-hand experience that is being provided can generate audience fear, shock, awe or excitement and still leave the spectators secure in the knowledge that they are not really moving from the cinema seat. Many writers about film have described this as a *voyeuristic* experience, meaning that the cinema spectator is experiencing the screen events as an invisible observer. The greater the element of realism that can be injected into even the most fantastic scenes, the greater will be the sense of spectator voyeuristic participation.

Some sets draw such favourable audience reaction that it becomes sound economics to use similar settings for future films. The Western is one example of a genre that has been established around well known settings.

These Western frontier settings have largely been replaced by the space frontier, but the way in which they context the performances remains similar. The frontier is the arena in which the characters must perform and they perform as they do largely because of the constraints of frontier existence. The performers must be self-reliant, they must eventually control their environment and they must bring with them their set of cultural values so that the hostile environment is made more comfortable. True deed will be as well rewarded as true love. Alien creatures who threaten the culture will be exterminated, whilst those with more culturally endearing qualities will be accommodated. This is the audience's cultural expectation and it is quite predictable. Into the predictability must be injected some novelty otherwise the potential spectator will find another way to spend the sizeable cost of a cinema ticket. The exotic settings certainly provide a great deal of the novelty.

From The Outlaw Josey Wales (1976)

From *Star Treck III: The Search for Spock* (1983)

Setting: conclusion

Fictional Hollywood type films depend a great deal upon 'realism' for their appeal. Sets are important in the construction of the realism, for even the sets of the fantasy films have to be convincing. The spectators must believe that they are stepping into the past, or on to a far flung planet. When 'real' or location settings are used, a strong suggestion of the exotic is still retained because the sleazy, the gawdy or the remote are preferred to the familiarity of middle class suburbia.

Finally, and most importantly, sets create a context in many ways. They become an arena for the type of action and conflict that can occur. The arenas of the general hospital and the American mid-west determine quite different types of conflicts and performances. The sets do not only limit performance, but also support the actor by providing many of the motives for the action and the mood of a performance. A sophisticated restaurant set will encourage intimate dialogue between a few performers whereas a cafeteria scene will be more conducive towards cross-dialogue between numbers of actors. It thus becomes apparent that we do have expectations about the sorts of actions that sets can engender. That is, we even inject our values into the arenas for the performances. For this reason, the sets comprise a very important part of the symbolic codes.

Other symbolic codes

At the beginning of this chapter, it was stated that the meaning conveyed in a feature film through use of costumes and objects was sufficiently important to warrant specialised personnel. The property person, the wardrobe people and the art director will all work with the director and will have many conferences about the style, size and arrangements of sets. Even location sets will be altered or properties added so that the desired meaning is injected. These frequent consultations make it quite apparent that the symbolic messages are being conveyed through interaction of the various elements.

All of the symbolic codes that have been examined so far are further controlled by the lighting that is chosen for the film. Lighting was discussed as part of the technical codes, an arbitrary decision that was made because

Clothing as symbols — Bette Davis in *Now, Voyager (1942):* (1) Matronly (2) Fashionable
(3) Sophisticated

lighting is a technical construction. However, it is impossible to divorce light from colour, which is considered as a symbolic code. Though the colours may already exist in the properties and costume and are therefore capable of carrying their own symbolic meaning, the director of photography can light a set so that particular colours are emphasised, distorted or even changed. The back cover of this book provides one example of a set that has been lit and in the process, particular colours have been emphasised.

Symbolic codes: conclusion

The symbolic codes refer to the parts of film language that are contained within the image that appears upon the screen. They are more dependent upon our culture for their meaning than are the technical elements of construction.

It is apparent that the symbolic codes do not operate in isolation from each other. Although in the large scale business of film making the tasks of managing the properties, costumes, sets and lighting have been divided into various departments, the activities are co-ordinated so that the meaning that the

spectator gains from each is consistent. The spectator may not be aware that the meaning is being received from an object on a mantelpiece, a frayed collar or a dimly lit corner, but such elements are not there by chance and they do affect the interpretation of events that are projected onto the screen.

Similarly, the technical and symbolic codes do not generate meaning in isolation. The illustration of lighting/colour working at both the technical and symbolic level is one example.

If the various codes, or hidden meanings, interact as they do, then the purpose of identifying each of the small components could be questioned. It is done so that the sources of meaning can be identified. By doing this, the informed spectator is still able to enjoy the fiction that has been created, but also will have the ability to reflect upon the experience and transfer some of the messages that have been received, from the subconscious to the conscious level.

Interpretation of the technical and the symbolic codes of film have now been considered. In diagrammatic form, the steps that have been taken towards film interpretation to this stage are:

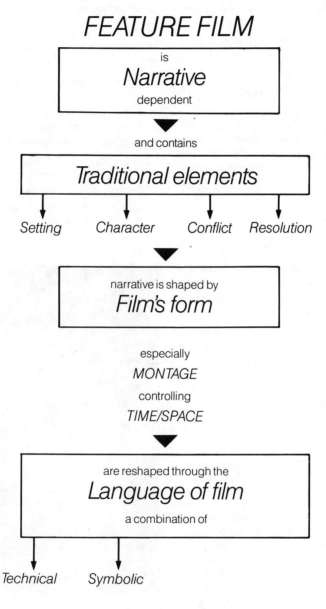

FEATURE FILM

is
Narrative
dependent

and contains

Traditional elements

Setting   Character   Conflict   Resolution

narrative is shaped by
Film's form

especially
MONTAGE
controlling
TIME/SPACE

are reshaped through the
Language of film
a combination of

Technical   Symbolic

codes and conventions

Analysis and research

Choose a star you know well and whose performances you enjoy. Find out as much as you can about this person from magazines and books. At the same time find out about the types of characters played by this star.

Is there a consistency in the parts played by this star?

Is there any relationship between the real life personality of the star and the characters he/she portrays? What aspects of his/her personality do the fan magazines and news articles concentrate upon? Can you suggest any reasons why these traits are given emphasis?

Discussion

1 View a feature film or at least 20 minutes of a feature film. Concentrate on one character throughout.
   - How is the character's personality conveyed to the audience?
   - Read Richard Dyer's list of character signs (p. 31). Describe the relative importance of each in constructing the character.

2 It has been argued that the range of roles which a film actor can play successfully is usually very much narrower than that of a stage actor.

'On the stage the great actor is often unrecognizable from part to part: there is no finding the Laurence Olivier of Oedipus in the Laurence Olivier of Justice Shollow ... On the screen the complete transformation of personality is rare; in the American cinema so rare as to be almost non-existent.' (Delys Powell in the *Sunday Times*, 31 March 1946.)

This statement was made nearly forty years ago. Do you think it is still true today? What examples can you offer to refute this observation?

Written response

Read the article about Rob Lowe, a young actor, which appeared in *Cosmopolitan*, February 1984, then answer the questions below:
- What image of the actor emerges? Support your answer by reference to the article.
- This actor has played the romantic lead in every film in which he has acted. What is the relationship between his acting history and the image of him developed in the article?
- Rob Lowe is depicted as valuing certain things in life. What things does the article suggest he values? Do you think this is a full picture of the man?

Actor Rob Lowe

□ "People are always making such a big deal about the way I look," Rob Lowe says, just a little wearily. But the 19-year-old American actor, star of the comedy *Class* and the forthcoming *The Hotel New Hampshire*, is resigned to the fact. He has to be. (When you're tall and sinewy, with chiselled features and glinting blue eyes, why fight it?)

Rob's had acting fever since the age of 10, when he was living in Ohio, and saw a touring company of the musical *Oliver*. At 12 he moved to Los Angeles, and from then on has pursued his craft relentlessly — making rounds of film and TV auditions, doing guest shots, and keeping abreast of casting trends.

"Right now, the trend is toward 'boy next door'," he comments, "— people you wouldn't look at twice if they walked down the street" — parts in which Rob Lowe is not usually cast. And because he's on a hot streak, with three movies shot virtually back-to-back, he's wary of anything that might get in his way. "I like this success," he says with a smile.

Still, there's more to Rob's life than just career — girls, for one thing. "I've *always* been in love with them," he says. During

than the other partner would like."

The two are still together, however. "We've gone back to the dating stage, the point at which we started," says Rob "— hard to do, but it was the only way. The choice was either retreat or break up, and I didn't want that at all. I really enjoy Melissa, so she's still my girlfriend — maybe not the only one, but a girlfriend for sure." (Nastassia has apparently gone on to other sets.)

Another attachment Rob formed on the *Hotel* set was with Jodie Foster, who plays his sister, Franny, in the film. He insists, however, that this bond wasn't romantic; the two are just "really good buddies".

"Jodie and I are a lot alike," he says. "We both went through our parents' divorces and started acting at a young age; we're easy-going, very 'California', and have the same attitude towards acting — go in, do the work, head home, and have some fun. So we just mentally clicked."

This emotional link obviously helped the two interpret what is definitely the film's trickiest sub-plot: The growing obsession of brother and sister, culminating in a fully realised incestuous act. Playing the scene didn't seem to

ROB LOWE
More Than Just A Hunk

Look out, Warren Beatty! Here comes a dazzling young rival who's gorgeous, talented and aims to produce movies as well as perform in them. By Laurie Werner.

his teens, he had a string of romances. The longest-running one is still current — a two-year relationship with actress Melissa Gilbert of *Little House On The Prairie* fame whom he met in LA.

"Immediately after that, we started dating," Rob explains, "and it got pretty serious. In this business, though, it's hard to keep a relationship going. I was away on location for a few months at a time; she was working long days on her *Little House* series. And we were meeting other people all the time . . ."

One of the people he met was Nastassia Kinski, the young German actress cast opposite Rob in *The Hotel New Hampshire*. He plays John Berry, sensitive son in an unorthodox family; she the mysterious Austrian he befriends.

"Sometimes a role can just take you over," he says. "I didn't expect anything to happen with Nastassia, but often these things are out of your hands."

Meanwhile, Melissa was keeping tabs on her boyfriend from the set in Los Angeles. Wasn't she the least bit jealous? "Well . . ." Rob searches for words. "Sometimes a relationship is more open

throw Rob and Jodie who knew instinctively how it should be performed.

"The two simply love each other very, very much and unfortunately are fated to be brother and sister," Rob explains. "Incest is pretty bizarre, of course, but John and Franny do survive . . . fall in love with other people, progress."

For Rob, survival means hoping this interview doesn't get him into more trouble with Melissa. He also hopes that in his late 20s or early 30s he'll marry and have two or three children — a boy first: "I want the other kids to have an older brother, so they can lean on him, the way my three brothers do on me," he explains.

Now, on this foggy morning, Rob checks himself in the mirror to see if his standard outfit — white T-shirt, black jeans, black leather boots — looks presentable for the business meeting he has later in town; he's optioning a script with an eye to becoming a producer as well as an actor. His role model is another "not just a pretty face" who proved that you can be taken seriously and succeed young in Hollywood: If Warren Beatty did it, he thinks, so can Rob Lowe. ▣

61

Practical exercise

Here is an extract from the novel *Rumble Fish* by S. E. Hinton. Read the extract and list some of the character traits of Rusty James and Steve.

I ran into Steve a couple of days ago. He was real surprised to see me. We hadn't seen each other for a long time.

I was sitting on the beach and he come up to me and said, "Rusty-James?"

I said, "Yeah?" because I didn't recognize him right off. My memory's screwed up some.

"It's me," he said. "It's Steve Hays."

Then I remembered and got up, brushing sand off. "Hey, yeah."

"What are you doing here?" he kept saying, looking at me like he couldn't believe it.

"I live here," I said. "What are you doin' here?"

"I'm on vacation. I'm going to college here."

"Yeah?" I said. "What you goin' to college for?"

"I'm going to teach when I get out. High school, probably. I can't believe it! I never thought I'd see you again. And here of all places!"

I figured I had as much chance of being here as he did, even if we were a long way from where we'd seen each other last. People get excited over the weirdest things. I wondered why I wasn't glad to see him.

"You're goin' to be a teacher, huh?" I said. It figured. He was always reading and stuff.

"What do you do here?" he asked.

"Nothin'. Bum around," I answered. Bumming around is a real popular profession here. You could paint, write, barkeep, or bum around. I tried barkeeping once and didn't much like it.

"Lord, Rusty-James," he said. "How long has it been now?"

I thought for a minute and said, "Five or six years." Math ain't never been my strong point.

"How did you get here?" He just couldn't seem to get over it.

"Me and a friend of mine, Alex, a guy I met in the reformatory, we just started knockin' around after we got out. We been here awhile."

"No kidding?" Steve hadn't changed much. He looked about the same, except for the moustache that made him look like a little kid going to a Halloween party. But a lot of people are growing moustaches these days. I never went in for them myself.

"How long were you in for?" he asked. "I never found out. We moved, you know, right after . . ."

"Five years," I said. I can't remember much about it. Like I said, my memory's screwed up some. If somebody says something to remind me, I can remember things. But if I'm left alone I don't seem to be able to. Sometimes Alex'll say something that brings back the reformatory, but mostly he don't. He don't like remembering it either.

"They put me in solitary once," I said, because Steve seemed to be waiting for something.

He looked at me strangely and said, "Oh? I'm sorry."

He was staring at a scar that runs down my side. It looks like a raised white line. It don't get tan, either.

"I got that in a knife fight," I told him. "A long time ago."

"I know, I was there."

"Yeah," I said, "you were."

For a second I remembered the fight. It was like seeing a movie of it. Steve glanced away for a second. I could tell he was trying not to look for the other scars. They're not real noticeable, but they're not that hard to see either, if you know where to look.

"Hey," he said, too sudden, like he was trying to change the subject. "I want you to meet my girl friend. She won't believe it. I haven't seen you since we were thirteen? Fourteen? I don't know though" — he gave me a look that was half kidding.

1 a From your group, choose the most appropriate actors to play these parts. Acting ability is not the prime consideration. Take into account dialogue delivery, mannerisms and physical characteristics.

b You now have the raw material for a film drama based on this extract. You need to develop the characters through the use of appropriate symbols. Consider clothing, hairstyle, make-up (scars? tattoos?), dialogue delivery, body language.

c As this is a condensed extract, the beach setting may not be appropriate. You need to develop a setting that will quickly develop further understandings about the characters. Decide upon an alternative setting that is practical and loaded with meaning. (Pool room? Back alley?)

d Decide upon the additional properties that you will need. Some properties may be part of the set. Others may be used by the performers.

e Are there any 'atmosphere characters' who are seen but not heard? Add these into your planning.

f Is there any appropriate music that could add to the atmosphere that you have been trying to create?

2 Allocate tasks to various members of your group. Make sure you have a script for everyone.

3 Shoot your film.

4 Review your efforts and discuss the effects that you have achieved.

5 Show your film to others and as a result of their responses, discuss whether you have effectively manipulated the symbolic codes. What response will you give to those in your audience who say that your film is different from the book?

References

Richard Bare, *The Film Director: A Practical Guide to Motion Picture and Television Techniques*, ch.3, (New York: Macmillan, 1971).

David Bordwell and Kristin Thompson, *Film Art: An Introduction* (Massachusetts: Addison-Wesley, 1980).

David Cook, *A History of Narrative Film* (New York: Norton & Co., 1981).

Richard Dyer, *Stars* (London: British Film Institute, 1979).

Charles Eidsvik, *Cineliteracy: Film Among the Arts*, ch 6, (New York: Random House, 1978).

Desmond Morris, *Gestures: Their Origins and Distribution* (London: Triad, 1979).

David Thompson, *America in the Dark: The Impact of Hollywood Films on American Culture* (New York: William Morrow, 1977).

Chapter 8

Audio Codes

A problem posed

You have been commissioned to make a low budget costume drama about the Australian goldfields in the 1850s.

Location shooting will be limited because of costs, so you have to centre most of your action around a tent that has been constructed in a wooded area.

Through the use of music and sound effects, you need to create an illusion that the tent is located on the goldfields, not far from the road into the fields and not far from the commercial activity. What sort of sounds and music will you add? What measures will you take to ensure that you do not overdo the effects that you create?

The components of the technical, written and symbolic film codes have their equivalents in the still photograph. It is true that some modifications have been necessary in order to analyse an image that moves, so attention has to be given to montage and performance, but many of the photographic codes remain quite consistent. The audio codes, however, add a dimension to cinema that is not present in still photographs.

It is an important premise in this book that the inventors, developers and present feature film makers have all sought to develop the most accurate representation of a reality that is possible. There are film makers who deliberately choose an abstract, *avant garde*, film making style but they operate outside the mainstream because the films do not appeal to mass audiences. Even films that create a fantasy world go to great lengths to make the audience believe in the fantasy. The spectator suspends disbelief and accepts the fantasy as the reality. Scores of artificial devices have been created by the film maker in order to create and sustain the illusion of reality. The various audio codes that can be used add to the film maker's weaponry. The film maker can use music, sound effects or dialogue in order to generate a greater sense of reality. Television employs additional sub-codes of

laugh or applause tracks but these are unusual in feature films.

```
Audio code
— music
— sfx
— dialogue
```

Music

Films were never silent. Before synchronised dialogue revolutionised film in the late 1920s, feature films were screened with some form of musical accompaniment. The smaller cinemas had a pianist who watched both screen and printed music and played the appropriate score. Some of the larger city cinemas boasted orchestras that were able to give a heightened sense of drama to the screen events. It is probably from these traditions that we have inherited the convention of film music. Certainly the emotive value of music has been known to civilisation for thousands of years, so there is some logic in using this quite artificial device to generate the appropriate emotions in the spectator.

One use of film music is to allow the musical score to imitate or reinforce what is being shown on the screen. Thus a moment of great tension or drama would be accompanied with very heavy 'melodramatic' music. Similarly a love scene will be backgrounded by violins playing something soft and sentimental. The intention in using this sort of music is to inflate the impact of the screen image but often the effect is the reverse. Music that simply repeats what is already visible on the screen can be quite redundant or *pleonastic*. The spectator is overloaded and can become quite conscious of the film music. The spectator's desired state of mind is not realised because the musical cliché has made the spectator too conscious of one of the operating codes. Once a code has been broken, it ceases to be effective!

A better use of music is to develop a musical score that will *interact* rather than imitate. In this more subtle film making, only the most significant moments will be intensified by an original musical score and clichéd scores will be avoided. More importantly, in the course of the film, the music will add elements that are not consistently apparent in the visuals. For example, a selection of songs from a particular era or location may remind the audience of place or time without having to consistently do so through the visuals. The film *Merry Christmas Mr Lawrence* attempted to portray situations that arose from a clash of Japanese and European values. The theme was reinforced through a musical score that contained suggestions of both western and eastern music. The music *interacted* with the events on the screen rather than imitated the events.

It is not possible to draw a clear line between pleonastic and interactive film music. Indeed some interactive film music, such as that in *2001, A Space Odyssey*, was so effective that it was seized upon by many others whenever they wished to suggest grandeur. Through repetition in advertisements, television spoofs and in some serious dramas, the music became a cliché and its impact was lost. The terms interactive and pleonastic are therefore terms of degree and they are also partly subjective.

It can be seen that the use of music in films is one interesting example of the film maker's art in creating a 'reality' in a highly artificial manner. The spectator needs to become mentally and emotionally involved if he/she is to enter the 'reality' of the film. The use of music is one way in which the emotional impact of the film can be heightened. However, heavy-handed use, or pleonastic music may have the reverse effect. In addition to strengthening the emotional impact, music can also inform. A familiar song may advise that it is a particular time of the year (what sort of songs would signal Christmas?) or a particular era (name a song to indicate 1970s). The use of music as information depends upon a shared spectator cultural experience. Our personal reactions to 'Jingle Bells' may vary a little, but culturally, it has a common meaning.

Sound effects

Many of the sounds of everyday life are not consciously detected. At this moment you are surrounded by a sound environment that has gone unnoticed. Only the breaks in the regular noises have consciously registered. Try for two minutes to create a classroom without any sound at all and listen to all of the sounds that are filtering in from outside. When you list the sounds that you hear and compare your list with others, the list is quite impressive! For a short time, you have elevated the sounds from the subconscious to the conscious level.

A world without the sorts of sounds that you have just experienced would 'sound' strange. For this reason, sound recordists on film locations record *ambient* sound tracks. That is, the sorts of surrounding noises that you heard when you sat and listened are recorded for later use. Each location will have its own unique sound environment, so the process needs to be repeated for each location.

When the film is shown, the audience will not be conscious of the ambient sound, but it will be affecting them subconsciously.

In addition to, and sometimes instead of, ambient sound, the film maker will create particular sound effects. Just as in everyday life, some of these will register at the conscious level, whilst others will be absorbed subconsciously. Either way, the effects carry meaning and are an important part of the language of film.

Convenient labels for this mixture of consciously and subconsciously perceived sounds in the environment are *justified* and *atmospheric*. Most, but not all, atmospheric sounds operate close to the subconscious level. If the spectator chooses, the sounds can be brought to the conscious level, but mostly it is the visuals and dialogue that will occupy spectator attention.

Atmospheric sound effects can create a large part of the environment for the performers. For example, two performers may be seated in a car (perhaps on a sound stage) and a whole range of street noises (car horns blaring, buses accelerating, police sirens wailing) are created on the sound track to place the performers in a busy city. In the film *Elephant Man*, a fairground was created by the use of sound. The audience could hear, but not see, the wild animals roaring, the musical roundabouts, the stall attendants who enticed the fairground visitors to try their luck. Similarly in *Gallipoli*, the Australian soldiers walk through a bazaar that is largely heard rather than seen. Traders haggling, dishes clashing, snake charmers playing, horses shuffling, dogs barking are some of the atmospheric sound effects that have been created. Atmospheric sound effects are able to inject a greater sense of reality into a film and also save a lot of money and time. It would cost many thousands to build an authentic looking nineteenth century fairground or an Egyptian bazaar. For the camera to dwell on these settings may also be unnecessary in the story's development, therefore telling the story through the use of atmospheric sound is more appropriate.

Fred Astaire and Ginger Rogers in *Top Hat* (1935). The Hollywood musical is the film genre that reverses the relationship between the visuals and the music. Instead of affecting the audience almost subconsciously, the musical score is the central focus of the film. For this reason, high quality sound is achieved by pre-recording the singing. A suggestion of 'reality' is then achieved by the method of playback synchronisation, which requires the actors to mime the words in front of the camera. In some of the classical Hollywood musicals, the actor's singing voice was actually replaced by one regarded as more appropriate.

Justified sounds are those sounds that have some visual justification. For example, we see and hear a gun being fired, we see and hear a vase smashing on the ground. Sometimes these sounds are recorded at the time of the action (synchronised sound). On other occasions the justified sound is artificially created (as when a fist hits a jaw). Justified sounds tend to operate at the conscious level. The audience expects to hear the sounds and would be jolted if they did not occur. A film director may play upon this audience expectation if an exceptional effect is required. For example, in a dream sequence there may be no sound to accompany splashing water or there may be car crashes without any noise.

Early sound films used quite primitive technology and this limited the collection of appropriate sounds for later use. As a substitute for this 'wild' sound, artificial sound effects were created. Over the years many of the artificial sounds have been 'naturalised' by the spectators to the extent that if the real sound was now substituted, it would seem unnatural and therefore distracting to the audience. The sounds of fists hitting jaws in a bar-room brawl is one example of a quite unnatural sound being accepted as normal.

Present sound effects tracks usually comprise a mixture of off-the-shelf recordings and collected wild tracks. The development of audio tape technology has permitted more

Justified sound effect from *Breaker Morant* (1980)

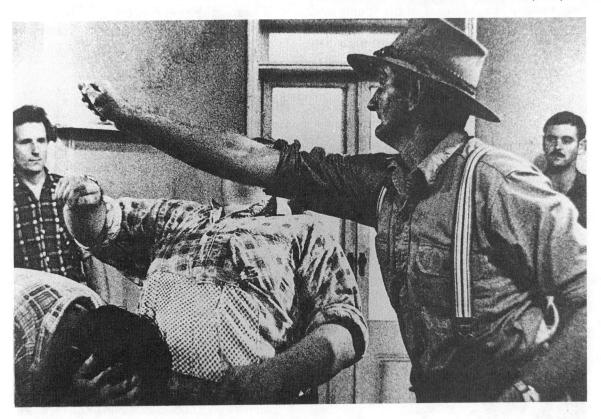

A fist blow on a face is an artificially created sound that bears only a slight resemblance to the actual sound. Now it is quite 'naturalised'. (From *Sunday Too Far Away*, 1975)

efficient collection of sounds and more complicated mixing of the required sounds. It is now possible to have over twenty different sound tracks being mixed into one final track for audience consumption. These tracks could include music, synchronised dialogue, ambience tracks and special effects. Such control affords the film maker a great deal of power over the reactions of the cinema spectator because a great proportion of the created sound environment is being absorbed subconsciously. Various meanings are being provided without the spectator being aware of it. The effect of the well constructed sound track will be increased if the film is viewed in a modern indoor cinema where there is likely to be a sophisticated sound reproduction system. If the sound track is being heard through an external speaker at a drive-in theatre or through the speaker in a television set, many of the subtleties of the sound track will be lost.

The naturalisation process mentioned previously means that the viewing audience tends to take sound for granted and dismiss its function in the creation of the narrative. Attention to the types of sound used in a film and their function in the total film will give you a greater understanding of the narrative. When considering the function of sound in a film ask yourself the following questions:

- What sounds can be identified — music, sound effects, speech? Is the sound track dense, that is many sounds mixed together, or thin with only a few sounds? What can be noticed about the qualities of the sound — its loudness, pitch and timbre?
- Is the sound rhythmic and is the rhythm in accordance with the rhythm of the visuals? What is the effect of the rhythm?
- Where is the sound coming from? Is it coming from within the story or from without? How does this affect the space we perceive?
- When is the sound occurring? Is it being used to foreshadow events by coming in earlier than the visuals or is it a memory device by coming later?

Exercise 8.A Atmosphere

A film's setting is constructed by the sound track as well as through visuals. The sound track can suggest a life occurring beyond the frame. In addition to these audio cues about a larger world, the sound track also promotes an atmosphere.

1 Examine the still from *Zelig* (1983) and identify what incidental things could be happening outside the frame.
2 Make a list of the sounds that you would associate with these.
3 Suggest a piece of modern music that would be appropriate and would add pace to the film.
4 Suggest a piece of music that would be quite pleonastic in this scene.
5 What justified sound effects would need to be added to the sound track?
6 Compare your conclusions with those of others.
7 Discuss as a group, the ways in which the mood that has been created could be changed.

Dialogue

Synchronised sound was first used in Hollywood feature films in the late 1920s. Almost overnight, audiences turned away from the 'silents' and flocked to experience the added 'reality' afforded by synchronised sound.

The preferred form of dialogue in feature films is synchronised. 'Voice over' in which a narration is given by someone who is not seen on the screen is rarely used in feature films. It is more common in news film that was made for cinemas and in modern film or television advertisements. On some occasions, a voice over was used when a film commenced with a dramatic moment, then the central character narrated over events leading up to that time. The technique of starting films at the end then recounting events is no longer popular, although *Phar Lap* used this ploy. However, *Phar Lap* did not use a voice over during the recount of the events that preceded Phar Lap's death.

Synchronised dialogue is the form of speech that allows the audience to identify the speaker at the time of delivery of the lines. Most of the lines are perfectly synchronised, so that the spectator sees the lips move and the words match perfectly. Once the speakers have been established, it is possible to have some lines

Use of off-screen dialogue is another manipulation of the audio codes. (From *Sunday Too Far Away*, 1975)

delivered by a performer who is not seen on screen. This modification to the technique is made during the editing stages of the film.

Early synchronised dialogue was quite *theatrical* in its presentation, that is, performers delivered their lines as though they were on a theatre stage acting for a live audience. It was not surprising that the actors adopted the live theatre tradition of delivering the dramatic facts quite explicitly in what sounded like a well prepared speech. When theatrical dialogue was and is used, action virtually ceases so that the audience can concentrate upon each word. Early sound films did not have very sophisticated microphones. Actors had to speak directly to microphones that were strategically 'planted' on the set. These technical limitations also encouraged the development of theatrical dialogue.

As the equipment became more sophisticated, film makers were able to be more flexible in its use. Actors were not pinned to one spot for their line delivery. The astute film makers also recognised that the large screen and the use of close-up allowed a lot of statements to be made visually. The stories did not have to be heavily dependent on words. Sometimes it was more important how the lines were delivered rather than what was said. This *mood dialogue* is not as precise and does not address any fundamental issue. It is expressive and reveals a lot more than the words say. Two of the screen's legendary actors, James Dean and Marlon Brando, carried this form of delivery to an extreme. Many of the audience (particularly those outside the United States) were only able to pick up the occasional word as they mumbled through their lines, yet the manner of delivery was sufficiently expressive to make them screen idols.

The theatrical dialogue of old and the mood dialogue in which the style of delivery contains all of the meaning, are the extremes. Both occur in modern cinema, but only infrequently at the extreme level. Theatrical dialogue may be used to mark the death of a great person. For example, in *Robin and*

Marian, an ageing Robin Hood is shown to be dying in the presence of Maid Marian. The death of a legendary character warrants the use of theatrical dialogue in Marian's farewell speech to Robin Hood. Marian's speech is low key and almost whispered in a way that would not be possible on a live theatre stage, but it is still recognisable as a speech. Other special moments that may warrant the use of theatrical dialogue are the achievement of some highly sought prize or goal or when the speaker is in a situation where a formal speech is appropriate. A police lieutenant addressing patrol men would be one such occasion.

James Dean is no longer alive to deliver his mumbled mood dialogue and Marlon Brando's speech seems to have become clearer as he has aged, but mood dialogue has not disappeared. Some modern films with examples of mood dialogue are *M.A.S.H.* (the movie) and *The Deer Hunter*. The characters in the operating theatre in *M.A.S.H.* continually conduct cross-conversations as they perform their operations. Their instructions to the nurses are confused by conversations about their recreational activities. The effect is to give a sense of bustle and chaos to the proceedings — which is what film maker Robert Altman intended. *The Deer Hunter* features a wedding scene which contains quite inconsequential dialogue. Characters order and buy beers, ask each other for dances amid the general confusion of music and other talk. It is the atmosphere of the wedding that is important, not the dialogue that is being delivered.

Most modern cinema dialogue lies somewhere between the extremes that have been outlined. The words are important, so need to be heard, yet a great deal of the meaning is delivered to the audience by the manner as well as the content of the delivery. Cinema dialogue, like mood dialogue, is more related to everyday speech, but it is not everyday speech. It is more economic in its choice of words and more coherent than the words we use to each other.

Two shot (from *Winter of Our Dreams*, 1981)

The large screen makes it possible to supplement dialogue with other codes; it is understandable yet seems to be 'real', and finally, it suits the method by which the speech is recorded by film makers. The latter requires some explanation.

With film, sound is recorded separately from the visuals. A tape recorder records the sound and the visuals are photographed on film. It is common practice to record a whole scene, then follow up by shooting close-ups. When sound film developed, the 'Hollywood two shot' developed along with it. The two actors were shown in discussion, then cuts were made from one actor to the other. The audience was able to accept that they were still talking.

Cinema dialogue, that compromise between theatrical and mood dialogue, evolved partly because it suited this style of film cutting, and partly because it has elements of precision and everyday reality.

In summary:

Audio code
— music
— sfx
— dialogue

Exercise 8.B Theatrical and cinematic dialogue

Cinema dialogue has a different delivery form from dialogue that is delivered in a live theatre. Cinema dialogue is sometimes used to generate a mood rather than give information. [*Special equipment: Audio or video tape recorders, preferably a sample extract of mood dialogue*]

Read the typewritten extract from a film script. It is a scene where various people are meeting for the first time.

1 Assign parts to members of your group.

2 Rehearse then read the script as a theatrical piece of dialogue — that is, the meaning of each word is important, therefore each line must be read clearly so that it is understood.

3 Record your efforts, preferably on video tape, but alternatively on to audio cassette recorders.

4 Now consider what it would be like if a large, informal group of people did come across each other for the first time. Re-examine the script and consider the possibility for overlapping comments. That is, the *mood* of friendliness is the important meaning that you

are trying to create. The meaning in the words is not significant. Rehearse again, concentrating upon this mood of warmth, friendliness amidst confusion.

5 Record your attempt to create this mood dialogue.

6 Replay both of your efforts and discuss the ways in which different meanings have been created.

7 If either is available, view the wedding scene in *The Deer Hunter* or the introductory scene in *M.A.S.H.* (the movie). Compare your efforts with those of the professionals.

8 If neither of these films is available, conduct your own search for examples of mood dialogue in films. Make a similar comparison.

SCRIPT

H. Eye:	Captain Hawk-Eye Pearce. [Hawk-Eye whistles]
H. Eye:	Are you leaving?
Lieutenant:	Yes I am.
Col. Blake:	Captain Hawk-Eye Pearce.
H. Eye:	Well good afternoon Lieutenant Dish. [He puts out his hand to shake]
Lieutenant:	Good afternoon Captain.
Col. Blake:	Captain Hawk-Eye Pearce. I have a twix about you. It seems that you stole a jeep over at headquarters.
H. Eye:	No, no, no sir. No I didn't steal a jeep. No it's right outside, right there.
Col. Blake:	Oh so it is. Capt. Forrest don't you know that when you report to your new duty station you go to your commanding officer with a copy of your orders?
Capt. Forrest:	Uh Capt. Pearce is it. Capt. Pearce and me have been boozing all day and we're . . .
Col. Blake:	Good, good you've been working close to the front. We have our slack periods here but when the action starts you'll get more work in twelve hours than the rest . . .

H. Eye:	How many nurses do we have on the base sir?
Col. Blake:	17.
H. Eye:	How many nurses will there be in my...
Col. Blake:	4. Now a brilliant surgeon...
H. Eye:	How many young girls come in?
Col. Blake:	A dozen a month.
H. Eye:	Good cause I can use them...
Col. Blake:	Yes I think it could be arranged.
H. Eye:	... and the blonde.
Col. Blake:	Oh Father Mulcody. I'd like you to meet Capt. Pearce our new surgeon. This is our Catholic chaplain and here's Capt. Forrest.
Fr Mulcody:	Ego Red.
H. Eye:	Ego Red.
Col. Blake:	Capt. Woldowsky. Our dental assistant.
Capt. Woldowsky:	Better known as painless pull...painless pull. I'm the dentist here. Duke? Welcome.
Voice off:	I don't doubt it. I'll be passing through.
Capt. Forrest:	Hi. Thank you.
H. Eye	Glad to meet you.
Voice off:	It's very funny. I'll be passing through.
Fr Mulcody:	If you have any problems my tent is right over. I'm saying if you boys have any...
Col. Blake:	Radar.
Radar:	Gentlemen. I'm Corporal O'Reilly. They call me Radar. You'll be staying in Major Burns' tent. I'll take your things over there now. Don't worry about the jeep, I'll change the numbers.
Col. Blake:	Take your gear and oh change the numbers on that jeep.

Conclusion

Modern feature films have quite complex sound tracks that are a mixture of dialogue, music and sound effects. Each of the three audio codes has the potential to be used with great subtlety so that meaning is generated both consciously and subconsciously. When music is used, the meaning that is injected is quite clearly derived from our culture. We associate different types of music with different feelings and events. Music from other cultures sounds strange to our ears.

Although dialogue and sound effects seem to be more a part of 'reality' than music, these too are carefully manipulated so that the desired meaning is created. Many of the conventions that have emerged are quite artific-

ial, but because they have been used so often (that is, they are convention) the spectator accepts them as being 'natural'. This process of naturalisation makes the cinema experience of the spectator more pleasurable because it allows her/him to become immersed in the 'reality' of the film. The pleasure is not reduced if the spectator is educated in these audio subterfuges. The educated spectator is able to enjoy, but also able to reflect upon the meanings that have been created. The meanings then become like other people's opinions. They can be assessed and rejected or accepted depending upon their perceived worth.

In diagrammatic form, the steps that have been taken towards understanding film to this stage are:

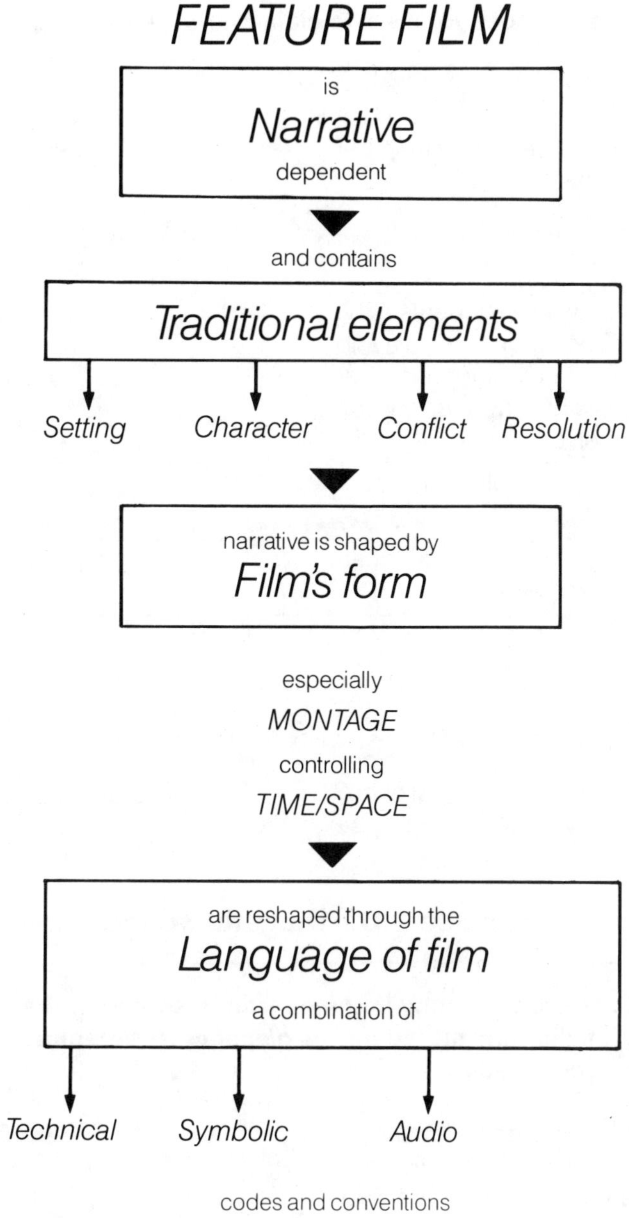

FEATURE FILM

is
Narrative
dependent

▼

and contains

Traditional elements

Setting   Character   Conflict   Resolution

▼

narrative is shaped by
Film's form

especially

MONTAGE

controlling

TIME/SPACE

▼

are reshaped through the
Language of film
a combination of

Technical   Symbolic   Audio

codes and conventions

Exercise 8.C   Audience attention

By manipulating the acoustic qualities of sound — loudness, pitch and timbre — the film maker is able to direct audiences to specific elements of the action.

1 The possibilities of adding and creating sound are almost endless. Outline the audio track for the scene breakdown below. Remember that you are trying to use sound to specifically direct audience attention.

Visuals	Audio
A classroom of about twenty students. The teacher is absent. One group is playing cards, a couple of boys are sniggering over a comic book, a transistor plays, a few are reading, a large number chattering.	
The camera selects the card playing group. They do not speak.	
The camera pans across a small group chattering, to rest on a girl reading.	
The door opens and the teacher enters. Every head looks up.	

2 Compare your notes with others. Are there any significant differences in your choices of audio tracks? Have you used silence? Suggest ways in which silence could be effective.

3 If you have an opportunity, try to video-tape this scene a couple of times using different audio tracks and compare the results.

Exercise 8.D   Diegetic sound

Sound has a spatial dimension because it comes from a source. If the source is a character or object in the story of the film the sound is *diegetic*. If the source is outside the story space of the film it is non-diegetic.

1 The still opposite shows the baby Tarzan in the arms of the ape mother. To establish the physical appearance of the mother ape and her relationship with the human baby the film maker has relied on medium shots and close-ups. At the same time the film maker needs to create the impression of a huge off-screen space — the jungle.

2 List the diegetic sounds you would use to create the off-screen space. List any non-diegetic sound you might use.

3 How will you select and order your sounds so that they are not heard as a cacophony? Use arrows as below to indicate relative loudness of sound.

'Music ↓ whistles ↑ voices ↓ whistles = music low under whistles and voices, whistles drop'

Still from *Greystoke, The Legend of Tarzan* (1984)

Analysis and research

1 *Musicals*: if Hollywood is a dream factory, then the musical must be its greatest accomplishment, for it would appear to be the most escapist of all genres.

View a modern musical.

- To what extent is it fantasy? To what extent does the musical that you have seen reflect a reality? Consider the events portrayed, the emotions expressed by the characters. Are they lifelike or larger than life?
- If the musical has elements of fantasy, what codes create the fantasy?
- Are the performances of the songs justified by the narrative (for example, are they depicted as occurring upon the stage or do they demand additional spectator fantasy? How important is spectacle in the staging of these songs?) How does the staging compare with video clips of songs? Consider shot length, special effects. If there is a difference, can this be explained?
- One film critic (Richard Dyer in *Movie*, no 24) has suggested that the characters in musicals are usually shown making a utopia, or perfect world, but it is essentially the men who do the making. To what extent is this true of the musical that you have viewed?

Library research

- M.G.M. was the studio most noted for its musicals. Research in the library and make a list of some M.G.M. musicals (include an approximate date for each film). Find as many stills as you can from these films. Examine the codes in these stills closely. Write down some generalisations about the characters and settings in these musicals. Is there any evidence that there has been a change of pattern over the years?

  Compare the characters and settings of the M.G.M. musicals with the animated characters and settings of Walt Disney musicals. What similarities and differences do they have? How does the evidence that you have gained from the stills compare with the codes present in a movie that you have seen recently?

2 *American Graffitti* used well known songs of the 1960s in the sound track. This gave the film a greater 1960s (or was it 1950s?) feeling. Since then, many other films have successfully used the technique, perhaps one of the most effective being *The Big Chill*. This sort of music, although well known to the audience, is *non-diegetic*, that is, it is accepted by the audience as being quite artificially independent of the visuals. The audience does not expect to see someone singing the songs in the course of the narrative. Occasionally, non-diegetic sound such as this is made diegetic by having the characters walk into a milk-bar where a juke box is playing. Justified sound like this, is *diegetic* sound.

- Analyse the sound track of a film that uses well known songs in order to evoke an era. To what extent are the moods of the songs reflected in the narrative? Are there any occasions in which apparently non-diegetic music becomes diegetic?

  To what extent is music (or sound effects) used to 'lead in' the visuals? That is, to what extent is the sound for the new sequence of visuals heard before the visuals appear on the screen? What is the effect upon the spectator when the sound track precedes the visuals?

  To what extent can the idea of montage be applied to sound? If there is such a thing as a sound montage, how is it similar to and different from a visual montage?

Written response

1 Post-synchronisation of sound, that has allowed many different sound sources to be mixed, has been a liberating force for the art of film. It has also enabled increased manipulation of meaning. Discuss.

2 'Only with colour as an available resource can we regard the use of black-and-white photography as the result of a conscious artistic decision. Only in sound film can a director use silence for dramatic effect.' (Perkins in *Film as Film*, p. 54.)

Discuss the value of silence in dramatic film.

Practical exercise

[*Special equipment: video replay equipment, video of feature film, sound effects records, record player, music cassette recorders*]

1 Select 10 minutes of film that are relatively unremarkable in that they do not feature any dramatic high points. (It is preferable that the extract is not heavily dialogue dependent.) Play the extract with the volume turned right down.

2 Discuss ways in which the meaning of the extract could be changed by the use of quite different sound tracks. For example, certain sounds and music could suggest a sense of foreboding while a different combination could imply romance.

3 Divide into two groups, each with the task of creating one of the moods that has been nominated. Create your sound track on an audio cassette tape. Use music and sound effects, with an absolute minimum of dialogue (no dialogue would be even better).

4 Re-form as one group and play your attempts to each other. Discuss the results.

5 Play the extract again, this time with the sound turned up. Give particular attention to the mood that has been created and the way in which it was done. What effects were the professionals able to achieve that you were not able to do with the equipment available to you? To what extent do you think the sound track creates meaning? Alternatively, does it merely support the meaning that is present in the visuals?

References

Christian Metz, *Film Language: A Semiotics of the Cinema* (New York: Oxford University Press, 1974).

Christian Metz, *Language and Cinema* (The Hague: Mailor, 1974).

Christian Metz, 'Current Problems in Film Theory', in *Screen*, vol. 14, no. 2, Spring/Summer 1973 (London: SEFT 1973).

V.F. Perkins, *Film as Film: Understanding and Judging Movies* (London: Penguin, 1972).

Chapter 9
Written Codes

A problem posed

You have access to a silent Super 8 movie camera and wish to make a film. One way to create your meaning without using dialogue is to revert to the pre-1927 silent era and cut written dialogue statements into your scenes.

Your film is a serious drama. What are your chances of producing an effective film by using this technique?

New media tend to inherit many of their early conventions from established media. It is not surprising, therefore, that early films showed marked similarities to the content of live music hall performances. Similarly, it is to be expected that the moving image was likened to the still photograph, which was almost invariably accompanied by a written text. The pattern of the silent feature film, of interspersing visuals with abbreviated written statements or dialogue, is a consequence of picture story book mentality. The technology existed that would have enabled films to be subtitled in a similar manner to the method now used in foreign films, but the more familiar convention was automatically adopted.

Early silent film dramas were shorter than modern feature length and carried no written text at all. The action had to speak for itself because most of the audience in the major American inner cities were newly arrived immigrants who spoke in many different languages and did not share English as a common language. Even though the audience quickly widened, a precedent had been established that confined the use of a written text to a minor role. Interspersing the visual sequences with written captions also had a jarring effect upon the audience who were immersed in the 'reality' that the film was portraying through the use of moving images. The static written information interrupted the flow of the visuals.

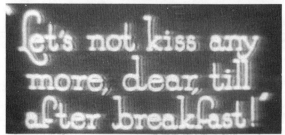

The silents

Modern subtitles are less jarring because they are contained within the image, but generally subtitled films are not popular commercially. It seems that most cinema goers are not prepared to give the extra concentration to mentally translate the written words into the performers' mouths. Foreign films with dubbed dialogue have proved to be more successful commercially.

The written codes in modern mainstream cinema are now confined to credits, film identification and pre-or post-film statements.

If the credits occur at the beginning of the film, the style of presentation will help set the mood of the film. In early post-war comedy and light romance films, there was a convention of using credits that resembled story book print. The use of animation within the credits of these types of films is an extension of the convention. In contrast, the dramatic or highly 'realistic' films tend to inject the credits into the visual footage of the film. In this way, the audience is being conditioned for the drama even while the credits are being projected.

Even at the conclusion of the film, the credits can form part of the total film experience. Sombre, white titles over a dramatic freeze frame or black background can intensify any shock value there might be in the final scenes of a film. In the Superman films, the credits zoom through the galaxies in a manner that allows the audience to briefly relive the excitement of flying with the hero.

Written pre-film statements are becoming less common as more sophisticated methods have now been found for introducing the relevant background information to the audience. Films that purported to show a slice of a well known historical event, such as a war, were often preceded by an introductory written statement. The statement gave some degree of authority to the events that were subsequently shown, particularly if it was established that the characters or incidents actually existed or occurred.

Written statements at the conclusion of a film are still occasionally seen. Again, the

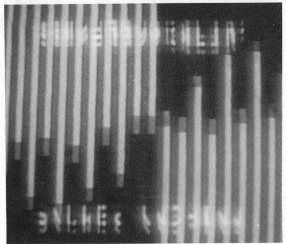

Hitchcock's thriller *Psycho* (1960) set a psychological mood with the opening credits. The fractured writing was in keeping with the split-personality drama that was to follow.

effect is to give credibility to the screen events. The statement becomes a link between the screen life and real life. In *American Graffiti* we learn what happened to the characters in the film once they grew up. The Australian film *Sunday Too Far Away* concludes with the shearing team that has been the central focus of the story going on strike. A written statement then advises the audience about the outcome of the strike. Some film critics have claimed that this highlights the weakness in many Australian film scripts, that so many have to conclude with a written statement to 'round off' the film. Argument against this is that the 'loose' ending which is

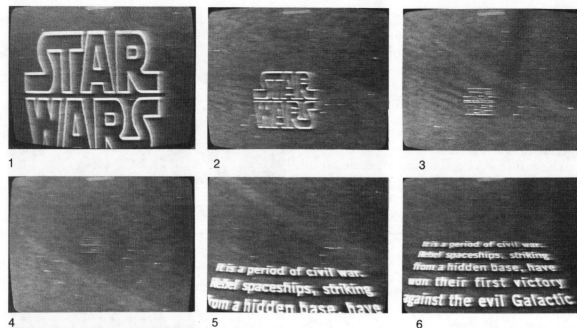

1　2　3

4　5　6

7

Star Wars (1977) opening credits: a combination of written story codes and modern cinema techniques. The credits set the mood for the adventure to follow.

a characteristic of many Australian films is closer to the 'reality' of everyday life. If this argument is accepted, then the post-film written statement is a useful device for assisting the transition from screen to everyday reality.

Conclusion

The written codes are not as significant as the other codes but they do carry meaning.

The written statement before or after the film is highly credible because our culture has conditioned us to respect the printed word. Film makers are obliged to give credit to the performers and to those who have helped make the film. They usually make the obliga-

tion work to their advantage by using the credits to assist the audience to settle in to the 'reality' of the film. End credits can similarly assist the transition back to real life — a transition that apparently occurs quite quickly, because by the time the end credits are concluded, the cinema is almost empty!

> Written code
> — titles
> — credits

The written codes do not fit so comfortably with the other cinematic codes and they appear to be more appropriate for other forms of expression. However, they do occur and like the other codes, work in a co-operative manner. Written messages on the screen are accompanied by music or superimposed on visuals. Because they play only a minor role in the total film experience, there is a risk that the meanings that they generate will become quite invisible. Therefore they warrant some attention.

In diagrammatic form, the steps taken so far towards film interpretation are:

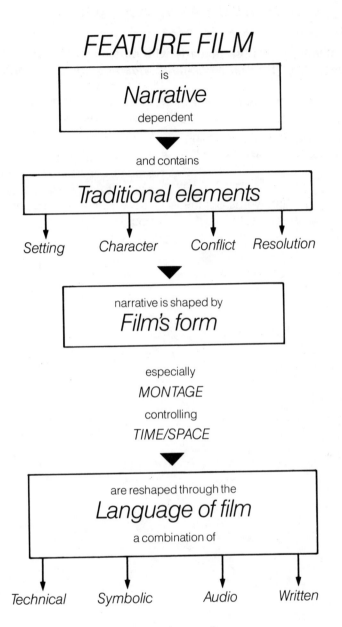

FEATURE FILM

is
Narrative
dependent

▼

and contains

Traditional elements

Setting   Character   Conflict   Resolution

▼

narrative is shaped by
Film's form

especially
MONTAGE
controlling
TIME/SPACE

▼

are reshaped through the
Language of film
a combination of

Technical   Symbolic   Audio   Written

codes and conventions

Exercise 9.A Written codes

Written codes interact with others (particularly with music), mainly at the beginning and end of a film, to create meaning. [*Special equipment*: *video equipment, feature film video tape*]

1 View the opening and end credits of a film.

2 Comment upon the images in the opening credits. What expectations do they create for the audience?

3 Examine the print style (not the words but the style). What does the style suggest?

4 To what extent does the music reinforce the impressions that you have gained from the other codes?

5 To what degree are the opening and end credits consistent? Are they sufficiently consistent to suggest a degree of completeness in the film, like the opening and closing of a book?

Chapter 10
Film Language

Diegetic effect

The earlier chapters have shown that feature film is a medium that is well disposed towards the creation of strong narratives. These narratives draw from life's experiences in various ways. Sometimes the relationship between screen events and life events is quite obvious. At other times, such as in costume dramas or science fiction films, the relationship to real life is less evident. However, these films, like those that are set in modern suburbia, still draw upon accepted cultural values, which are demonstrated particularly through the actions of the characters. Although they have already been touched upon, the cultural messages are so significant to understanding film as a language, that the issue will again be addressed later in this chapter.

It was also shown in earlier chapters that film has derived some of its narrative elements from other media, particularly the novel and the stage play. Four useful concepts that help in understanding film, but which are not peculiar to that medium, are setting, character, conflict and resolution.

Although there are similarities between narratives in film and those in other media the differences are greater, and for the student of film, they are more interesting. Film has developed its own language — a language that has made it a most distinctive and powerful medium. At the heart of that language is montage, the procedure by which images and sounds are strung together to make a cohesive narrative. It is through montage that time and space are manipulated in the narrative. It is through montage that a psychological dimension is established. It is through montage that the 'reality' is created.

Within and around the montage, a coded film language operates. For the convenience of critical analysis, the divisions of technical, symbolic, audio and written have been chosen. These categories are useful as tools of analysis; they are not divine laws of nature. The codes provide the meaning in the sequences, a meaning that is drawn from culture and convention. Thus, a frilly dress has been culturally determined to mean feminism and grainy film has now been accepted as suggesting 'seediness'.

What is the purpose of all of the effort that goes into making a feature film? That really depends upon where you are standing! If you are standing in a queue in front of a cinema box-office, the purpose is to entertain you. A film maker who successfully employs the language of film will entertain you, even though the original subject matter may not have been very promising. *Chariots of Fire* is an example of such a film. The basic ingredients of the narrative were one man who perceived a conflict between his love of running and his love of God, and another who had a 'chip on his shoulder' and was out to prove himself. Skilful montage, a brilliant sound track and artful symbolic constructions however, transform the banal content into a highly entertaining film. Most of those who stood in front of that box-office and paid their money felt that it was money well spent.

If you are standing on a film set as a significant creator of the feature film (say, as the director) then perhaps your purpose is to create something that is artistically satisfying (though you may have trouble in defining just what that is). Perhaps is a key word here, because there are some who would argue that many or most of the creators are required to work in a tradesmanlike fashion, with little perception or vision that they may be creating a great work of art.

If you have been involved in financing the film and the film has succeeded in creating large queues of people standing in front of the box-office, then you will be 'standing in front of your bank' about to make a huge deposit. It is this stance that is crucial in understanding the feature film industry, for above all else it is an industry. The outlay on each product is huge but there is great reward if the product is handled correctly. Correct handling involves skilful merchandising as well as expert production. This is why it is so important for the producers to create an appealing narrative image. The right context must be created so that profits can be made.

Though the perspectives of financier, artisan and spectator may be different, the positions are not incompatible, in fact the reverse is true. If the spectator is satisfied, the financier will make money and the reputation of the creators will spread. To do this, the film must create a *diegetic effect*. A diegetic effect is one when the spectator is willing to suspend the external reality and become immersed in the film's narrative. A strong diegetic effect will allow the cinema goer to ignore the hard seat and the popcorn being munched two rows further back and become immersed in the screen's reality. In spite of the hard seat and popcorn, the cinema context is far more likely to create a strong diegetic effect than the lounge-room context for a video movie.

The term *diegesis* requires a little more explanation, for it is not one that can be found in a dictionary. It is a term that was first used by Christian Metz, a French film theorist, who described the diegesis as the sum of all the parts of the film: the narration, the manipulation of space and time, the dimensions of character and landscape, the events and any other elements that give us information. Others have advanced this definition, describing how all of these elements synthesise, giving a close proximity to life. Most lifelike of all are the manipulations of time and space. It has already been shown that although these manipulations create a lifelike effect, they are not in themselves lifelike. That is, they create a reality, they are not 'real'.

It would be convenient to avoid the difficult term of diegesis and use instead something like 'compelling narrative', but this simplification would probably be misleading. Although narrative is usually an important part of the diegesis, a diegetic effect can occur without a strong traditional narrative structure.

Although you may not previously have heard of the descriptive term, if you have been to a cinema more than once, it is likely that your return was occasioned by the diegetic effect. *You were willing to suspend your disbelief.* You were willing to forget that you were seeing flat images upon a screen and accept the screen events as a life in which you were involved as an invisible spectator. This diegetic effect is the crucial thread that binds spectator, producer and creator. The film maker is trying to make money by creating it; the spectator is prepared to pay to experience it and the producers reap the rewards of the film makers' efforts and the spectators' satisfaction.

The earlier chapters have stressed that it is important to distinguish between the illusion of reality and reality itself. The filmic codes create an illusion of reality, not reality. Thus when speaking of diegesis being dependent upon lifelike occurrences upon the screen, it is important that lifelike is equated with illusion rather than reality. It is true that techniques that seem to approximate life situations may add to the diegetic effect. For example, the development of synchronised sound in film seemed to give audiences a greater diegetic effect. People talk in real life and we can see it happening. When this dimension was developed in film, audiences quickly abandoned the cinemas where the silents were playing.

It could similarly be argued that music is quite an anomaly if lifelike is equated with

Synchronised sound has gone well beyond the apparent 'reality' of the Hollywood two shot in which we see each of the performers who deliver dialogue. Sound tracks are manipulated so that we hear off-screen voices, we hear performers speaking before we see them, we even occasionally have sound effects mixed with words (for example, computer 'creatures'). These quite contrived, quite artificial uses of sound create a very lifelike situation for the audience. (From *High Road to China*, 1982)

real. Music will add to the audience's sense of emotive reality, but there is nothing 'real' if music accompanies every action. If music had to be real, then we should expect to see the orchestra playing an accompaniment to every screen murder! This is patently absurd because the audience has accepted the quite artificial contrivance of music in the diegesis.

To sum up, the diegesis is what the film maker is working towards. The aim is to create a product that encourages a willingness in the cinema spectator to suspend disbelief and become immersed in the film. Artfully used film language will create a strong diegetic effect. The film will be popular, which will in turn fill the coffers of the producers.

Film art

Already we have established that the term a 'good' film is highly problematic. It begs the question good for what, good for whom? If it is good for the producer then it will be a money spinner; if it is good for the crew then it probably means job satisfaction; if it is good for the audience it means they had a pleasant evening out. To speak of a good film then is to say little. However, can we discuss film art or film viewing as an aesthetic experience?

Film is different from other works often referred to as art such as poetry, the novel, painting, sculpture or even photography.

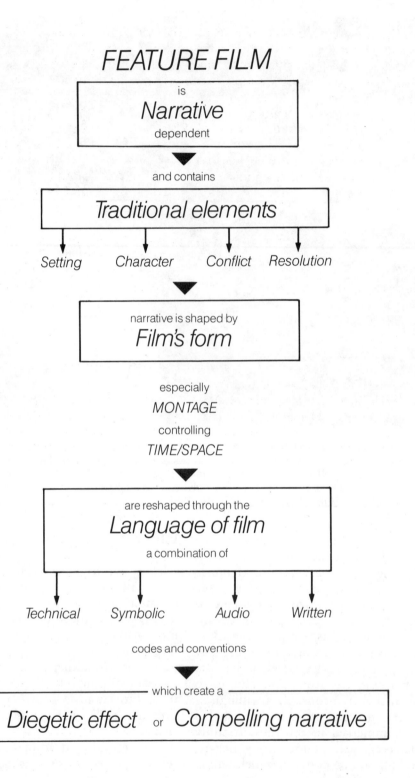

FEATURE FILM

is
Narrative
dependent

and contains

Traditional elements

Setting   Character   Conflict   Resolution

narrative is shaped by
Film's form

especially
MONTAGE
controlling
TIME/SPACE

are reshaped through the
Language of film
a combination of

Technical   Symbolic   Audio   Written

codes and conventions

which create a
Diegetic effect   or   **Compelling narrative**

Film, similar to a performed play or a piece of music, is a temporal event. It communicates with the audience only so long as it is on the screen and the viewer, short of walking out, has no control over the time spent with it. This is unlike the reader of a poem or the viewer of a sculpture. The temporal nature of film is important to remember when discussing the aesthetic experience of film because we can only ever be talking about the immediate experience of the viewer. Eidsvik sums this up when he says 'Great art may have to be for all time. But a good movie must, first of all, make tonight more interesting.'

Innovation

This puts the focus on the audience. What are the elements of a film that make it for us, the viewer, an aesthetic experience? One element is innovation. Cinema is a popular art that is consumed by a mass audience and so it must continually seek new subjects, new forms, new ways of showing old material if it is to keep its audience enthralled. This appetite for something new has meant that the cinema's dominant pattern is a continual updating of old forms and structures, a continual stretching of established genres and conventions to reproduce something new. To include innovation as an essential element of the film aesthetics allows us to see both *Citizen Kane* and *Raiders of the Lost Ark* as having some claim to being art. *Citizen Kane* was not a 'good' film in that it made money because it has still not made a profit. It is not a 'good' film in that it succeeded in entertaining masses of people because obviously it did not — otherwise it would show a profit. It may have some claim to being art, however, because its original and innovative manipulation of the codes added to our culture's reservoir of film understanding and appreciation. It led cinema beyond the bounds that it had previously known. Similarly *Raiders of the Lost Ark* could be said to do the same. This film manipulated the adventure genre into a novel pattern. Although the episodic style was well known to Saturday matinee audiences forty years ago, Spielberg, through creative and original manipulation of the codes, updated and re-created the style. In the process he managed to create an extremely entertaining film which assured him of box-office success. Innovation alone cannot be the sole criterion to be met for a film to be pleasing aesthetically. Many films could be singled out as using innovative techniques yet be generally classed as poor cinema. Pornography continually experiments with new camera angles, new ways of presenting fairly common subject matter and yet there are few if any pornographic films that are renowned as being art. Innovation then is only one element of the aesthetic experience and not a sufficient condition in itself.

Unpredictability

Unpredictability (entropy) is another element of the aesthetic experience. Audiences have conscious and subconscious expectations when they attend a film. The narrative image and their foreknowledge of actors, plot and genre affect these expectations. A film may not meet all these expectations and by deviating from the norm, may raise itself above our everyday experience. The unpredictable way in which the film manipulates the codes and conventions within its text may set it apart from other similar films and turn the film experience into an aesthetic experience. Such was the case with *Raiders*, another adventure movie that stands above thousands of forgettable adventure films. Deviating from the norm will not automatically make a film great. Mel Brooks, in *Silent Movie*, deviated from the norm in making a modern film without dialogue but the film flopped badly. It was rejected by mass audiences and film critics alike. Neither innovation nor unpredictability are in themselves sufficient conditions for a film to be regarded as aesthetically pleasing.

Complexity

The third element to be considered when looking at film art is complexity. Complexity is closely connected to unpredictability but is used here to refer to elements *within* the narrative rather than the construction of the narrative. Complexity within the narrative demands audience involvement. The audience cannot remain the passive viewer but must become intellectually active in experiencing the film. The construction of the character of Karen Silkwood in *Silkwood* is an example of such complexity. The Silkwood character is coded as lover, crusader, slut, mother, worker. Within the film all aspects of the character continually exist. In the course of the narrative one or other trait will be dominant but the others are never lost. Disorder and confusion could have been the outcome of this. The performer's skill, however, is such that the attempt succeeds and Silkwood emerges as a character whom the audience is continually and actively trying to understand. The ambiguities of her character have demanded audience involvement in the performance and so heightened the aesthetic experience. Ambiguity will only add to the aesthetic experience when it requires the audience to be intellectually active in a fulfilling way. If the audience does not find it fulfilling then complexity within plot and character will be rejected as confusing and non-sensical.

The three elements of the aesthetic experience which have been identified — innovation, unpredictability and complexity — are not preconditions for a film to be regarded as art. Perhaps all we can say is that if these elements are present and used in a particular way then the film is more likely to offer an aesthetic experience for the viewer. All of the elements are dependent upon established codes and these codes derive their meaning from the culture. Film art is not something that is frozen in time. (Consider how we laugh at some old films.) It is dynamic because a film is a discrete, temporal event that can only become art when it is in direct communication with the audience. The value of studying the aesthetics of film probably lies more in the activity than in the findings.

When we try to establish what makes a particular film stand out from the rest we are focusing upon such key issues as:
- what are the codes of meaning?
- how are they being reworked in the film?
- how does the manipulation of the codes relate to the culture which created them?
- what new view of the world is the film offering?
- what reassessment of our own position does the film demand?

These questions are subsumed in the crucial question: 'What relationship do the codes have to the culture which created them?'

Exercise 10.A   Film aesthetics

Innovation, unpredictability and complexity have been identified as being important elements of the film aesthetics. To what extent does a film you consider to be 'good' possess these elements?

1 Think of a film you know well, which you enjoyed and considered highly. Fill in the required information on the chart below.

Film title: _____

Innovation: To what extent does this film add to our culture's understanding of film?

Technical devices	Sound	Plot	Performance
(Give examples)	(Give examples)		

Unpredictability: In what ways has the film manipulated the codes and conventions that set it apart from other similar films?

Technical code	Plot structure	Characterisation
(Examples)	(Examples)	(Examples)

Complexity: To what extent does the film demand a fulfilling intellectual response on the part of the viewer?

Character construction	Conflict	Resolution

2 Look again at the information in the chart.

- Is any element — complexity, unpredictability, innovation, not present?
- Are there any categories not listed here that you consider to be important in determining that the film is a good film?

- Which element do you consider to be *most* significant in determining that the film you have selected is a good film?

3 Using the information collated above prepare notes that could be used to argue that this is a 'great' film.

Exercise 10.B   Codes of meaning

Some key issues that should be considered when discussing the value of a film are:
- **the codes of meaning**
- **the manipulation of the codes**
- **the view of the world presented in the film**
- **the reassessment of our position, views demanded by the film.**
[*Special equipment: TV monitor, video tapes, video replay*]

Here is a list of films described by one writer (Eidsvik) as being decisive in changing the direction of mainstream cinema.

Bonnie and Clyde	*Love and Anarchy*
Easy Rider	*Blow-Up*
The Graduate	*Jules and Jim*
Five Easy Pieces	*Seven Beauties*

All of these films were box-office successes. Nearly all are available on video.

1 View *one* of these films.

2 Use the issues summarised above and note headings and write down the pertinent details about the film under these headings.

3 After you have made your notes discuss:
- All of these films are between ten and twenty years old. Did the film you watched appear out of date? Why/why not?
- Why do you think Eidsvik nominated this film as being decisive in changing the course of mainstream cinema? Consider its level of innovation.
- Can you name any recent films that have employed the same techniques?

Above and right: From *Blow-Up* (1966)

From *Bonnie and Clyde* (1967)

From *Easy Rider* (1969)

Meaning

Film is a very complex language system, which can be used to create an unlimited number of narratives. It is a very complex language, yet we did not have to spend years learning it, as we did when learning to read and write. We have absorbed subconsciously what we need to know in order to understand most stories. If the story content was all that was important, there would be no point in studying the language of film, because the story can be understood without study. However, study of the medium is important, because there are other levels of meaning in addition to 'story meaning'.

It is possible to absorb film language subconsciously because the symbols used obtain their meaning from the culture that is shared by film maker and audience. Each piece of information that is seen or heard has symbolic significance. It is there to suggest meaning to the viewers, but that meaning depends on the viewers relating what is seen to their own cultural experience. The viewers are not just sitting and passively absorbing the information.

The viewers have to process the screen information and place it in a context. For example, a piece of cloth wrapped around the waist is a piece of clothing. The viewers' experience within their culture gives the cloth meaning and value. If the film is an ancient Roman epic, the cloth is interpreted as a toga on a male Roman citizen. It could be part of a constructed image of manliness. If the context was changed and the cloth was seen on an actress in a modern romance, the image could be one of gracefulness and femininity. If the cloth was draped around a present-day man, the man's sexuality would be open to question. Each viewer is engaged individually in this mental process, but the audience as a whole will interpret the meaning in much the same way. This is because they share the same culture.

The shared, or dominant, culture will determine the most generally acceptable meaning, but subcultural interpretations are also possible. Take again the example of the present-day man in a dress. The dominant reading of this image is of an effeminate man. If the man was a rock star, the dominant group may 'read' the costume as outlandish, even offensive, while the subcultural group of rock fans 'read' the image as zany and anti-Establishment. Meaning is not fixed at the time the film is made but is negotiated by viewers in accordance with their cultural and subcultural allegiances.

In summary, the symbols that we use derive their meaning from the values that are present in a given society. The symbols or codes may structure the meaning for the audience, but they can do this only because there is a shared set of values. Film makers create their stories within the parameters of society's values. The audience creates the meaning. 'Story meaning', therefore, is created by the use of symbols that have a fairly common meaning within a given culture. Sequences of symbolically loaded information are created (edited together) to create the final 'story meaning'.

It has been seen that 'cultural meaning' is used to create 'story meaning'. It follows that stories can be examined in order to understand more about our culture and the way that we create meaning. This is why the study of popular media is so important. The rules and meanings we live by seem normal and right because they are with us all the time, but they are constructed patterns, not natural ones. Once the process is understood, we can choose to accept, reject or change the meanings.

Film does not just reflect meanings. It is an active agent in reworking meanings and values. Examples of this process will be given later.

Meaning is created through selection and sequencing

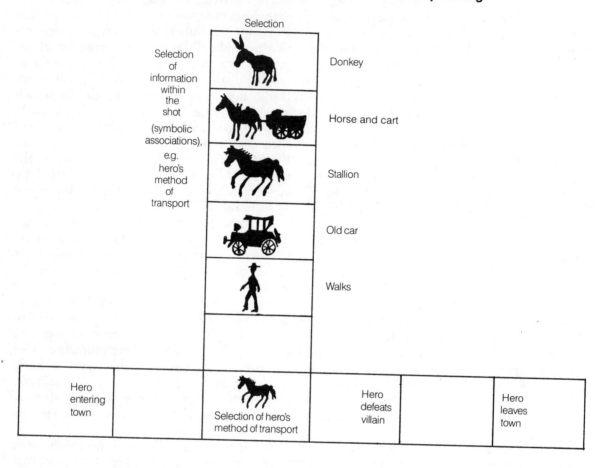

Selection

Selection of information within the shot (symbolic associations), e.g. hero's method of transport		Donkey
		Horse and cart
		Stallion
		Old car
		Walks

| Hero entering town | | Selection of hero's method of transport | Hero defeats villain | | Hero leaves town |

Assembly of sequences: Sequence of the *shots*, their *order* and *duration* (editing)

→ Sequence →

Exercise 10.C   Meaning

Meaning is a product of society. The symbols we use derive their meaning from the values placed upon them by society.

We are able to read the symbols or codes in the stills from *The Birds* and *Rio Bravo* because there exists a shared set of values in society. You can check this by comparing your reading of the symbols with that of others.

1 For each still shown prepare a chart similar to the one on the next page. The first still has been partially analysed for you as a guide. Complete the chart for still 1 and then repeat the process for the other stills.

In which country is the film set?

Are any of these symbols outdated, that is, no longer used in the same way?

Still 1

Code	Items	Meaning
Clothing	Slouch hats, rolled up sleeves, boots, calf-length dress	Working men, outback Australia, heat Set in the past
Body language Facial expression	Linked arms of man and woman, squinting, hands in pockets	Close relationship Hot glare of sun relaxed, casual
Lighting Objects Setting	Deep shadows Draught horses Dusty road	Strong sunlight ? ?

2 Complete similar charts for the other stills.

3 Swap your charts with another class member.
- Are there any symbols you have interpreted differently? Why might this be so?

4 What symbols are dependent on knowing the film genre?

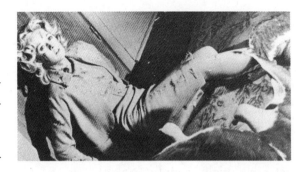
From *The Birds* (1963)

From *Rio Bravo* (1959)

From *The Irishman* (1978)

From *The Term of His Natural Life* (1927)

Recognising meaning

Outlined below are the steps which should help you come to an understanding of a film's cultural values.

The first step is *identification*. It is necessary to identify the elements of the narrative which have significant cultural meaning. The commutation test will help you in this identification process. The commutation test involves exchanging one unit in the element under study for another different unit. If the exchange changes the meaning of the element then a cultural value has been revealed. For instance if a character in the film is seen driving a Mercedes Benz then we could test the 'meaning' of the Mercedes by mentally exchanging it for an old Ford. If this exchange changes our understanding of the character then the Mercedes is a unit of the narrative with significant cultural meaning.

The decision as to which units should be tested in this way can be aided by going back to the elements of the narrative: character, setting, conflict, resolution. In terms of character we might usefully look at:

    appearance
    strengths
    personality traits
    relationships with others
    goals

Let us apply the approach to a particular film and see the type of character profile that is built up. If we applied this to *Indiana Jones and The Temple of Doom* our analysis would probably look something like this:

- appearance — rugged, quite good-looking, physically well built
- strengths — leadership, attractive to women, 'nice'
- personality traits — quick thinker, brave
- relationships with others — a leader, looks after the other characters
- goals — to help people (the Indians), to fight evil.

We can check the importance of each of these characteristics within the narrative by asking ourselves would the meaning change if Indiana was weak and puny, or a coward, or very ugly. The answer must be 'yes'. However, if we asked ourselves would the meaning change if his eyes were green instead of blue then the answer is 'no'. Obviously in this film the colour of the central character's eyes does not have any significant cultural meaning.

Scene from *Raiders of the Lost Ark* (1981)

Do not attempt to interpret the meaning of this character yet. Continue to identify the significant cultural elements of the narrative.

Setting

In an effort to identify the cultural importance of setting we need to look at:

- place —
  - country
  - rural/city
  - nationality of characters

- time —
  - present
  - past
  - future

Again applying this approach, our analysis would look like this:

- place — foreign country, India? or some place like it?
  - setting in country, no large cities
  - people are foreign, bad people are swarthy, good people are Indians.
- time — the present day.

Apply the commutation test again. Would it change the meaning of the film if the starring people were in America instead of India? Obviously it would so it is important to the meaning of the narrative that India and not America is the setting.

Plot

Obviously plot must be highly significant in any narrative because we are usually talking about plot when we say 'The film was about . . .' In identifying the significant cultural elements of plot we will go back to the narrative devices talked about earlier: *conflict* and *resolution*. In conflict we could usefully look at:

- nature of conflict —
  - man vs. man
  - man vs. nature
  - man vs. himself

- motivation (i.e. what causes the action) —
  - crime
  - greed
  - love
  - revenge

In *Indiana Jones* the conflict involves man vs. man: Indiana Jones fights the evil devil worshippers.

- motivation — Indiana is motivated by pity for the starving Indians, sometimes love for the lady and little boy.

The plot must have a resolution to the conflict so we must look at:

- resolution —
  - who wins
  - who loses
  - rewards

and we find:

- winner — Indiana, the Indians
- loser — evil Indians
- rewards — Indiana gets the lady, the Indians find prosperity again and regain their children.

Again we can check for significance by doing a mental swap. Would the meaning change if the evil Indians won? Of course it would. Would the meaning of the film have changed if the starving Indians were left to starve? Again the answer is in the affirmative.

Audience placement

The final important step in the identification process is the identification of audience placement. Within a fictional narrative film there is invariably an attempt to 'place' the audience in relation to the characters and so place their actions. This placement is both in terms of the understanding we have of the characters and our feelings for them. At the most simple level the placement occurs in terms of our liking for or dislike of a character; our belief in the 'rightness' of their actions, our sympathy for them. To a certain extent we judge the characters on the extent to which they fit our assumptions of what members of that group are like. Within the narrative the audience is sure to dislike or disapprove of some characters or like and approve of others and this occurs through the endowment of characters with particular traits, through symbolic associations and through performance. In

Indiana Jones the placement of the audience is favourable towards Indiana and unfavourable towards the devil worshippers. This audience placement has important ramifications for the types of cultural values the audience will take from the film.

Interpretation

Interpretation is the next step in ascertaining the cultural values of the film. We must re-examine the data we have collected in step 1 of identification in the light of our knowledge of our culture and our other media experiences. Look again at the character profile of Indiana Jones that was built up in the identification process. He is a strong leader, he is motivated by 'good' feelings, he saves people weaker than himself and he is rewarded at the end by defeating his enemies and getting his lady love. This information allows us to see how well this character fits in with our knowledge of our culture. This character, it seems, is the typical hero figure in the mould of many of our other heroes such as King Arthur, Robin Hood, and Jesus Christ. Indiana Jones fits the heroic stereotype. The audience placement is positive. We are cued to approve of this character and his actions. This positive audience reaction coupled with the character and actions of Indiana Jones, points to some of the cultural values of the film. The audience is cued to approve of the values embodied in the Indiana Jones character and these values are those of the traditional hero: bravery, altruism and leadership.

Similarly, the other characters could be examined to see the extent to which they fit into pre-existent cultural categories and then how the audience is placed in relation to these characters.

Categories

A film, like the world in which we live, consists of a multitude of elements so vast that if we tried to understand each separately, they would never make sense. Some order can be achieved once we start to categorise the elements. For example, in an adventure film like *Indiana Jones and the Temple of Doom*, there are scores of adventures, incidents, characters and escapes from death. Categorising the people, events, settings etc. could result in perceptions like:

- The heroic journey of the hero, heroine and child could be seen as *the forces of good versus the forces of evil*.
- The hero, Indiana Jones, fits comfortably into the *traditional hero category*. He rescues maidens, children and those not able to fend for themselves.
- The heroine is very similar to helpless heroines that are common in other media. In fact she can be categorised even more specifically as the dumb blonde stereotype.
- The child fits well into the category of 'cute child' that we have seen so often on television.
- The resolution conforms with the predictable category of good triumphant over evil.

Having identified some of the categories, attention should be given to the ways in which the codes create meaning within the categories. Commutations are useful at this stage. It is also useful to examine the specific codings, then develop some generalisations. By now, you should certainly be able to do this on these images of the three lead characters, even if you have not seen the film. Make some notes on the coded meaning in the images before you proceed. Take as an example the codes that are used to develop several meanings about the female role. We can identify (from the film, not the photographs) several character traits that are consistent with the category that has been established. The consistencies between the actions of the heroine in this film and others in the 'dumb blonde' category are:

- she is not very intelligent
- wealth, particularly jewels, seem to be the focus of her attention
- she is preoccupied with her own beauty

- she is loyal (although sometimes reluctantly) to her man
- she doesn't initiate significant action, but rather responds to events
- she is admired for her beauty, which seems to be the justification for her existence.

It is a fairly certain bet that a category that is so identifiable, and has been for many years, contains some general and specific cultural values. There must be some underlying values that produce both surface and deep meaning. The general values that are represented reflect a perceived function of women as ornaments, as fairly passive responders to calls for action rather than as initiators. There are more specific cultural references in the image of the dumb blonde. Theorists have suggested that the dumb blonde stereotype was created at a time when white American masculine superiority was under threat from two sources. In the 1930s, when the stereotype became significant, females were demanding to be regarded as being rather more than baby breeders. Blacks were also denting the vision of white male superiority with evidence of their physical prowess (when they were given the opportunity). Hence the dumb blonde was an image that encapsulated a reverence for whiteness (blonde hair being an ultra-white symbol) and a model of an obedient plaything.

Although there is some possibility that the inexperienced film analyst, through a knowledge of the codes and an effective categorisation, may have arrived at some of the general cultural values that have been mentioned, it is unrealistic to expect those specific conclusions about the dumb blonde stereotype to be reached. Such conclusions are the result of a great deal of research by scholars who have the time and research background to develop the theories. However, their findings are available to those who are interested. This is why the search for 'deep meaning' is initially difficult, but becomes easier with practice. In the course of the search, the discoveries of others will be unearthed and tested against

From *Indiana Jones and the Temple of Doom* (1984)

your own theories. As your knowledge accumulates, your analytical abilities are sharpened.

Categorisation then, can lead to an understanding of some of the values that are significant in our society and reworked in our media. For categorisation to work it is necessary to draw from a foreknowledge of other media experiences. We have seen heroes and heroines in other films and draw from this experience to form categories. What happens

From *Indiana Jones and the Temple of Doom* (1984)

when an attempt is made to categorise and the content does not render itself comfortably into these moulds? *Silkwood* is an example of such a film. One complication is that the film is based upon the events in the life of a real person and it is not easy to categorise real people. This complication should quickly be dismissed because we are analysing the film, not the book about the real person or the person herself. A study of the relationship between the 'real' events and the film version of the events is quite a different study.

Silkwood is a story about a woman factory worker. The factory manufactures fuel pellets for nuclear reactors. In the course of her work she discovers some questionable procedures that she believes could jeopardise the health of the factory workers and thousands of other citizens. As the film progresses, she becomes increasingly interested in the safety issues and sacrifices more of her private life in the

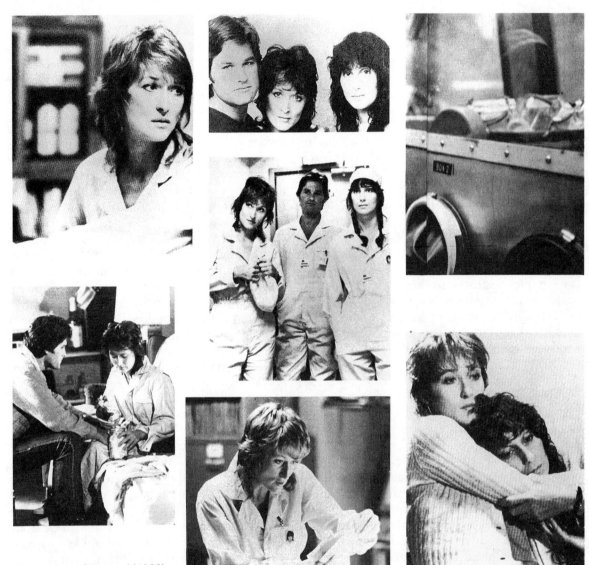

Scenes from *Silkwood* (1983)

process. This development is motivated in part by threats to her own health.

When attempts are made to categorise *Silkwood*, some problems occur. The forces of good and evil are not clearly identified. It would be convenient to say that the workers are good and the factory owners evil, but these classifications break down when we see the union structure as a highly organised force capable of similar worker manipulation. The character of Karen Silkwood is far more complex than that of the heroine in *Indiana Jones*. We see Karen Silkwood as factory worker, fleetingly as mother, as lover, as slut, as agitator, as a good friend. The categories that we can draw from our other media experiences are useful only in that they become measures against which we can test this film. When the attempt does not produce convenient answers, we need to look for other tools. The concept of *oppositions* can be of some help. (If the term 'oppositions' fails to give meaning, ambiguities is a close approximation.)

Oppositions

As a character, Karen Silkwood does not have a readily categorised set of symbols. True, she is part working girl, part lover, part friend and our media experience can give us categories for each of these. The essence of her representation however, is that she is only *part* of each and that these parts are in opposition. Her role as concerned worker is in opposition with her life as compliant lover. There is a further opposition between Silkwood's relationship with her boyfriend and her friendship for her lesbian flatmate. There are several less obvious oppositions within the Silkwood portrayal — her concern for people opposed to her erratic role of mother; her 'smartness' opposed to her lack of formal education; her obsession about her health when faced with the possibility of exposure to nuclear material as opposed to her heavy smoking habits.

The ways in which the codes develop these oppositions provide some of the film's meaning. For example, the sexual oppositions are full of meaning. It is clearly stated that Silkwood has a promiscuous past. She lives with a man out of wedlock and enjoys the company of a lesbian friend who rents a room in Silkwood's house. The values associated with these situations unfold through the symbols that create the sets, characters etc. and the narrative that develops. These manipulations do not place any negative value upon the *de facto* relationship, but compared with the friendship that exists between Silkwood and her lesbian friend, the *de facto* relationship is deficient. When the various oppositions about human relationships are examined it becomes apparent that the values from which the characters derive their meaning are somewhat novel. Unlike films that were produced under the influence of the Hayes Code of censorship, there are no negative values ascribed to relationships outside the cultural norm, whether *de facto* or homosexual. This could be an indication that attitudes are changing in these areas or it could mean that the film maker has misjudged the cultural expectations of the audience. If the latter is the case, then the values that are presented should reduce box-office receipts. People like to be shocked when they go to a cinema, but deep-seated offence is another matter! Silkwood is therefore a character whose coded construction represents a modern, 'liberated woman', but even if we create a new category for such people, she still does not fit comfortably. It is the oppositions rather than the category that reveal the values.

The character of Silkwood is one aspect of the film that reveals oppositions, but not all oppositions are confined to character (although they usually affect character motivation). We see the landscape of the oil areas opposed to the nuclear plant landscape, the refined northern cities opposed to the southern towns; the need to earn a living opposed to the concern for one's health. The attitudes that are constructed around the oppositions reveal values.

Point of view or perspective

The most significant of all oppositions is the perspective or point of view of any film. As film creates for the audience the role of invisible spectator, it possesses the potential to switch attention from one character to the next. In the course of a film this will be done many times, but in spite of these changes, there will be one person or at most a small group of people with whom the audience identifies and perceives as the person who generates the action. As the title suggests, Karen Silkwood is clearly this focus in *Silkwood*. *Indiana Jones* has three central characters, all of whom could provide a source of identification for different groups within the audience. Indeed this is probably the basis for selecting the symbol systems for each character. The three characters are a family of sorts and each has different appeal for the different members of the families who attend. Although the three exist as vehicles for identification, it is Indiana Jones whom we meet first; it is Jones who generates the action; it is Jones whom we already know from the previous film. The woman and the boy are both lovable but not as central. They react rather than activate.

Even though the audience may not approve of all of the actions of the character with whom they have identified for the duration of the film (and certainly aspects of Silkwood's character would be repugnant to many), there is a strong inclination to accept the values of the film as their own. It is even possible to reverse some strongly held beliefs for the film's duration. This happened in the German-American film *The Boat*. Audience identification was with the German U-boat crew, and the audience agonised on their side. The enemies were the elements and the British. However, although the audience was persuaded to switch allegiance from the British to the German side, the values that were portrayed were consistent (as were many of the images that generated these values). The German U-boat crew was loyal to family, country and skipper. Part of their fight was with bureaucracy just as it is in the lives of the audience. The German crew had to depend upon initiative and perseverance for their survival, and so on.

The issue is that point of view persuasively encourages acceptance of the associated values, providing that they are not too far out of kilter with the community's mainstream values. In summary, the significant person is identified, the symbols upon which that person is built are accepted as valid, so along with the symbols comes acceptance of the value system that created them.

The Boat (release date 1982)

The cinema spectator is well disposed towards accepting the transmitted point of view and associated values because whatever time period is being depicted upon the screen, for the viewer those events are happening *now*. This makes the emotional pull towards the screen events quite strong and adds credence to the film's version of reality. The strong pull is for the spectator to perceive the screen's reality as 'the reality'. Not only do the images seem real, but the emotions that they elicit are very real. As a film critic (and everyone should be one) it is important to recognise that point of view has this strong emotional dimension.

Preconceptions

The spectator's perception of screen events as 'now' has a second effect. This concerns issues rather than characters. When we see a film we subconsciously match the film's realities against preconceptions associated with the screen events. If we are viewing *Indiana Jones* we are matching our preconceptions of heroes, heroines, foreigners, the 1930s, religions etc. with those elements in the film. It is quite likely that our preconceptions have been drawn from other media experiences so it could well be that a great deal of recycling is occurring. It is important to realise that many preconceptions are simplistic. We cannot be walking encyclopedias on all subjects! If we have met a person from Afghanistan it is likely that the preconceptions that we bring to a film about Afghans will be heavily flavoured by whatever attitude that one person inspired. We generalise from the particular.

Similarly in film, there is not time to develop a detailed history of the screen events. For example, in a Western it may be relevant to show that the Indians are attacking the settlers because they are full of white man's whisky. It may be more pertinent to delve more deeply into history and discover that the Indians are hostile because they have been dispossessed of their land. As only

immediate cause is relevant to the narrative, quite a distorted view of the problem of a minority group is presented (perhaps no more distorted than a perception that is drawn from a non-mass media experience, but nevertheless, distorted). This distorted perspective is then recycled because it is the preconception that we bring to the next Western (or perhaps even the next film that depicts a different minority group). In such a way are values developed.

Hence, although it is difficult, when confronted with issues in a film it is important to examine our preconceptions, to test the film against those preconceptions, but more importantly, to ask how these preconceptions were created. The content and the omitted explanations of the film that you have just been watching may provide some clues. Occasionally a film may encourage you to rethink your preconceptions, but the tendency is for preconceptions to be reinforced, not shattered. It takes an enquiring mind and some degree of courage to question your own value system!

As we have seen, the commutation test is a useful device for detecting values. In the process of value exposure, preconceptions are revealed. In *Indiana Jones and the Temple of Doom*, what preconceptions did the commutation test reveal about goodies, baddies and victims? What value has been exposed in the process? Is it fair to judge the film as having racist elements on this evidence? If so, how do you account for the cute Japanese child as one of the heroic trio?

In summary, it is difficult but not impossible to understand more about film by searching for the 'deep meaning' that it contains. Some understanding will have to be drawn from those with more time, experience and expertise. As these opinions are sifted and incorporated into a personal perspective the task becomes easier, but the expertise of others is only valuable if it is based upon personal inquiry. There are a few directions that can be given that will help investigations. It is suggested that attention is paid to categorisation, oppositions (or ambiguities), point of view and pre-conceptions. The codes that are used in film will shed some light when categories and oppositions are considered. The commutation test will help in baring preconceptions.

Exercise 10.D   Symbols

A symbol is something regarded by most people in a culture as representing something else, for example, we all accept a smile as representing purity; a lion as representing courage. Often we automatically interpret symbols without being aware we are doing so.

1 Look at the posters for *Beau Geste, Don Q's Love Story, Tarzan 'Rescue'*, and *The Bells of St Mary's* (below and p. 146). For each, list the symbols the art designer has used and the meaning they represent. For example:

The Bells of St. Mary's   *Meaning*
clothing — nun's habit   religious order

2 Design a poster for a film to be made from your favourite book. Use symbols of clothing, body language, art work to suggest the film's meaning to the audience.

3 Display posters and discuss:
- Which symbols have been used by more than one person?
- What is a universal symbol? Is there any such thing as a universal symbol?
- What are the recurring symbols of the horror genre?
- Detective genre?
- Musical genre?
- Western genre?

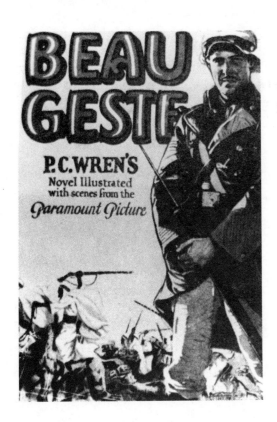

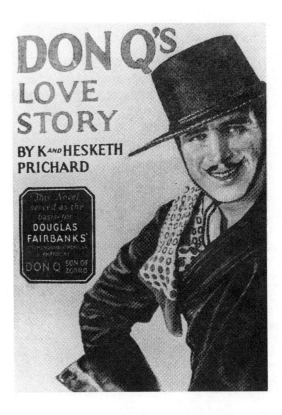

Exercise 10.E   Cultural meaning

Recognising the cultural meaning of a film is not an easy task but it is made simple if it is divided into manageable steps. The suggested steps are:

- **identification**
- **interpretation, then**
- **conclusion.**

The commutation test (read preceding pages) will help you determine which of the elements have significant cultural meaning.

1 Consider a film you have seen recently. Collect as much data — reviews, advertise-

ments, articles etc. — as you can find to help jog your memory.

2 Prepare an analysis chart similar to the one below.

a
Identification

Characters	Setting	Conflict/Resolution
Appearance	Time	Nature ....
Strengths	Place	Motivation ....
Traits		Winners ....
Relationship with others		Losers ....
Goals		Rewards ....

b Audience placement

    Favoured characters ....

    Valued/Favoured actions ....

3 The next step is to interpret your material in the light of your knowledge of the medium and your society. Can you categorise the film in terms of its plot or characterisation? For example: adventure story, love story, thriller, mystery, or goodies vs. baddies, hero saves the day. These are just a few possible categories, you should be able to think of many more. What generalisations can you make about the film in terms of the category into which it fits?

Conclusion

There have been three important considerations in this chapter. Attention has been given to the ways in which the language of film operates to create a diegetic effect upon the spectator. The diegetic effect was identified as the driving force of cinema. The eagerness of the spectator to experience the effect motivated payment of the admission price. This in turn encourages further investment in film which keeps the film maker paid and perhaps, artistically satisfied.

The second consideration addressed the difficult question of 'film art'. Is there such a thing as film art? If so, what is it? If a film aesthetic exists, then it is related to the degree of innovation, the potential to develop the unpredictable and the elements of ambiguity contained within the narrative. The film aesthetic is quite culturally dependent, for complexity, innovation and predictability all depend upon sets of cultural expectations. The value in searching for a film aesthetic lies in finding out more about the relationship between a film and the culture that views it. There is little point in creating a list of films that are highly desirable because of some 'intrinsic' worth.

Finally, and most importantly, the 'deep meaning' of film is important. Three levels of film understanding are identified. At the most superficial level there is simply the recounting of the narrative with a few embellishments regarding the actors' performances. More significant criticism is possible if attention is given to the structures operating within the medium, the various codes that are part of the narrative. The claim is made that the most significant level of criticism is one that recognises the interdependence of language and culture. Language draws its meaning from culture and the values that are present in the culture are transmitted through the language back to members of the culture. In the process, the values are reworked, re-emphasised. Because film is so heavily dependent upon a mass audience the values that are being transmitted through the language of film must have broad acceptance otherwise the values would be subconsciously rejected. The outcome would be a financially disastrous film.

Although the language is so heavily dependent for its meaning upon the culture that spawned it, the transmitted values are not apparent because they have been transmitted so often that they appear to be 'normal'. It is not apparent to the viewer that a different sort of culture would have produced a different sort of meaning. (Imagine the meanings that would be created in a film industry controlled by the American Indians or the Australian Aborigines.) One of the ways in which the process of naturalisation surfaces, is in our preconceptions about the various issues we see projected on to the screen. In the process of exposing the 'natural' as in reality being cultural, it is useful to tease out one's own preconceptions. Other tools in the values search are skills in categorisation, recognising oppositions and identifying points of view.

The process of recognition and comprehension of film will never be complete. Those who search for understanding will become progressively richer, but unlike Indiana Jones, they will never find the magical stone because there is none. However the search provides its own reward, for as understanding increases, so does the satisfaction. Those who know something about the language of film are rewarded with increased enjoyment from a greater number of films. The magic never disappears. May the diegesis stay with you!

Analysis and research

Library research

1 Feature film making is an industry that has many similarities to organisational structures in other industries. There is a hierarchy of management and there are specialists who perform particular tasks.

   a Find out the function of each of the following people on a feature film:
   - producer
   - director
   - executive producer
   - director of photography
   - editor
   - mixer
   - key grip
   - scriptwriter
   - special effects

   b What positions have been omitted from this list? Describe the function of these people.
   c This sort of specialisation means that some codes become the responsibility of one person (for example, lighting). What steps are taken to ensure that a coherent, unified message is delivered and the film does not result in a collection of contradictory coded messages?
   d With so many people involved in a feature film, is it possible to say that any one person is responsible for the meaning in a film? That is, does the film have an author? How does the notion of authorship in a film compare with a novel's authorship? Does the general public consider a film to have an author? How accurate is the perception?
   e *Follow-up activity*: make a habit of watching the end credits of feature films. In this way you will be able to add to the specialist list you have compiled. Such observations should reinforce for you an understanding of how meaning in a film is so carefully constructed.

2 The Hayes Code was a censorship code that applied to Hollywood feature films. It gained notoriety because of the extreme position it took regarding the ways in which male/female relationships could be depicted. Find out what you can about the Hayes Code. How influential was it? How did it affect the construction of film narratives? Was it only concerned with the depiction of sexual relationships? To what extent could the Hayes Code be regarded as a formal instrument for reinforcing the dominant values in American society?

Written response

1 'The history of film as an art form is mainly a history of films that lost money.'
(C. Eidsvik, *Cineliteracy*, p. 177.) This quote from Charles Eidsvik tells us a little about the way he defines film art. Prepare a case in support of or in opposition to his stance.

2 Write a review for a daily newspaper of your favourite film. In your review try to persuade your readers that this film in some way rises above others. You must try and persuade them that it is a 'good' film.

Practical exercise

Script and shoot a film that consciously attempts to identify and transmit some specific cultural values. Do not be heavy-handed. Consider setting up sets of oppositions (either oppositions to those that are customarily expected or oppositions within the film). Try also to establish a point of view.

It may not be possible to shoot all of your script. If it is not, shoot a section that you feel best incorporates some of these learning points.

View and criticise your own work. If possible, discuss your attempt with a more objective audience.

OR

Examine in detail (several screenings will be necessary) a section of a feature film that you have identified as projecting a value or values. Analyse the codes that have been used to construct this meaning.

Use the examination as a basis for a film of your own. Use similar characters and codes.

View and criticise your own work. If possible, discuss your attempt with a more objective audience.

References

Noel Burch, 'Narrative/Diegesis — Threshholds, Limits' in *Screen*, vol. 23, no 2, July/August 1982 (London: Society of Education in Film and Television, 1982).

Richard Dyer, *Stars* (London: British Film Institute, 1979).

Umberto Eco, *A Theory of Semiotics* (Bloomington: Indiana Press, 1979).

Charles Eidsvik, *Cineliteracy* (New York: Random House, 1978).

Stuart Hall, 'Rediscovery of "Ideology": Return of the repressed in media studies' in *Culture, Society and the Media*, M. Gurevitch et al. (eds) (Methuen: London, 1982).

Jurij Lotman, *Semiotics of Cinema* (Michigan: Ann Arbor 1976).

Christian Metz, 'Current Problems of Film Theory' in *Screen*, vol. 14, no 2, Spring/Summer 1973 (London: Society of Education in Film and Television, 1973).

Christian Metz, *Film Language: A Semiotics of Cinema* (New York: Oxford University Press, 1974).

Janet Woollacott, 'Messages and Meanings' in *Culture, Society and the Media*, M. Gurevitch et al. (eds), (Methuen: London, 1982).

Peter Wollen, *Signs and Meaning in the Cinema* (London: British Film Institute, 1972).

Part 2
Television

Chapter 11
Television's Form

A problem posed

You have been a successful film director and now find it necessary to transfer to television production.

What factors will you have to take into account in making the transition? In what ways are the media similar? How are they different? In what ways are these similarities and differences likely to affect the sorts of programmes that you are asked to direct? How will you change your directing methods to accommodate the perceived differences?

Part 1 of this book developed a structured approach towards film analysis. It is clear that there are similarities between film and television, so it is a reasonable assumption that the developed film analysis structure is valid for television. However, there are differences between the two media, not enough to warrant a completely new approach, but sufficient to require modifications to the suggested approach for film. Some modifications have to occur because the form of the television medium is different from that of film.

Television's form — a domestic medium

One significant difference in approach comes about because television is a broadcast medium that is viewed in a domestic situation. Attention will be given to the ways in which broadcast affects meaning, but first let us examine the context of the home viewer.

Narrative image

During the discussions on film, it was established that the film was contextualised for the cinema goer well before he/she entered the cinema. This occurred because a narrative image was created about the particular film. Marketers of television shows will not go to this trouble in establishing a narrative image for an individual programme, but they will attempt to establish public awareness about a new television series. Although some of the more glamorous aspects of media hype are not available for television series (for example, world premieres with super-stars in attendance), there are many ways in which a narrative image can be established. It should be realised that in Australia television companies also have other media interests, therefore they have ready access to both formal and informal publicity. Clearly too, it is also possible for television companies to publicise the forthcoming series on the screen itself.

Once a series has begun, it generates its own contextualising momentum. Each week the public will be shown snippets of the next episode, but really these serve only as a reminder to the public to tune in to their fancied characters again next week. The plot details are not as significant as the preferred format. That is, through viewer familiarity the series itself has created its own narrative image. The same is true of non-fiction television. For example, the content of the news may differ each night but the pattern is very familiar to the viewer. The style of news presentation on each channel is a little different, allowing the viewer to choose, then enjoy a loyalty to a particular news programme.

Creating a narrative image

Technical limitations

Because television has developed as a domestic medium, the television sets have been designed to sell to a mass market. It would have been possible to design larger sets with better images and higher quality sound, but this would have put the purchase price out of reach for most home dwellers. The sets that are in modern homes do vary a little, but essentially they have been designed to be in the price range of any family. We therefore have sets that have small screens when compared with a cinema screen and cheap speakers. Furthermore, the image on the screen is created by a single dot of light that flies across the lines on the screen many times each second. Image and audio quality are therefore inferior to cinema presentation. Consequently it is not surprising if a television presentation is less than overpowering. Even if a large television projection screen is used, the technical limitations on image quality remain because of the way in which the flying dot generates an image. The spaces between the lines along which the speck of light flies become greater, resulting in a larger, but less dense image.

Spectator position

Picture the typical family in front of the television set for an evening's viewing. The light is on so the eldest child in the family can do her homework while watching and this creates quite a rumpus when discovered. Mum is knitting and dad is trying to get his feet warm by the heater. The youngest member in the family was interested in the programme when it started but has lost

interest and is now checking his face to see if he has started to grow a beard (although he is not yet nine). The scene is domestic and the medium that entertains has to accommodate this. The set is a small part of the larger furniture pattern. The image does not fill the cone of vision for any spectator. The discussions, the dog and the homework all create distractions. Marketers provide television programmes to this household so that their eyeballs can be sold to an advertiser and so the domestic situation must be accounted for. Therefore, the programmes will not demand the same levels of attention that a cinema film demands. (Feature films are shown on television with quite a different impact because of the different viewing situation. This has been touched upon in earlier chapters.)

Exercise 11.A   Ratings

Commercial television's purpose is to make a profit for the owners of the television company. Costs are met by advertising. The surplus after costs is paid to those who own the company.

'Ratings' are a system that indicates the approximate number of viewers watching any programme. Higher ratings for a programme mean that advertisers can be charged more, thereby making profits greater.

Here is a sample set of ratings for television in one Australian capital city.

Time	Channel 2 (A.B.C.)	Channel 7	Channel 9	% of sets turned on
5.30 to 6.00	2	17 Family Feud	20 Bewitched	39
6.00 to 6.30	2	23	41 NEWS	66
6.30 to 7.00	2	37 NEWS	26 Young Doctors	65
7.00 to 7.30	11 NEWS	29 Happy Days	34 Sale of the Century	73
7.30 to 8.00	24 Butterflies	19 Trapper John MD	28 Sullivans	70
8.00 to 8.30	26 Are You Being Served?	18 Trapper John MD	29 Sullivans	73
8.30 to 9.00	17	20 Quincy	37 Prisoner	73
9.00 to 9.30	17	20	37	73
10.00 to 10.30	17	21 Not the 9 o'clock	26 Dallas	62
	2	20 News	26	47
	1	7	9	17

1 It is evident that the commercial channels out-rate the A.B.C. From your knowledge about narrative image, can you suggest why? What other factors might contribute towards higher commercial television ratings?

2 Do the ratings suggest that news is a community service or a significant money making programme?

3 Based upon the figures supplied, what types of programmes would you buy if you were given the task of lifting A.B.C. ratings? What are some of the objections that you might receive?

4 Which of the two commercial companies is likely to return the larger profit in the next trading period?

5 From your own knowledge of the programmes listed (or programme types) write briefly about the claim that television is a domestic medium that caters for a broad audience who give limited attention to the television screen.

Segmentation

There are several ways in which this domestic form has affected the content of television. The ways in which the codes are affected will be discussed later. At this stage, it is worth drawing attention to the *segmentation* that occurs to accommodate limited concentration spans. Segmentation is most noticeable on commercial channels. Episodes within the drama are separated by advertisements. This does not mean that the spectator concentrates only for the drama then mentally switches off for the advertisements. The advertisements provide a variety in content, pace and style. Indeed, you have probably experienced many occasions when your attention has wandered during a television drama, only to find that you have 'switched on' again for the advertisement.

This is not surprising when you consider the cost per second, for the advertisement is a far more expensive product than the cost of drama. At very high cost, techniques have been developed to arrest viewer attention. Even within a television drama, the action is segmented to accommodate an audience that may be giving only marginal attention to the small screen.

You can probably think of many drama series that show a scene at a local pub, then cut to different characters in the used car yard, then a third scene at the police station, again with different characters. These disparate segments may only overlap in the final segment when the lives of the various characters are shown to affect each other.

Segmentation is even more apparent in non-fiction television. News and current events programmes are very popular and are profitable forms of television entertainment that draw very high ratings. Even a superficial analysis of a popular television news programme will reveal how clearly segmented the various items are. Perhaps it is significant that each news item forms a segment that is not much different from an advertising segment (average time range is thirty seconds to two minutes). News has no natural or inherent length. The news item has been made to match the concentration span that advertisers have found to be most effective.

Sporting telecasts too, have been segmented in various ways. Some sports events have structures that encourage segmenting at particular points (for example, at the end of an over of cricket). Segments are also created by slow-motion replays, spectator scenes, scoreboard shots, and so on.

Exercise 11.B Segmentation

Television dramas are usually divided into segments. This allows the domestic viewer to concentrate for shorter periods of time on one aspect of the drama. Sometimes the segments are developed quite separately from each other, and the action associated with each only coincides in the final segment. [*Special equipment: television monitor, video replay equipment, access to an episode of a TV series*]

1 View an episode of a television series (for example, *Minder, Hill Street Blues*).

2 Identify the segments — those sections of the story that seem to have fairly self-contained characters and locations. This will be easier if you present the segments visually.

3 To what extent do we depend upon a fore-knowledge of the main characters for the segments to make some sense as a complete story?

4 British television series often contain a pub segment. Pub life is a feature of British life, but the pub segment is more than just a reflection of British life style. The pub scene is a very useful (and cheap) segment. What advantages and possibilities does a pub segment give creators of the series?

5 Segments are most noticeable on television. A film tends to be a more cohesive unit. Is there any indication that some form of segmentation occurs in film? Use examples to justify your answer.

Scenes from *Minder:* The pub segment

The visit segment

The garage segment

The apartment segment

Scheduling

These segments of television are linked together and organised into what we recognise as a television programme. Sometimes the segments are simply cumulative such as in a news broadcast or current affairs programme which will consist of perhaps a dozen discrete segments. But other segments are organised sequentially and repetitively in the form of a series or serial. This organisation into repetitive units involves *scheduling*. Scheduling is the way in which a day's or a week's programme is organised into particular time slots in an effort to attract the maximum number of viewers at any one time. Scheduling is closely related to the perceived behaviours of the family unit, thus children's programmes are scheduled for after school hours, women's programmes are scheduled for daytime viewing. Scheduling provides viewer familiarity in that we know our favourite programme will be on at the same time next week and probably each week after that.

The repetitive nature of television scheduling is partly an outcome of the greed of the medium. McLuhan described television as the 'hungry medium', meaning that it continually demanded new material. Television is 'on' for something like eighteen hours per day. This means that a huge amount of material is devoured every day by broadcast television. This voraciousness has two effects. First, it means that television must be repetitive if it is to produce sufficient material. So we have the news programme repeated every night, the quiz show twice every week, the current affairs programme every Sunday and so on. Secondly, the huge continuous output of television creates what Raymond Williams described as 'flow'. Although television operates in terms of segments linked together, the overwhelming impression for the viewer is one of continuous flow. Williams describes flow as a liquid process by which broadcast television tends to average the various programme forms in such a way that everything becomes like everything else, advertisements are much like the drama, as is news and so on. Perhaps this 'flow' effect accounts for why television viewers tend not to turn the switch on and off for discrete programmes; rather they leave it on and then select segments to be viewed from the 'flow'.

Many countries have both commercial and paternal television. Paternal television is television under the control of an independent authority and at least partly funded by government sources. The Australian Broadcasting Corporation and the British Broadcasting Corporation are examples of paternal television. Although paternal television does not play commercials for revenue, it is not free of commercials (for its own programmes and for public announcements) and these are used to create segments. The difference between commercial and paternal television is that the segments on the latter are longer. Within the programmes on paternal television, the segmentation is identical to the commercial counterparts.

Exercise 11.C Scheduling

Because television is a domestic medium, its programmes are arranged in accordance with the supposed activities of its viewers. Programmes are scheduled with the viewers in mind.
[*Special equipment: television guide*]

1 Below is an excerpt from a television guide for a weekday. Copy out the schedule and next to each programme suggest who might be the viewers in these time slots.

What changes might growing unemployment bring to daytime scheduling?

2 Take the television guide and look up any

weekday from 4 — 9 p.m. For each programme listed write down:
- the intended audience
- the relationship between family lifestyle and the scheduling of the programmes.

Consider your own domestic situation. What changes would you make if you had the power to decide television schedules?

2	7	9
8.00 Sesame Street	7.30 Bugs Bunny Show	7.00 The 7am Early News Report
9.00 Play School	8.00 Tom and Jerry Show	9.00 Here's Humphrey
9.30 Flip, Slide, Turn	8.30 All New Popeye Show	10.00 The Restless Years
9.50 Environmental Man	9.00 Fat Cat and Friends	11.00 The Richard Simmons Show
10.20 Ensemble	9.30 Flamingo Road	11.30 The 11.30 News Report
10.50 Words Fail Me	10.25 Holiday Island	12.00 The Mike Walsh Show
11.20 My Place, Your Place	11.15 Late Late Breakfast Show	1.35 MOVIE: Bitter Harvest (1963, PGR, rpt) ** Stars Janet Munro, John Stride, Anne Cunningham. A girl from an impoverished small town longs for something more. She sets out to find excitement but becomes engulfed in tragedy.
11.40 Words and Pictures	11.55 News Headlines	
1.05 For the Juniors: David, My Blind Cousin	12.00 Another World	
1.25 Lower Primary Science: Tooled Up	1.00 Days of Our Lives	
1.50 Playsport: Badminton	2.00 The Young and the Restless	
2.20 Insight: Magic	3.00 Wheel of Fortune	
2.40 A Visit From Captain Cook	3.25 News Headlines	
3.00 Sesame Street	3.30 The Flintstones	
4.00 Play School	4.00 Lassie	
4.30 Dr Snuggles	4.30 Shirl's Neighbourhood	3.30 Three's Company
	5.00 Happy Days	

Viewing habits

Unlike cinema, television is cheap to watch and the cost does not increase significantly with extended viewing. As a domestic medium, it is more likely to be watched when the inclination occurs, rather than as a special event. Occasionally there will be something special on television that demands to be watched at a particular time, but mostly, people decide that they will watch television, *then* decide what they will watch. One cynic has suggested that they thumb through the

television guide and select the least bad programme.

Before there was television, film going was a regular weekly event for most urban dwellers. Sometimes serials would be included as part of the film programme, particularly for the younger audiences. A serial was a drama that was divided into several parts and shown over successive weeks. Each week's episode would finish with a climactic moment, thus encouraging the audience to return the following week. Would the hero escape from the clutches of the villains? As indicated earlier, *Raiders of the Lost Ark*, though not a serial, captured the spirit of the genre. Serials were also a feature of radio before the advent of television.

Television still has its serials (mostly seen during the daytime soap operas) but the series programme is more popular. A series is a modification of the serial form. In a series the lead characters and formats are consistent but the viewer is able to understand each episode without reference to happenings in previous episodes. The series therefore, is more suited to the sporadic television viewing habits that have been indicated. The spectator is able to comfortably slot into the narrative and enjoy the unit as a total experience. The creators hope that the spectator will enjoy the experience enough to want to tune in again next week, but it will not be to find out if the hero escapes from the villain's clutches because each episode is self-contained. Previous episodes serve only as part of a developing narrative image about the series.

If you reflect upon the presentations of news and current events programmes, it will also become evident that these are also part of the series format.

Scenes from *Falcon Crest*: Identifying with characters encourages the audience to return for the next episode.

Exercise 11.D Mini-series

The television 'mini-series' is a combination of series and serial. It is possible to miss some episodes and still understand what is happening, but at the end of each episode there is an enigma that is not resolved. This encourages the audience to return for the next episode.

1 Select a mini-series that you are familiar with (for example, *Bodyline*, *Jewel in the Crown* or one that is current).

2 It is important to attract as many viewers as possible to the first episode of a serial type format. What sort of marketing occurred before the mini-series was screened?

3 Television mini-series are frequently developments of well known novels or events (for example, *Roots*: the book, or *Bodyline*: the infamous test cricket series). How does this help in attracting an audience to view episode 1 of the series?

4 How are the screenings scheduled to encourage people to watch as many of the episodes as possible? Ratings figures suggest that there is a large audience fall-off as a series progresses. To what extent is the scheduling an attempt to counteract this trend?

5 Is the mini-series a format that is admirably suited to the television medium or is it a contrived format that is more dependent upon marketing than inherent suitability for television?

The television 'special occasion' is confined largely to live happenings, particularly sporting events. The special attraction of these is discussed when the 'broadcast' aspect of the medium is considered. 'Special event' status used to be bestowed on feature films screened on television. Although the conditions for viewing are not as conducive as in a cinema, ratings were generally high for special film screenings. Feature films enjoy a production edge on most commercial television material because they are made with much higher budgets. Programmes that depend exclusively upon television exposure must be made with much smaller budgets. That is, feature films were the luxury items of broadcast television and this made them special. Feature films that are made exclusively for television (telemovies) do not enjoy such luxury expenditure and therefore do not warrant 'special' status. Telemovies also suffer because they do not have the legacy of a narrative image that was created for cinema patrons.

Since the video hire outlets have competed with broadcast television, ratings have dropped quite dramatically for this type of programming.

Exercise 11.E   Live telecasts

Audiences are attracted to live telecasts because they feel part of the event. Because the event coincides with the presentation of the event, there is a tendency to accept the presentation as unmediated — that is, as the reality rather than as a version of reality. [*Special requirements: access to television coverage of a live sporting event, access to television sports review programmes. Special equipment: television monitor, video replay facility*]

1 Analyse in detail 20 minutes of a live sports television coverage.

2 By using the knowledge that you have already gained about film codes, identify ways in which information has been selected for presentation. (Refer particularly to the technical and symbolic codes.) How have the audio codes been used to heighten the drama of the event? To what extent does the commentator direct the viewer perceptions of the event?

3 Compare the telecast of the live sporting event with an occasion when you have been present at a sporting spectacle. What is gained and what is lost in the telecast?

4 Television channels gain additional mileage from live events by showing highlights at a later time. Experts are brought in to comment on the action. Football review programmes are particularly popular. Len Masterman, a television theorist, believes that when review

programmes are time slotted well after the event, the 'experts' become the event, not the action. The football action only supports the live happening of the panel programme. Analyse in detail a review panel programme and detail evidence to support or deny Masterman's claim.

5 If you have argued that there is some validity in Masterman's claim, what other features are there in the sports review programme that create the review as a happening in its own right? How is the audience at home drawn into the 'event'? If you have argued against Masterman's claim, how do you explain the need for quizzes, highlights such as 'goal of the day', and competitions?

Television's form — a broadcast medium

Television, as we presently know it, is largely a broadcast medium and its form has been significantly determined by this fact. Though it is possible to receive images from video or cable sources, the predominant pattern is to use air waves. There are therefore some similarities between television and the other broadcast medium, radio.

Both radio and television are particularly suitable media for creating programmes at the time that an event occurs. Even when the broadcast is international, the message can be received almost simultaneously. The fact that the media 'happening' coincides with the actual 'happening' generates a greater sense of involvement than is possible with a recorded event. The spectator feels as if he/she is watching the actual event rather than a *mediated version* of it. This is why millions of people with only a marginal interest in athletics will spend hours in front of the set when the Olympic Games are on, or why millions will watch a live telecast of a royal wedding. There is a sense that the viewer is participating in a moment of history. Once the event has occurred, it is still possible to replay the proceedings, but this is not quite the same for the audience. Once the immediacy of the event has gone some of the magic disappears. Television therefore seems to have its greatest appeal at times of 'live' coverage, allowing a sense of immediacy to be generated by the spectator. The worldwide

ratings for international sporting events and the number of spectators at events such as royal weddings support this contention.

Marketers of television programmes have recognised the value that this sense of 'immediacy' has for attracting audiences. When a programme is not transmitted live, attempts will still be made to generate a sense of 'immediacy' for the spectator. Concerts or even situation comedies that have been recorded in front of a live audience are the most obvious examples of this manipulation. Although meaning is significantly re-created in the days after the live audience has departed, the lounge room spectator is given a sense of being part of that live audience. Shots are edited, new sound tracks laid, yet for the television viewer, it is all happening 'now'.

Quiz programmes are excellent examples of these pseudo-'live' events. A great deal of effort is made to create the illusion of a 'live' music hall event. The set is created to give the impression of a stage, the quiz master has music hall *bonhomie* and a bevy of beautiful girls to serve him in the traditionally sexist music hall manner. He is even given ogling rights in the same way as the music hall compere was allowed to be something of a lecherous character. However the modern form of lechery is far more clean-cut because the modern quiz master is a superstar in his (is it ever her?) own right. There is also a great degree of audience participation in the quiz programme, to the extent that on many programmes, the audience is encouraged to shout advice to the contestants. Floating lights, special sound effects and gaudy properties add to the 'aren't we all having fun together' atmosphere. The content of the quiz or contest must be very secondary compared with the atmosphere and the rags-to-riches human drama that is generated. Even if the lounge room spectator knows that it is common practice to record up to six of these programmes in a single day then telecast them over several weeks, when the programme begins on television there is a sense of live telecast, of immediacy about it.

Quiz programme, *Jeopardy*

Exercise 11.F   The 'happening'

Popular-music programmes, such as 'Countdown', are favourites with young audiences (and with older viewers who are sometimes reluctant to admit their interest). The programmes generate the sense of a happening that is occurring right now. The currency of the music helps, but the programmes are also staged to add to that sense of 'happening' and 'immediacy'. [*Special requirements*: *access to popular-music programme. Special equipment*: *television monitor, video replay facility*]

1 From knowledge (and preferably viewing) of a popular-music programme, identify the technical and symbolic codes that create the sense of 'happening' and 'immediacy' that is in the programme. Does the programme have a central character or superstar? How does this character add to the overall flavour of the programme?

2 View a couple of minutes of the programme with the volume turned down. How important is the sound track? Turn the sound up again and analyse the ways in which the audio codes heighten the 'happening' and the 'immediacy'.

3 What part does the live audience play? Do they contribute in any way or are they just decoration?

4 To what extent is the programme segmented? If the programme is segmented, identify the segments. If not, identify another television genre with a similar pattern. To what extent is the programme's pattern repeated each week? How is novelty injected into the repetitive pattern?

Other television programmes also exploit this sense of 'immediacy' but in less obvious ways. News coverages give you headlines that are phrased in the present tense. Library footage is presented in the context of recent events. News is selected on the basis of what is perceived to be of interest to the home viewer at this moment. The tendency in recent years has been for news to be presented in more frequent slots rather than only in the traditional early evening telecast. These news *updates* put the viewer in touch with what is happening *now*.

The same applies to current events programmes — the name speaks for itself. Again, ratings show that this type of programme is extremely popular. We are arguing that they are popular because they capitalise on the distinctive form of television: it is a broadcast medium and therefore encourages programmes that imply a sense of 'immediacy'.

The form that television drama takes can also be attributed to the broadcast nature of the medium to some degree. It has already been indicated that the most effective packaging of television drama is the series. Television series and the related genres of situation comedies and soap operas, provide continual updates in the lives of the screen characters. Very rarely is the history of the series referred to in a current episode, yet we accept that the characters do have a history, for we assume that the relationship between the characters will remain constant from one week to the next. Each week we are given an event that is occurring 'now'. If the programme is a comedy, then the laugh track will confirm that we are experiencing the events as a performance (yet we still 'believe' the events). Further reference will be made to television drama's capacity to develop a sense of 'immediacy' when television narrative is discussed.

Conclusion

The significant characteristics of television as a medium are that its message is *broadcast* into a *domestic* environment. Though it is possible to receive television images from video or cable sources, broadcast is still the major mode of transmission. For this reason the content that is most appropriate to television is that which takes advantage of the immediacy of broadcast. In this sense there are parallels with radio. Live coverage, on-the-spot reports and simulated live telecasts (quizzes and 'happenings') are some formats that television either shares with radio or has usurped from radio once television became the significant mass medium. The effect of broadcast upon dramas, particularly series and

---

TELEVISION'S FORM

Television is a domestic medium

Encourages	Immediate establishment of a narrative image
	Segmentation
	Repetitive scheduling
	Constant programme output
Favours	Series over serials
	Specials

Television is a broadcast medium

Encourages	'Live' programmes
	'Immediacy' programmes
	'Happenings'

situation comedies, is not quite as obvious. Further attention will be given to this issue in a later chapter.

The domestic environment for audience reception has affected the presentation formats and the specific content of television. The tendency to segment programmes is one illustration of the way in which the domestic situation has been accommodated. The notion of domesticity goes further however. It is common to hear about television being 'family entertainment'. The example that was given earlier in the chapter of mum, dad and the children is an illustration of the family being entertained. It is a popularly held concept of a family, even though less than half of the families in this country conform to that stereotype. This concept of the balanced nuclear family influences the sorts of programmes that are presented and when they are presented. Hence, the notion of a domestic medium goes beyond the way in which programmes are structured to satisfy a partly attentive audience watching a marginal quality image on a television set. It also determines the content that is deemed to be 'appropriate'.

These two aspects of television — broadcast, and domesticity — affect the content of television and consequently the ways in which meaning is created.

Analysis and research

1 a Analyse in detail one television news programme. Identify all of the ways in which a sense of 'immediacy' is injected into the programme. Consider:

- The regular features such as introduction, newsreader's opening lines, station identification.
- The characters — newsreader/s, reporters. How do they deliver their lines? Consider the various codes.
- The individual stories. How recent? How topical? How visual?

b Television news contains segments, then segments within segments. Identify the segments and sub-segments within a news programme. Are any of the sub-segments more likely to appeal to particular members of the family audience? Although segments can be identified, efforts are made to link them together. What devices are used to link the segments?

c How do television companies create a narrative image about their news programmes?

Library research

2 Many of television's programme genres have been drawn from radio rather than film. This is not surprising as they are both broadcast media. News, soap operas and quiz shows are only a few examples.

- Research in your library and then try to outline a typical evening's radio programme *before* television became a household medium. (If you have difficulty in obtaining the information in the library, ask some of the middle-aged and elderly members of the community. You will be surprised how much detail they can provide about programmes and time slots.)
- Compare your constructed radio programme with an evening's television programme.
- If it is possible, take the comparison further so that weekday and weekend radio and television programmes can be compared.
- Write or discuss in detail the similarities in pre-television radio programming and modern television planning. How do you account for these similarities and differences?

3 Cable television is an alternative to broadcast television in some parts of the world, particularly in North America.

Research in your library to find out as much as you can about cable television — the sorts of programmes that it provides, the choice that it offers, the cost to the users, the degree of saturation it has in urban areas.

- On the basis of your research, discuss or write in detail about the similarities and differences between cable television and broadcast television. Consider the audience sense of immediacy in each, the ability of each to target specific members of a family, the number of viewers necessary to make a programme viable. Is it likely that cable television will eventually eliminate broadcast television? Justify your answer. How does the potential for television via satellite affect the cable/broadcast debate? Is the *form* of television likely to change as a result of these developments?

Written response

1 'Perhaps the most serious threat to television, as an art to be taken seriously is its direction ... to the bitch Goddesses Mammon and Mass Appeal, who of course go hand in hand.' (Halliwell, *Halliwell's Television Companion*, p. x)

Consider earlier arguments about film aesthetics and suggest what modifications need to be made to the arguments to develop a case for a television aesthetic. How significant are Mammon (money, ratings etc.) and *mass* appeal in the development of television as an art form?

2 Given the form of television that has been identified, what will the weekly television guide feature in twenty years time? Which programme types will be most popular, and which of the present programme types will disappear? How will news presentations have changed in the twenty years?

Practical exercise

[*Special equipment: video portapak*]
School lessons and school assemblies have developed a form that is most appropriate for the medium — the school. If the medium was changed, the form of the lesson or assembly would have to change.

Take a mundane school lesson or school assembly and rework it so that it is suitable for television. Reconstruct your lead and support characters to accommodate television's form. Rework the settings and the delivery style so that your programme has a sense of 'immediacy'. Remember that you no longer have a captive audience so you must inject pace in order to capture ratings.

- Prepare a 20-minute script, also indicating the appropriate commercial breaks.
- Organise your crew and cast, then create your programme. (It may not be possible to shoot all 20 minutes.)
- Review your efforts. Consider the potential audience age range and consider the presentation style.

Have you tended to comply with an existing television genre when developing your presentation? What improvements could be made to make your programme more marketable? How could a broader audience age range be attracted? What precautions have you taken to ensure that your audience does not switch off during the advertisements?

References

John Ellis, *Visible Fictions: Cinema: Television: Video* (London: Routledge and Kegan Paul, 1982).
Lesley Halliwell, *Halliwell's Television Companion*, 2nd edn (London: Granada, 1982).
Len Masterman, *Teaching About Television* (London: Macmillan, 1980).
Raymond Williams, *Culture* (London: Fontana, 1981).
Herb Zettl, 'Television Aesthetics' in *Understanding Television: Essays on Television as a Social and Cultural Force*, R. Adler (ed.) (New York: Praeger, 1981).

Chapter 12
Television Content

A problem posed

As a television producer, you have been given the out-takes (leftovers) of a spy film. You now have to create a spy series by using the out-takes for novelty and studio sets as the consistent images. How many sets can you afford if you are working within the parameters of a 'normal' budget? What instructions will you give to your script writers about the sets? What are the sets? How are they to be used? What are your instructions to the script writers regarding character development? What can and cannot happen to the characters?

In the previous chapter the distinctive form of television was discussed in some detail. The characteristics of television as a mass medium, its domestic nature, its perception of its audience as a family group and its hunger for material distinguishes the narrative patterns of television from those of film.

The model of narrative development discussed in the film section is generally applicable to television but the distinctive features of television narrative must be taken into account. For the purposes of this discussion there is no need to distinguish between fact and fiction television. Television dramas, news programmes, current affairs programmes, quiz shows and such like share the same narrative form. The differences between fiction television and non-fiction television lie in the origin of the material that is used (whether or not it purports to be true), not in the structure or presentation of the material.

Repetition

A glance at the weekly television programme guide reveals that television repeats itself. This repetition occurs at all levels. The programmes are repeated either on a daily or weekly basis usually at exactly the same time. Few of us now even bother to look up the guide to find out when our favourite programme is showing.

We can be confident that if we saw it last Monday at nine o'clock then it will be on next Monday at the same time. Formats, too, are repetitive. The presentation of the news is identical every night of the week; the quiz show host will bounce on to the set and tell a joke at the start of every show; the comedy always begins with the credits, theme music and the entrance of the central character. If there was a radical change one night and the quiz show host did not run on and joke with the audience, viewers' first reaction would be that they had the wrong channel switched on. Similarly, within the individual programmes the characters and plot lines are repeated from show to show. When a viewer switches on one of his/her favourite dramas it is not to see who will appear this week but to see what adventure his/her favourite character is involved in. Many of the genre programmes repeat plot lines and so we are confident that a police drama will always deal with crime, a hospital drama with a medical emergency.

The repetitive nature of television means that there is a high degree of viewer familiarity with the material. This viewer familiarity with formats, characters and plots means that characterisation in a television programme is minimal. Viewers are intimately acquainted with the characters so it is unnecessary after the first programme to devote much space within the show to developing character.

MONDAY

| | 2 | 7 | 9 |

Pick of the flicks

Judith McGrath (above), as Officer Colleen Powell, is one of the characters in Nine's 8.35pm soapie, *Prisoner*, who finds her life shattered by Carol Colsen's murder case and her colleague Joan's involvement in it. Seven has a *State Affair Special* at 7.35 on artificial conception and surrogate motherhood. It is titled *The Baby Makers*. ABC-TV starts Ronnie Barker's new series, *Open All Hours*, at 7.55.

Tonight at a glance

	2	7	9
6	Cartoons	State Affair	News and Weather
	Monkey		
		News and Weather	
7	Take Five	Sons and Daughters	Sale of the Century
	News and Weather		
	Let There Be Love	News Headlines	Willesee
		State Affair Special	
8	Open All Hours	MOVIE: High Ice	Arthur C. Clarke's Mysterious World
	Nationwide		News Break
			Prisoner
9	Minder		
10	News	Quincy	
	Burrows		

2

8.00 **Sesame Street**
9.00 **Play School**
9.50 **Flip, Slide, Turn**
10.10 **A Search for Solutions:** Investigation
10.50 **Northern Australian Documentaries:** The Spirit of Uncle Edward
11.10 **Maths in a Box**
11.30 **For the Juniors**
12.00 **Four Corners**
12.30 **Open File:** Aren't the Thursday Ladies Fat?
1.05 **A Tale of Bhutan**
1.45 **Countrywide**
2.15 **Detective**
3.00 **Sesame Street**
3.55 **Dr Snuggles**
4.00 **Play School**
4.30 **Mr Squiggle and Friends**
5.00 **Secret Valley**
5.25 **Danger Mouse**
5.30 **Inspector Gadget**
5.55 **Come and Get It**
5.58 **News Headlines**
6.00 **Cartoons**
6.10 **Monkey**
6.55 **Take Five**
7.00 **News and Weather**
7.30 **Let There Be Love:** Dad's the Word. Timothy is still intent on marrying Judy and has accepted that she has three children. He has not considered what to do with them when he and Judy go on their honeymoon.
7.55 **Open All Hours.** Arkwright is more dedicated than ever to his twin business objectives — to get his grasping hands on the public's money and to brow-beat his nephew Granville into being a worthy heir to his commercial empire.
8.25 **Nationwide**
9.00 **Minder:** Back in Good Old England. Robber Jack Ragg returns to England after eight years with a lot of money and an account to settle.
9.50 **Late News and Weather**
10.00 **The Burrows Collection:** Pearce Pickering. Don Burrows features two pioneers of Australian jazz, Tom Pickering and Ian Pearce. Pickering and Pearce's musical relationship goes back to the mid 30s.
10.55 **All Star Soccer**
11.55 **Close**

§ **Supertext subtitles**
# **Stereo transmission**
Programs correct at time of going to press. Stations may change programs after publication date.

7

7.00 **Bugs Bunny**
7.25 **Tom and Jerry Show**
7.55 **Famous Adventures of Mr Magoo**
8.25 **Hong Kong Phooey**
8.50 **Here's Lucy**
9.20 **Fat Cat and Friends**
9.50 **Too Close For Comfort**
10.20 **White Shadow**
11.15 **The Late Late Breakfast Show**
11.55 **News Headlines**
12.00 **Another World**
1.00 **Days of Our Lives**
2.00 **The Young and the Restless**
2.55 **News Headlines**
3.00 **Wheel of Fortune**
3.30 **The Flintstones**
4.00 **Wombat**
4.30 **Lassie**
5.00 **Happy Days**
5.30 **The New Price is Right**
6.00 **State Affair**
6.30 **News and Weather**
7.00 § **Sons and Daughters.** Karen decides what to do about Todd. Leanne tries to help Jeff overcome his drinking problem. Stars Rowena Wallace, Tom Richards, Pat McDonald.
7.30 **News Headlines**
7.35 **State Affair Special:** The Baby Makers. Looks at the greatest moral dilemma facing Australian society — the artificial conception of human life.
8.00 **MOVIE: High Ice** (1980, PGR) ** Stars David Janssen, James G. Richardson, Tony Musanti. Two couples on a weekend mountain climb are caught in an avalanche. One person dies — the others are trapped on a tiny ledge in cold, raw weather.
9.55 **Quincy.** During the television taping of his nightclub act, an entertainer is consumed by flames. Stars Jack Klugman, John S. Ragin, Robert Ito, Anita Gillette.
11.00 **T.J. Hooker:** Too Late for Love. Hooker and Romano clash when Hooker suspects that Romano's girlfriend may be feeding information to a gang of fur thieves. Stars William Shatner, Adrian Zmed, Heather Locklear, Richard Herd.
12.00 **Lou Grant.** Stars Edward Asner, Robert Walden, Linda Kelsey.
1.00 **State Affair.** Repeat of the 6pm program.
1.30 **Close**

9

6.00 **The Life and Legend of Wyatt Earp**
6.30 **Victory at Sea**
7.00 **The 7am Early News Report**
9.00 **Here's Humphrey**
10.00 **Rainbow**
10.30 **The Streets of San Francisco**
11.30 **The 11.30 News Report**
12.00 **The Mike Walsh Show**
1.35 **MOVIE: Kiss Them For Me** (1957, G, rpt) *½ Stars Cary Grant, Suzy Parker, Jayne Mansfield. Some naval air officers find romance on a four-day leave in San Francisco.
3.30 **Magilla Gorilla**
4.00 **Simon Townsend's Wonder World**
4.30 # **The Ossie Ostrich Video Show**
5.00 **Diff'rent Strokes**
5.30 **Joanie loves Chachi**
6.00 **News and Weather**
7.00 # **Sale of the Century.** Hosted by Tony Barber and Delvene Delaney.
7.30 **Willesee**
8.00 **Arthur C. Clarke's Mysterious World:** Dragons, Dinosaurs and Giant Snakes. In 1900, an unidentified monkey was photographed by a Swiss geologist — but no trace of the creatures has since been found. A zoologist searches for the world's "newest" big creature and an American professor investigates reports on pterodactyls in Africa.
8.30 **News Break**
8.35 **Prisoner.** Joan's involvement in Carol Colsen's murder case has shattering repercussions. Stars Maggie Kirkpatrick, Judith McGrath.
10.35 **The Streets of San Francisco:** Blockade. Two men — one meek and the other a burly animal type — are involved in the rape-murder of a waitress. Stars Karl Malden, Ida Lupino, Michael Douglas.
11.35 **Tonight With Bert Newton**
12.40 **MOVIE: Guns of the Revolution** (1970, PGR) ** Stars Ernest Borgnine, Padre Humberto, Harry Harris.
2.25 **MOVIE: The L-Shaped Room** (1963, AO, b/w) **½ Stars Leslie Caron, Tom Bell, Brock Peters. An unwed mother-to-be, living in a squalid boarding house, finds companionship and love.
4.35 **Animal World**
5.05 **Bonanza**

NEWS Mon-Fri 6·30

MONDAY

Pick of the flicks

Jack Klugman (above), as Quincy, gets married in tonight's special, two-hour edition of *Quincy* (Seven, 8.35). Being Quincy, he manages to combine his nuptials with the investigation of an old woman who claims to have murdered her husband. Nine also bowls up a double serving — a two-hour episode of *Prisoner*, from 9.35pm. ABC-TV has *Let There Be Love* at 7.30pm, followed by *Open All Hours* at 7.55pm.

Tonight at a glance

	2	7	9
6	Cartoons Monkey	State Affair	News and Weather
		News and Weather	
7	Take Five News and Weather	Sons and Daughters	Sale of the Century
	Let There Be Love	News Headlines TV's Funniest Game Show Moments	Willesee
8	Open All Hours		Arthur C. Clarke's Mysterious World
	Nationwide	Quincy	News Break Cut That Out
9	Minder		
			News Break Prisoner
10	News Burrows		

2

8.00 **Sesame Street**
9.00 **Play School**
9.50 **Flip, Slide, Turn:** Symmetry — Mathematical Monsters
10.10 **A Search for Solutions:** Evidence
10.50 **Northern Australian Documentaries:** Darwin — City on the Move
11.10 **Maths in a Box**
11.30 **For the Juniors**
12.00 **Four Corners**
12.30 **Open File:** A Different Sort of System
1.05 **A Tale of Bhutan**
1.25 **Music Time**
1.45 **Countrywide**
2.15 **Detective**
3.00 **Sesame Street**
3.55 **Dr Snuggles**
4.00 **Play School**
4.30 **Mr Squiggle and Friends**
5.00 **Secret Valley:** The Monster
5.25 **Danger Mouse**
5.30 **Inspector Gadget**
5.55 **Come and Get It.** With Peter Russell-Clarke.
5.58 **News Headlines**
6.00 **Cartoons**
6.10 **Monkey**
6.55 **Take Five**
7.00 **News and Weather**
7.30 **Let There Be Love:** Man and Super Man. When his mother-in-law turns up, Timothy finds himself compared with Judy's late husband.
7.55 **Open All Hours.** Arkwright improves the sale of an overstocked commodity with spellbinding efficiency, while Granville's bid for power is thwarted again. Stars Ronnie Barker, David Jason.
8.25 **Nationwide**
9.00 **Minder:** In. A shady deal involving a hot car lands Arthur in trouble. A German police inspector tries to nail him as "the Fulham Connection" for an international drug ring. Somehow, Terry has to arrange Arthur's release.
9.55 **Late News and Weather**
10.05 **The Burrows Collection:** The Brazilians. Two brilliant contemporary Brazilian musicians, Nana Vasconcelos and Egberto Gismonti, were recorded in concert at the Festival of Perth. Gismonti plays eight and 12-string guitar while Vasconcelos produces extraordinary sounds playing a berimbau, an ancient, one-stringed African instrument.
11.10 **All Star Soccer**
12.10 **Close**

7

7.00 **Bugs Bunny**
7.25 **Tom and Jerry Show**
7.55 **Famous Adventures of Mr Magoo**
8.25 **Hong Kong Phooey:** Gold Fisher
8.50 **Here's Lucy:** Rudy Vallee
9.20 **Fat Cat and Friends**
9.50 **Happy Days:** A Place of His Own
10.20 **White Shadow:** Trial and Error
11.15 **The Late Late Breakfast Show**
11.55 **News Headlines**
12.00 **Another World**
1.00 **Days of Our Lives**
2.00 **The Young and the Restless**
2.55 **News Headlines**
3.00 **Wheel of Fortune**
3.30 **The Flintstones**
4.00 **Wombat**
4.30 **Lassie**
5.00 **Happy Days:** Breaking Up is Hard to Do
5.30 **The New Price is Right.** Hosted by Ian Turpie.
6.00 **State Affair.** Hosted by Tony Murphy.
6.30 **News and Weather**
7.00 § **Sons and Daughters.** Nat's decision forces Karen to choose between him and Wayne. A potentially violent friend of Terry's falls in love with Amanda. Stars Rowena Wallace, Tom Richards, Pat McDonald.
7.30 **News Headlines**
7.35 **TV's Funniest Game Show Moments.** Hosted by William Shatner.
8.35 **Quincy:** Quincy's Wedding. Even Quincy's wedding can't keep him away from an investigation into an elderly woman who claims to have murdered her husband. Despite an angry confrontation, Quincy and his fiancee finally take their walk down the aisle. Stars Jack Klugman, John S. Ragin, Robert Ito, Anita Gillette.
10.35 **Not the Nine O'clock News.** Stars Pamela Stephenson, Rowan Atkinson, Mel Smith, Chris Langham.
11.35 **Cagney and Lacey:** You Call this Plain Clothes? Cagney and Lacey pose as prostitutes to act as decoys for a deranged killer who has murdered three women.
12.35 **State Affair.** Hosted by Tony Murphy.
1.05 **Close**

9

6.00 **The Life and Legend of Wyatt Earp**
6.30 **You Asked For It**
7.00 **The 7am Early News Report**
9.00 **Here's Humphrey**
10.00 **Rainbow**
10.30 **The Streets of San Francisco**
11.30 **The 11.30 News Report**
12.00 **The Mike Walsh Show**
1.35 **MOVIE: Hombre** (1967, PGR, rpt)*** Stars Paul Newman, Diane Cilento, Cameron Mitchell. In Arizona in 1880, eight people board a stagecoach headed south. They are attacked by bandits who kidnap one passenger's wife and leave the others to die in the desert.
3.35 **Magilla Gorilla**
4.00 **Simon Townsend's Wonder World**
4.30 # **The Ossie Ostrich Video Show**
5.00 **Diff'rent Strokes**
5.30 **Joanie Loves Chachi**
6.00 **News and Weather**
7.00 # **Sale of the Century**
7.30 **Willesee**
8.00 **Arthur C. Clarke's Mysterious World:** Monsters of the Deep. From the seven seas come spine-chilling tales of monsters of the deep.
8.30 **News Break**
8.35 **Cut That Out**
9.30 **News Break**
9.35 **Prisoner.** Joan's involvement in Carol Colsen's murder case has shattering repercussions. Phyllis takes advantage of Brandy's vulnerable schizophrenic state. Roxanne realises the legal position she's in as a surrogate mother.
11.35 **Tonight With Bert Newton**
12.45 **MOVIE: Rush It** (1979, PGR) ** Stars Judy Kahan, Tom Berenger, Jill Eikenberry. Catherine is a messenger for the Rush It messenger service. She is an intelligent, humorous young woman doing a job she likes. She experiences many adventures as she crisscrosses New York.
2.10 **MOVIE:The Tunnel of Love** (1958, PGR, b/w, rpt)**½ Stars Doris Day, Richard Widmark, Gig Young. A suburban couple who, after five years of marriage, have a charming home but no baby, decide to adopt a child.
3.50 **MOVIE: The Strangers in 7A** (1972, PGR, rpt)**½ Stars Andy Griffith, Ida Lupino.
5.05 **Bonanza**

Viewer familiarity is recognised and promoted by the programmers. In the earlier television programme guides (see channel 2, 7.30 pm), the writer has obviously assumed that the reader will be familiar with the character to the extent that he, Timothy, is referred to by his first name and the reader's impression is that we are simply catching up with what Timothy is up to this week.

If viewer familiarity with the television programmes was total, however, then there would be no reason to watch television. Into this pattern of repetition, television programmers must find a way to inject novelty to ensure that the audience continues to watch the programmes.

'The basic principle remains the same: to bring interesting individuals in remote, isolated areas of Australia into the living rooms of the city people'

The Big Country Air

A Big Country goes into its sixteenth year.

Novelty

Into the repetitive format of television must be injected novelty that will keep the audience interested. It is the expectation of novelty that makes us watch the same series more than once. So in the television drama there must be developed in every episode a new dilemma. In the news, there must be a new scandal or a new disaster. It is the novelty aspect to which we are referring usually when we discuss 'what the show was about'. This novelty in itself becomes part of the repetitive process of television because just as we have total confidence in the same characters appearing week after week, we have equal confidence that we will be provided with the spectacle of a new adventure for these characters. The injection of novelty into the repetitive structure of television produces one novel aspect of television narrative, which is its open-endedness.

Open-endedness

In the discussion of film narrative a lot of space was given to the narrative devices of resolution and closure. Television narrative lacks the resolution of film narrative. Because television programmes are both continuous (broadcast over many nights) and episodic (frequently self-contained and not serialised), the programmes tend to lack a final narrative resolution. This can best be explained through example. In a hospital drama the desperately ill patient may indeed be saved by the skills of our hero, the surgeon, yet the central enigma — that of illness and death in society — will not be resolved. The programme rests upon the generalised plot line that illness and disease exist and so this enigma, a problem, carries over from week to week.

Similarly, in a police drama the criminals will undoubtedly be caught and brought to justice but the central problem upon which the programme is based — that of crime in our society — is not solved. This lack of final resolution is even more obvious in situation comedies. Where would *Fame* be if the students graduated from the school of performing arts? What would next week's show be about if Gilligan and his friends finally managed to get off *Gilligan's Island*? The open-ended nature of television narrative is quite different from that of film narrative. Resolution in a film is closely connected with the development of the problematic, the central conflict; whilst television depends upon the non-resolution of the central conflict.

The lack of the final resolution in television narrative means that each individual programme in a series offers the viewer a sense of immediacy. We, the viewers, update ourselves each week as to what the characters are up to now, secure in the knowledge that the central problem in the show was not solved last week and is not likely to be this week.

Immediacy

Television series, fiction and non-fiction, are characterised by the slice-of-life approach. The lack of a final resolution in any one programme means that neither the characters within the show nor the viewer needs to remember what happened last week. (This is not true of a serial which tends to keep its crisis until the final moments of the programme in the belief that you will tune in next week to find out what happened.) Characters never refer to the behaviour of other characters last week and rarely bring up events of past plots. Rather, there is a sense when we switch on the programme of an update, a 'what are they up to now' feeling. This is enhanced by the novelty of a new dilemma, the consistency of sets and characters and the use of such devices as laugh tracks. All of these elements provide the viewer with a sense of immediacy. Even when we know a series is ten years old the episode we are currently watching appears to be happening now. There is little or nothing in the drama itself that tells us the show was made a decade ago.

Expansion

Film narrative tends to work in casual progression, that is, one event leads to another and so on until the final resolution. It is fairly linear in its development. Television narrative, however, operates in the opposite way. Television narrative concentrates on multiplicity and the expansion of issues. So in news coverage we see a talking head describing the event, then probably a film clip of the event and perhaps some related interviews. The single news event has been expanded for the viewer and presented in a number of modes. Within television drama there is a similar construction. Characters' conversations are used to expand the event of the drama, movement from place to place is detailed, numbers of characters are shown in simultaneous action. A classic example is the hospital drama. The patient/victim is shown suffering; the medical characters are shown discussing his/her condition and agonising over a crucial decision; the nurses on another set are commenting upon the action; the parents/lover are shown worrying in another room and in the cafeteria the sub-plot of a love affair between the junior nurse and the registrar is developing.

This expansion of the narrative means that there is greater emphasis on what characters are saying than in a film and structure provides for a number of mini-climaxes after which an advertisement can be inserted. It

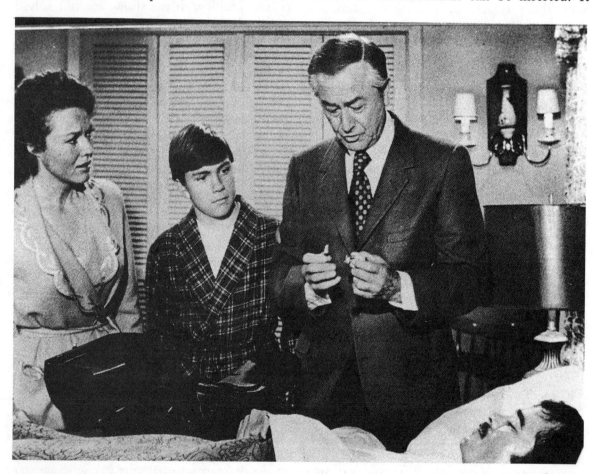

Scene from *Marcus Welby M.D.*

might be expected that the multiplicity of characters, situations and mini-climaxes would destroy the unity of the programme (not to mention the advertisements breaking in every fifteen minutes) but in reality this is not so. The unity of the television programme does not rest on the coherence of events so much as it does in film but rather upon the audience's recognition of and familiarity with the characters and patterns of the narrative. There is a circularity of structure too within a television programme that helps to give it this unity.

Circularity

Within each television programme there will be an opening stable state. This opening state sees the sets and characters very much as we left them last week. It can be thought of as being the norm. This stability will be disrupted by the issues of the plot, perhaps a crime in a police show, perhaps the introduc-tion of a guest character in a situation comedy, perhaps a disaster in a news coverage, perhaps an argument in a soap opera. Whatever the issue, it will introduce novelty into the stable situation. In the course of the show this issue will be resolved (the crime will be solved, the guest character will leave or the argument will be patched up) and the characters will return to the stable state they shared at the opening of the programme. The return to this stable state means that next week a new issue/dilemma/conflict can be introduced and the pattern repeated.

Film narrative, as we have seen earlier, does not work in a circular fashion but in a linear mode. The final state of characters in a film is never identical to the opening state.

The characteristics of repetition, novelty, open-endedness, immediacy and circularity dominate the narrative structure of television. Together they serve to restructure for television the classical narrative devices of set, character and conflict into a form particular to television.

Exercise 12.A Establishing a narrative image

Repetition within the narrative structure of television means there exists a high degree of viewer familiarity with the characters. Into this repetition must come novelty otherwise the viewers would get bored. The novelty usually appears in the form of a dilemma, a problem the central character must solve.

Television does not produce strong narrative images in the way film does because it depends upon the viewers already knowing the characters. However, before the start of a new series a narrative image is sometimes established. [*Special equipment: drawing materials*]

1 You are a television producer and have arranged to sell one of your series overseas. The overseas audience knows nothing about the series but you, of course, know it well. It is your task to design a single page newspaper advertisement for this series to appear prior to it being released.

2 Choose a drama, quiz or current affairs programme for this series that will act as a narrative image. Your advertisement should tell its audience something about the central character, something about the sort of show it is — action packed, intellectual, fun etc. and of course, the time and station on which it will be aired.

3 Compare your poster with those created by others in your group. The comparison should be about the extent to which the narrative

pattern is identified, not the quality of the artwork.

- What unique claims are made about the programme?
- To what extent does this new programme 'slot in' to audience perceptions of other programmes within the genre?
- What images could possibly be picked up and developed by the television gossip magazines?

Exercise 12.B Narrative development

Television narrative is characterised by repetition of characters and formats, immediacy, expansion and circularity. It has been stated earlier that these characteristics are common to both fiction and non-fiction television. [*Special equipment: television set, video recorder*]

1 Determine the degree of accuracy of the above statement by conducting a detailed analysis of one evening's half-hour news programme and a half-hour drama episode on a commercial station.

2 Prepare an analysis chart similar to the one below.

3 From the material you have assembled prepare some answers to these questions:
- How do news programmes expand their material?
- How do news programmes promote a sense of immediacy?
- How is a sense of immediacy achieved in a television drama?
- What is the relationship between the opening moments of each programme and its closing moments?

	News	Drama
Major characters		
Problems/Conflicts/ Events		
Major segments (give each segment between advertisements a letter of the alphabet)		
Segments within segments (e.g. one news story might have three segments — a talking head, a film clip, an interview. A drama might have a chase, a shoot-out and a capture.)		

Setting

Setting has been described earlier as the time and place within which the action occurs. This definition is quite adequate for the television medium, but in television setting is a constant. The setting for a programme tends to be same from night to night or week to week. Often the viewer is cued in to the setting during the title sequence. The same shots of the location are used every week under the titles and this serves as the narrative image for the programme. The viewer expectations are aroused and focused by the narrative image just as they are by a film's narrative image but, in the case of television, viewer recognition plays a key part. Within the programme sets tend to be repeated. This

The evil J.R. is ready for a night out. He's got his cane and he's got a saddlebag full of dirty money. You never know when you're gonna have to make a bribe or rap a stray dog.

is primarily a factor of budget and time. There is neither time nor money to build elaborate sets for each episode so the same sets are used again and again. Hence we tend to see the central character either in his lounge room or his office or the local bar. (Some sets such as the local bar serve as neutral areas into which other characters can be introduced.) Time and place are constants in a television programme.

Setting in a television show can be thought of as an arena which confines the action and determines its nature. For example, a police drama invariably has as its setting the city. It can be any city but it must be large enough to provide believably a sufficient number of crimes to form the plot of the show. Consequently, we see numerous police dramas such as *Starsky and Hutch, The Sweeney, The Streets of San Francisco, Quincy* and *The Professionals* being acted out on the streets of a large often unidentified city. The city arena acts in itself as a kind of narrative image for the viewer, raising our expectations as to the sort of drama we can expect.

Characterisation

Characterisation in television dramas tends to be static. Once established, characters operate entirely within the parameters of the assigned character traits. The character traits remain constant from week to week and little or no development of character occurs. This is not to say the character never changes; we can all think of the 'bad egg' who changed his ways or the reformed tough guy figure, but the character traits remain essentially the same. This tends to make the characters appear fairly one-dimensional because their characteristic behaviour is the same in every episode. It also has the effect of increasing viewer intimacy because we feel we know (and we probably do) all there is to know about the character. The overall effect of the one-dimensionality and singularity of television characters is that, far more than film, television lends itself to the 'typage' of characters.

Exercise 12.C   Restrictions on narrative

The settings of television shows are usually very limited and repeated every week. Budget restrictions and time would make it very difficult to build elaborate sets for each new show. [*Special equipment: drawing materials*]

1 As the director/producer of a new television series you are planning such details as the sets. Budget requirements limit you to four permanent sets. You will occasionally be able to build others as the story requires but these four will provide the basis of your action. The series outline tells you that the show is about a family of two parents and twin daughters. It is a situation comedy built around the funny situations the twin teenage daughters get themselves into with their boyfriends. Mother is a housewife, father is a doctor.

2 Outline in detail (or draw if you are able) the four sets you would choose to have built.

Work within these limitations:
- A family meeting place where all the characters can come together
- A place where the girls can be seen alone
- A place where new characters can be introduced
- A place where we can see the mother and the father in relation to their occupations
- A place the girls can go to with their boyfriends.

3 Discuss with others in your group, or with your teacher:
- The potential that these sets provide for plot development. What sorts of plots are possible? What should be ruled out (for example, fire)?
- What occasional characters would be appropriate in these settings?
- What objects, artifacts could be included in the settings to further enlighten us about the lead characters?

Exercise 12.D   Characters in narrative

Characters and plots in television series change only marginally from week to week. Although the actual details of the plots will vary each week the characters' attributes will not change. [*Special equipment: television guide, video, television, access to favourite television programme*]

1 Choose two of your favourite prime time adventure programmes. For each programme draw a chart similar to the one below.

Programme:		Time:	
Name of lead characters	**Problems/ dilemmas**	**Method of solution**	**Traits, skills possessed**

2 Watch the programmes you have selected and during your viewing, carefully monitor the action of the leading characters. Note each problem the character is faced with and the attributes or skills the character possesses that allow him/her to solve the problems presented.

3 After your viewing, fill in the appropriate information on the chart. Compare your findings with others in the class especially those who have chosen to watch different shows. From the comparisons try to come up with some generalisations about the following:
- The types of problems presented in adventure shows
- The character types of the central figures
  — their skills
  — their appearance
  — their attributes
- Common methods of problem solving presented in the drama programmes.

4 Compare your findings with those of others in your group.

Typage

In an earlier chapter typage was discussed in terms of the films of Eisenstein and Pudovkin. Typage occurs in a similar manner in television drama. Certain types of performers invariably play the heroes, a different type plays the antagonist and a different type again will play the *femme fatale* role. This typage of characters can be most easily observed by analysing the lead characters in a variety of soap operas, family situation comedies and adventure dramas. Because television shows are essentially about the characters rather than action it is not surprising that certain types predominate. Television is a money making enterprise and those character types that are found to be successful will be repeated over and over again. The plots of each episode will be written around the major character types of the series.

Plot

Plot in television dramas is largely a function of character and is designed to provide novelty in each episode. The plots in many if not most television shows are usually anticipated by the viewer. The real interest lies not in what will happen but how the central characters will behave; the methods the central characters will use to cope with the situation and the devices the narrative might employ such as car chases, gun fights, escapes, lures, blackmail etc. In the less sophisticated television dramas the plot is often unveiled in the first few minutes and the remainder of the programme is devoted to the machinations of the central character in his/her efforts to achieve the mini-resolution. The mini-resolution is necessary to allow the return of both the character and the situation to the opening, stable state.

The nature of the plots preferred by television dramas offers some insight into the cultural beliefs of the society in which we live. It was earlier stated that television is a domestic medium. In simple terms this means that it is designed for people sitting in a family group at home watching the television. Television's perception of its audience as the family group leads it to develop narratives around the perceived beliefs and preoccupations of the nuclear family. It matters little that the nuclear family is an almost mythical entity because television acts as if it were a reality. This has resulted in a plethora of television narratives built around the myths of romance stability, health, domesticity (women), strength and leadership (men), innocence of children and the justification of authority. In its dramatisation of these myths television is partly reflecting the preoccupations of its viewing audience but also directing and restructuring the audience's understanding both by its repetition of these themes and its treatment of them.

Conclusion

The narrative structure of television has much in common with film in that it constructs settings, characters and plots for our entertainment. However, the distinctive nature of television means that the narrative structures it employs have some unique characteristics. These unique characteristics are its use of repetition, its open-ended story form, its sense of immediacy, its expansive story structure and its circular pattern of story development.

Characters in television narratives take precedence over the other elements of setting, conflict and resolution. Television shows tend to be about people and the plots are fairly incidental. Plots in television narrative become a case of 'what the characters are up to this week' and not the defining characteristic of the programme. The material that forms the basis of television plots is repetitive and closely reflects the perceived interest of the audience.

TELEVISION NARRATIVES

Characteristics

Format repetition
Novelty within repetitive format
Open resolutions
Sense of immediacy
Expansion of simple issues
Character emphasis
Circularity

Construction

Settings	Quickly established arena /a physical and psychological constraint
Character	Tendencies: static, typage
Plot	Character dependent Mini-resolutions Return to stable state Domestic themes

Exercise 12.E   Narrative and values

Television presents us with a view of the world. It presents us with its own version of reality in such a way that this version seems quite natural. [*Special equipment: television guide*]

1 Read the television guide on pages 168-9. Put an asterisk next to all of the programmes that you know well and watch regularly.

2 Now select a number of these shows that have a woman as the main character. How is this female character presented in the programme? Circle the appropriate description and add others as you feel it necessary.

- home/work
- mother/friend/lover
- follower/leader
- attractive/unattractive

3 The article 'The oh-so-naughty girls of Special Squad' claims that there is now increased scope for female performers. Has your analysis found any information to support this?

The oh-so-naughty girls of Special Squad

If you're a beautiful girl in TV's toughest show you'll most likely be a baddie

PRISONER aside, there have been very few television series made in Australia which have offered actresses the opportunity to play villains.

But Special Squad, Network 10's new series of self-contained police dramas, is turning out to be literally a showcase for female crooks.

From the first episode, Duel, it was a woman who led the men of the Special Squad a merry dance, destroying their sophisticated communications system, planting car bombs and staging daring robberies.

And, to top it off, she turned out to be a policewoman who had failed in an attempt to become part of the squad.

The role was played by Nina Landis, an actress who has studied extensively overseas and whose previous television credits include Prisoner, A Country Practice, Cop Shop, The Sullivans and Skyways.

And the role was typical of many written for actresses who have already been seen in Special Squad, or who will guest star in future episodes.

In the main, they will be the bad girls of the series, or at least they will be

Page 14—TV WEEK—SEPTEMBER 8, 1984

ABOVE: Two sides of Nina Landis . . . as Lisa Ryan, the rogue policewoman, being arrested by the Special Squad's Detective Senior Sergeant Greg Smith (Anthony Hawkins) in the first episode of the series and (right) in a far more glamorous pose away from the set. LEFT: Beautiful actress and singer Jeanette Leigh. She is one of the few actresses to guest star in Special Squad as a character on the right side of the law.

playing roles which ''are not the light and fluffy parts women usually are given in Australian series,'' as one spokesman for Special Squad explained it.

Lorna Lesley, an actress who has packed a wealth of experience into a relatively short career, will play a

(continued)

Television Content   179

everything from Certain Women to Number 96 to A Town Like Alice, was also a star of movies such as Caddie, Newsfront, and Chain Reaction.

Newcomer Susie Lindeman already has made an enormous impression playing street kid Lindy Sharpe.

She wound up on the run from both the underworld and the police in a recent episode called Easy Street.

A big future is predicted for the attractive young actress, who by the way, speaks four languages — English, French, German and Italian.

Stunning Antoinette Byron will play Jasmin, the girlfriend of a shady character called Jimmy Hadden, in an up-coming episode called Golden Run.

Antoinette, who studied drama at Flinders University and the National Institute of Dramatic Arts (NIDA) in Sydney, is probably best known for her 16-month run with the original Australian cast of The Rocky Horror Show, in which she played Janet.

Her movie credits include Winter Of Our Dreams and the current youth film Fast Talking, and on television she has appeared in shows such as Prisoner, Scales Of Justice and Kings.

Antoinette also is the "Scarlett O'Hara" seen rushing down a stairway only to be rebuffed with a "Frankly, my dear, I don't give a damn" by her "Rhett Butler" in a commercial for a brand of television set.

It seems Jeanette Leigh is one of the few actresses who will guest in Special Squad as a goodie.

She will be seen as a computer operator who helps the Squad track down a criminal in an episode called Business As Usual.

Jeanette, also an accomplished singer, has been seen in shows such as Skyways and Cop Shop and has a role in the up-coming comedy movie Melvin, Son Of Alvin.

Lawrie Masterson

TOP: Lorna Lesley brings a wealth of experience to her role as a kidnapper in a Special Squad episode called Same Time Friday.
ABOVE: Newcomer Susie Lindeman as street kid Lindy Sharpe in the recent episode Easy Street.
RIGHT: Dark-haired Antoinette Byron is Jasmin, the girlfriend of a rather shifty character with whom the Squad becomes involved in an episode titled Golden Run.

kidnapper in an episode called Same Time Friday.

Her victim will be another of Australia's top actresses, Carmen Duncan, who plays the role of a political commentator.

Lorna, whose TV credits include

SEPTEMBER 8, 1984
—TV WEEK—Page 15

Analysis and research

American series have a slightly different structure from English series because of the allowances for advertisements. American series tend to have a short prologue wherein the plot is established, two or three acts where the plot is worked through and an epilogue where loose ends are tied up. Each major section is usually self-contained to allow for advertisement breaks. Watch a couple of episodes of an American television series and a couple of English-made episodes. Visually represent (for example, in a graph) the structure of each type of programme and compare the differences.

Written response

1 Using your knowledge of the form of cinema and the form of television narrative suggest some distinctive forms that home video recorders might develop. In your answer consider the nature of the medium, the position of the audience, family use of video and your own experiences with the medium.

2 John Ellis in *Visible Fictions* says that television 'foregrounds family life'. By this he means the central concern of many television programmes is family life. Through reference to both fiction and non-fiction television programmes prepare an argument in favour or against Ellis' contention.

3 'Broadcast news and the police series have much in common' (Fiske and Hartley, *Reading Television*, p. 189). By this statement Fiske and Hartley are implying that television news and police drama series such as *The Sweeney*, *Starsky and Hutch* and *Cop Shop* have some elements in common. Assess the degree of commonality of these two types of shows through reference to their narrative structures, their plots/themes, their characters.

4 Imagine that all television programmes are written and produced by a totalitarian group called the 'Ministry of Public Education' whose job it is to teach the public about acceptable and desirable modes of behaviour. Either think back over your last week's television viewing or devote some time to watching keeping this 'fact' in mind. What sorts of things do you think the Ministry of Public Education is trying to teach people in your State? Do not base your answer on one programme but consider the messages of the television dramas, the quiz shows, the news and the current affairs programmes and the advertisements.

Practical exercise

Here are the written guidelines for a Western television series, *Bonanza*.

These "rules" for *Bonanza* writers appeared in Nancy Vogel, "'Bonanza' Scripts," *Writer's Digest*, Vol. 48, No. 12 (December 1968), 62–64, 93, 95.

1. Absolutely no railroad stories, or yarns which require mine interiors, floods, blizzards or fires.

2. Because of the color requirements, exterior night shots should be avoided if possible, with the exception of the Ponderosa ranch house and barn, which are located on stage.

3. Stories must *always* deeply involve the Cartwrights. We do not want the Cartwrights "looking in" on the problems of someone else. At times we have used, and will continue to use, guest stars of considerable stature, but when we do the problem is still to be a Cartwright problem and the solution a Cartwright solution.

4. The Cartwrights must never be cast as "do-gooders." In other words, the problem should never become a Cartwright problem merely by having the Cartwrights push their way into it.

5. We often have a surfeit of Indian stories. Forget, too, any stories concerning a "wife" showing up, or someone claiming to own the Ponderosa, or the young, misunderstood rebel who regenerates because of the Cartwrights' tolerance and example.

6. We have many stories submitted in which the townspeople "turn against" the Cartwrights. Unless the story is truly unique and believable, this area should be avoided. The Cartwrights are too intelligent in their behavior, too respected and too prominent to have such a thing happen.

7. What we do want is Western action and Western adventure, concerning a worthy and dramatic problem for the Cartwrights, and strong opponents. We want human drama built around a specific locale and specific period in the country's history; simple, basic stories as seen through the eyes of Ben, Hoss, and Little Joe Cartwright, and Candy.

1 Refer to the section 'A problem posed' at the start of this chapter.

2 Given the information that you have gained from this chapter, develop the spy series outlined in 'A problem posed'.

3 When you have thought out the details about character and setting, create a set of written guidelines for your spy series.

4 In order to help your writers understand the narrative image of your series, collect a portfolio of images (sets and characters) that are appropriate for your series. Make the appropriate notes underneath.

References

Tony Bennett et al, *Popular Television and Film* (London: The Open University Press, 1981).

John Ellis, *Visible Fictions: Cinema: Television: Video* (London: Routledge and Kegan Paul, 1982).

John Fiske and John Hartley, *Reading Television* (London: Methuen, 1978).

Roger Silverstone, *The Message of Television* (London: Heinemann Educational Books, 1981).

Raymond Williams, *Television Technology and Cultural Form* (London: Fontana Collins, 1974).

Chapter 13
Television Codes

A problem posed

You have been trained as a radio news and current events producer. You now have the opportunity to develop your own current events programme for television. What aspects of your previous training will you be able to take into your new job? How will you manage to convey information on complex matters and still entertain your audience? What are the most appropriate elements to draw from existing current affairs programmes such as 60 Minutes?

In chapter 5, 'Film's Conventions and Codes', it was indicated that a very complex language has been developed in order to convey meaning. Some of the meaning inherent in the conventions and codes is consciously perceived by the audience, while some codes go unnoticed. In both cases meaning is transmitted to an audience who, either consciously or subconsciously, quickly learn the language. Chapter 5 also emphasised the need to be aware of the ways in which the codes and conventions construct meaning because members of modern societies depend so much upon the media for a coded version of the world. This coded meaning is transmitted not only in news and current events, but also in the fictions — the dramas, soap operas and situation comedies. Significant cultural values are reworked and re-energised in the process of reconstruction for the modern mass media. The codes and conventions are the active agents in this process.

The same basic structure will be used to analyse the codes and conventions of television. As before, 'codes' will be the abbreviation used to represent both aspects of the language. The convenient divisions of technical, symbolic, audio and written codes will again be used. It may be valuable at this stage to refer back to chapter 5 and reacquaint yourself with the definitions and limitations of these categories as the task in this chapter is to identify modifications necessary for

television, not to repeat the earlier information. There is a slight difference in the ways that the television codes operate because the form of television is different.

The previous chapter analysed some of the significant aspects of form and gave particular attention to the domestic and broadcast elements. It is now necessary to explore ways in which these affect the technical, symbolic, audio and written codes.

Technical codes

The technical codes identified in Part 1 of the book were:

Framing
— camera distance
— lens choice
— camera angle/movement
Shot duration
Film choice
Lighting
Special effects

Framing — camera distance

The pattern in cinema has been to establish a scene in long or medium shot, then use the close-up for emphasis. The smaller television screen has necessitated a rethink about shot distances. The long shot, in which the environment dominates the actors, was very effective on the large screen. John Ford was a director who used the long shot particularly well in many of his Westerns. The western deserts of America were most appropriate settings for the drama. They provided spectacular images, but also some degree of scale for the human conflict. Such long shots do not work on the small television screen, because, although the mountains and gorges may be identifiable, the cowboys and Indians are reduced to ant-like specks. The medium shot has replaced the long shot as a means of establishing a relationship between the characters and the environment. To make matters even more confusing, some scripts and texts have retained the term 'long shot' for television, but have changed the meaning of the term. A television long shot would roughly equate to a film medium shot.

On television, the close-up is used as the norm rather than as emphasis. The close-up is the only time that the television image size corresponds with life size. Perhaps this is part of its attraction. Certainly, the close-up relieves the spectator of having to peer intently at the screen for detail, and as the screen is often watched only in a casual manner, this is important. Use of close-ups is further encouraged in low budget dramas such as soap operas, because they eliminate the need for elaborate sets.

Emphasis upon close-ups (mostly faces) encourages a focus upon the human elements in a television presentation, rather than upon spectacle. Some of the great screen spectacles and costume dramas suffer when shown on television for this reason. If a television drama does require a spectacular set, the detail must be provided in close-ups. There is not sufficient space on the screen for the set to speak for itself. However, television directors have to be careful here because a succession of close-ups upon scenery rather than human action could destroy the focus of the narrative.

Long shot (from *Against the Wind*)

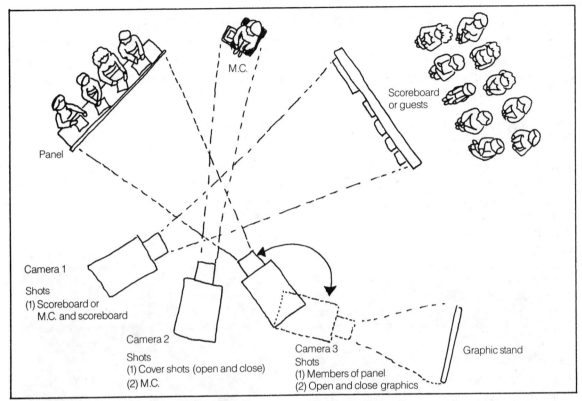

Figure labels:
- M.C.
- Panel
- Scoreboard or guests
- Camera 1 / Shots / (1) Scoreboard or M.C. and scoreboard
- Camera 2 / Shots / (1) Cover shots (open and close) / (2) M.C.
- Camera 3 / Shots / (1) Members of panel / (2) Open and close graphics
- Graphic stand

After McRae *et al, Television Production: An Introduction* (London: Methuen, 1973)

There are some live events, such as Olympic Games and Royal occasions, that are renowned for their spectacle and do attract vast television audiences. These examples would appear to negate the claim that television's form encourages the human element rather than spectacle. A closer examination of these spectacular events will show that the close-ups are providing the drama — the close-up of the strain on the high jumper's face, the tears of joy upon success. These are the riveting moments of television. The massive auditorium with its thousands of spectators is merely background for this engaging human drama. The television audience is given a privileged insight into the emotions of the central character. It is an insight that is not available to the spectators in the auditorium. The medium, in this sense, is quite personalised.

Increased emphasis upon close-ups must clearly affect understandings of montage. The close-up directs audience attention quite specifically, unlike some of the medium shots seen on a giant wide screen that allow some degree of information selection by the spectator. The montage style will tend to be more static, with specific information shown in close-up sequences. Two and three camera set-ups that are used in television studios tend to reinforce this pattern. Each camera focuses upon one element of the action. The camera images are previewed and the most appropriate is selected for transmission.

It can become quite confusing for the television director if the studio camera operators attempt to create 'flowing' shots. They work very closely under the instructions of the director, and camera movement is usually limited to a few well rehearsed dollies. The result is a presentation style that is more akin to films of the 1930s and 1940s rather than the more 'cinematic' films of recent years.

Exercise 13.A   The television close-up

Close-ups on television are the norm rather than the exception. The drama is advanced through use of close-ups, unlike in film where the close-up is reserved for the most dramatic moments.

Here is a series of stills from *Days of Our Lives*. The dialogue is paraphrased under each still.

1 Compared with film, which codes retain their importance when the close-up is used so persistently? Which codes become less important?

2 To what extent can the narrative be understood through the images? How important are the words?

3 *The Young and the Restless* goes to air five days each week. How does this coded system help producers and performers meet such a heavy schedule?

4 To what extent is the claim that this sort of television is 'radio with a few pictures' justified?

She: David, darling, you don't ever have to pay us back for that. We did it because we loved you and we wanted you to be free.

He: I am going to pay back all my debts. I know how much money you spent trying to get me cleared.

He: Very careless of you. My son must have had a valid reason for not granting you that divorce.

She: You know Tony only married me to get American citizenship, and he only stayed married to me all this time so that it would come in handy some day, and needless to say that day arrived.

Framing

Lens choice — zooms

Some of the significant developments that have occurred in television technology have been associated with sporting telecasts. Sports fans are a very large audience who are likely to give their attention to the screen for large amounts of time. This makes their eyeballs very marketable to the advertisers. Many developments, including video tape development, action replay and the zoom lens have been developed and improved so that the sports enthusiasts will retain their loyalty. The zoom lens is particularly useful in sporting telecasts because it is not possible to mount cameras on the sporting field or at all of the potential areas of interest. The zoom lens overcomes the problem as it can be used as a medium shot lens, a close-up lens or can combine the two into one shot — the shot starts with a medium shot then the operator zooms into close-up without stopping the shot.

Although it is an unnatural movement for the eye, the audience has now accepted the zoom as part of television language, not only in sporting events but also in other programmes. Zooms are short cuts in news coverage; they are used to inject artificial movement into many advertisements; they are becoming more frequent in television dramas. It seems that the zoom is the television replacement for the cinematic shot. It does not require the preparation and staging that are necessary for the cinematic shot and is therefore more appropriate for a medium that is gluttonous in respect of programme content. Zooms are quick, easy and therefore appropriate.

Shot duration

There is a tendency to hold shots longer on television than on film. This tendency can also be traced to the need to produce a lot of content for a very hungry medium. The amount of television material that is shot on film then transferred to television, is rapidly diminishing. Even footage that is shot on film is now frequently edited on video. It is therefore logical to expect that the traditions associated with film editing will become less important.

This generalisation should be modified to recognise the variations within television genres. Television dramas have tended to mimic film dramas, though there is a slow move towards longer takes on television. Shot duration in live coverages will vary according to the cost of production, the equipment available and the choices available for camera positions. (In a marathon race there may be only one camera covering a particular section of a race, so there is no choice other than to hold the shot.) Because the event is live, interest can be sustained in a single shot for a longer period of time, though the viewer will feel cheated if there is no zoom, or close-up to capture the human element of the live action.

Advertisements enjoy a production edge over most other programmes. They are constructed with much higher budgets if programme duration is used as a bench mark. The commercials are carefully researched and constructed in fine detail. It is a useful technique to cram many short shots into a sixty-second commercial, as a means of attracting audience attention. Within the television commercial genre are many sub-genres, each with its own presentation style. The soft drink sub-genre aims to inject pace by quick cutting. The used car sub-genre seems to prefer the longer take, perhaps because the budget does not allow the luxury of the Coca-Cola type advertisement.

The key question about shot duration has been 'How long can a shot hold interest?' Before the interest dies, the shot should cease. Television seems to be conditioning its audience to sustain interest for longer periods. The human element provided by the close-up helps to do this, which is fortunate for those whose task it is to produce a great deal of product in a comparatively short period of time.

All of the above suggests that there is a strong element of expedience about shot duration on television and certainly shot duration varies according to genre. However, as with film, the duration of a shot still affects the audience's sense of time.

Exercise 13.B   Advertising pace

Soft drink commercials tend to inject pace into their advertisements by using a fast cutting technique. [*Special equipment: video, television monitor, two soft drink commercials, one bank or finance company commercial*]

1 Select two different soft drink commercials that you are able to analyse in depth.

2 Count and graph the shots in each, for example:

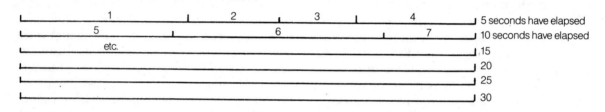

3 How many shots are there in each commercial? To what extent is the pattern similar or different?

4 Does each commercial have a narrative element? If so, what is happening? If not, what holds the interest?

5 What are the other levels of interest apart from the narrative? How do the technical codes contribute to this interest? Framing? What is framed and why is it interesting?

6 What is the implied relationship between the product and the images in the commercial? Is this a valid relationship? View a commercial for a finance company (bank, insurance, society) and compare the pace of this advertisement with the soft drink commercials. Why is there a difference? What would happen if the two sub-genres swapped techniques?

Film choice

Video tape did not exist during the early days of television. Early television programmes had to be transmitted live or recorded on film, then projected for the television cameras.

There were even dramas that went to air live. The British series *Z Cars* is quite famous for the quality it was able to achieve under these conditions. Exterior shots would be recorded beforehand on film. The interior shots would go to air live, interspersed with the telecined film footage.

Once developed, video tape became quickly popular because it dramatically reduced costs. It soon became apparent that the limiting factor was not the tape but the technology surrounding its use. Cameras were too bulky to be carried by operators, even if they could find batteries small enough to operate them. Early video tape editing was imprecise when compared with film. The result of these and other factors was reduced image quality when video tape was used instead of film. However technological development has been rapid. Portable cameras are now available and editing

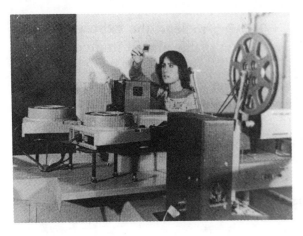
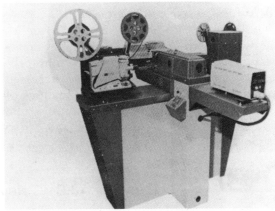

Telecine chains

has undergone computerisation. The result has been increased efficiency and improved image quality. The development has been so rapid that in the space of ten years, video has become the preferred medium to such an extent that many industry people are predicting the complete demise of film. 'Prestige' products such as television series and some advertisements are still using film, but video tape has become increasingly popular in the other areas of television production.

Lighting

When film was being discussed in Part 1, lighting was identified as one of the very significant ways in which meaning was developed. Lighting remains as important in television but the meanings cannot be developed in such subtle ways. The small, lower quality image restricts some possibilities even if time was available to create detailed meaning through lighting. Visibility, clarity, then effectiveness is the most appropriate order of priorities for the television lighting crew.

Special effects

Electronically-produced images are generally cheaper to manipulate than film images. Colours, backgrounds, screen shapes can all be changed at the flick of a switch. Computer technology

has also enabled the range of special effects to increase. The quickly generated captions of modern news programmes and the station identification logos are two examples of computer technology affecting television's codes. Split screen, a special effect in the cinema of yesteryear, has been revamped for sporting telecasts. On the small screen it is sometimes difficult to simultaneously show detail and suggest spectacle. Producers have reverted to a version of the split screen to suggest a larger arena. Sometimes the screen is split down the centre or sometimes part of the action is inserted into a corner of the screen. This can be done at will by the vision mixer as the action is occurring.

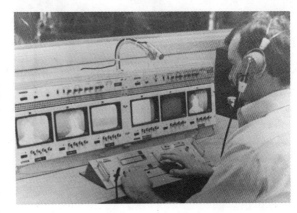

Vision mixer

Technical codes: conclusion

The ways in which the technical codes create meaning in television are similar to film techniques. The differences that have occurred can be attributed to the different qualities of a television set and to the possibilities that have been created by electronic and video technology. In some ways the developed technology has made the image maker's task easier. In other cases, the limitations of the set have encouraged the television people to revert to a presentation style that has more in common with past cinematic practice than with modern cinema. One general effect upon the meanings that have been constructed is to switch the emphasis from the spectacle to the personal.

Exercise 13.C Television technical codes

The technical codes in television bear some similarities to those in film. There are also some differences that result from the difference in form between film and television.

The stills from *Minder* illustrate some of the technical codes that have been used in the television programme.

1 Examine the codes by using this outline:
Framing
— camera distance
— lens choice
— camera angle
Shot duration
Film choice
Lighting
Special effects

2 Eliminate the aspects that you cannot comment upon when you are examining stills for evidence.

3 Make notes on the other codes, mentioning particularly any cases where you think there would be a difference between the way the codes are used in film and television.

4 Use your notes as a basis for discussion with your group or teacher.

Scenes from *Minder*

Symbolic codes

The symbolic codes refer to the parts of the language that are contained within the image as opposed to the technical codes associated with the construction of the image. Chapter 7 outlined the symbolic codes that operate in film. Therefore it is not necessary to elaborate in detail upon the effect the small screen has on each symbolic code. However, it is worthwhile for the reader to do just this, before proceeding.

Having completed this mental exercise, it will become apparent that the symbolic codes have to act with greater specificity if they are to generate the appropriate meanings. If the colour red is important, then the audience will have to see it quite clearly displayed on the screen. If a bowler hat is intended to symbolise Britishness, then the performer's actions need to direct audience attention to the hat. There will tend to be fewer symbolic channels of meaning, but those that are used will be given specific attention.

Rather than elaborate further upon the fact that codes generate meaning, it will be useful to gain further insights into how they create this meaning. To do this, it is necessary to understand about metaphor and metonymy.

Metaphor

A metaphor is a means of communication whereby something that was unknown is made known by drawing upon something already familiar. An example in speech is, 'Mary was a pillar of strength'. The unknown is the sort of strength that Mary possesses. It is made known by referring to a pillar, which is something recognised as solid and immovable. For the metaphor to work, we must know something about pillars, not only physically but also how they are perceived culturally. This cultural perception becomes more evident when animate objects are used as analogies, for example, 'Bill's lion-hearted display led the team to victory'. Our culture perceives the lion to be an animal of courage. Whether or not the lion has more courage than a cockroach is irrelevant. The courage of the lion is a known *cultural* fact, that is transferred to Bill. We now know more about Bill's efforts. (What would happen if the metaphor was changed to 'Bill's cockroach-hearted display ...?') The aim of a metaphor is always to gain the maximum meaning by describing one thing in terms of another.

Television commercials communicate the unknown in terms of the known. When a soft drink is manufactured it is quite anonymous. It is not very different from the other drinks made at other factories. Why should people buy that particular drink? The marketers give them a reason by making this unknown product become known in accordance with some cultural myths. One brand of soft drink will become known through analogy with the outdoors/fun and games, another through the family life, and so on. Through this analogy, a *displacement* has occurred. The meaning of outdoor recreation has been shifted or displaced. Particular aspects of recreation are now associated with the previously anonymous soft drink. When the analogy of cool drink and healthy outdoor life is analysed it makes little sense. How could one use a cultural myth that suggests health and vitality to convey meaning to a basically unhealthy product? The displacement gives a different emphasis to the values. Within the commercial there is emphasis on smiles, muscles, free flowing hair, shiny teeth and so on.

Viewer attention is redirected in the same way that a magician redirects audience attention away from the hat before the rabbit is extracted. Displacement is the equivalent of the conjuror's trick. Through the displacements that work within the advertising metaphor, the drink companies are able to avoid accusations of false advertising. It has not been overtly stated that the brand of cool drink will create a healthy, outdoor, extroverted life for you. The cultural weapons that are used are more subtle and more powerful because of that subtlety.

The metaphor is also a powerful means of transferring meaning in television drama. We have seen that the symbolic codes include setting and performance. For the viewers, various settings are loaded with cultural meaning. The inner city slum has a different meaning from the middle class neighbourhood, which again differs from the outback, and so on. When characters are put into these culturally familiar settings, meaning is transferred from the setting to the comparatively unknown characters. The settings will then determine the parameters of behaviour for the characters. There are similar metaphors at work in the costume of the characters. The clothes have a cultural significance which is used to describe the personality of the characters. It is significant that the preferred forms of television drama are the series and the situation comedies. Programmes within these genres have consistent settings and costumes. The television medium does not allow time to establish then re-establish character traits. The traits must be easily recognisable and quickly reidentified each week. Thus the metaphoric mode of communicating meaning from the culturally known settings and clothing is most appropriate.

Exercise 13.D   Television's symbolic codes

Television's symbolic codes have to be used with greater specificity than film's symbolic codes. Attention needs to be drawn to the significant symbolic elements.

View the stills from *Special Squad*.

1 Make notes on the significant symbolic codes in each still. Use the following framework.
   - objects
   - setting
   - clothing
   - performance (body language)
   - colour

2 How do you think the significant symbols have been emphasised so they are discerned by television viewers?

3 Use your notes as a basis for discussion about the ways in which the symbolic codes develop character.
   - Which woman is likely to be the 'goodie'? Why?

- How much of the symbolic meaning would be lost on a black/white television set?
- Given the symbolic meaning that has been created, what possibilities are available for character development? What sort of characters can they become? What sort of actions would be out of character?

Metonymy

The other fundamental way in which meaning is communicated is through metonymy. In a sense, metonymy is the opposite of metaphor. A metaphor takes a world of shared cultural experience and concertinas it to explain a particular unknown. A metonym takes a particular known thing and transfers meaning from this to become representative of a broader issue. In the spoken word metonymy is the substitution of the name of a thing for the name of something else which it is taken to represent, for example, 'crown' for king, authority, constitution; 'red tape' for bureaucracy, officialdom. The example of the setting used earlier can be used to illustrate how each works in opposite directions. The slum street scene is a metaphor that helps explain the character that we see. Seedy street suggests seedy character (with a few displacements added). However the street scene can also be seen as a metonym for the city. Seedy street (known) suggests evil city (unknown). That is:

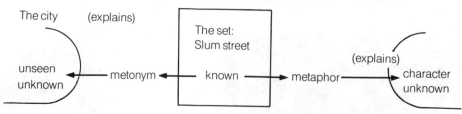

The slum street set is both metaphor and metonym.

The most obvious example of the metonym at work on television is in the performer's use of body language. A clenched fist is a known symbol that can be used to convey a broader set of meanings that may include anxiety and aggression. Images, too, can be used as metonyms. The meaning of a broken mirror is known and therefore the mirror can be used symbolically to convey despair or shattered hopes. The metonym works because the spectator is given a little information and has to make an effort to construct the rest for her/himself. By actively enticing the spectator into the communication process, the viewer is encouraged to believe that she/he is responsible for the perceived meaning. Thus metonymy is a very persuasive form of communication.

One example of the way in which the spectator is invited into the construction of meaning then left with the impression that the meaning results from the spectator's interpretation, is the perimeter advertising at sporting events. A superficial analysis would suggest that an advertisement at a televised sporting event giving only a brand name is a waste of the company's money. A brand name is a metonym for a fantasy that has been metaphorically created through other advertisements. The brand name is read in conjunction with these other elements of communication. These several trains of suggestion are *condensed* into a single representation. The brand name has become an indispensable part of that representation. When we think of test cricket we think of ? company. When we think of football we think of ? company.

The condensation that has occurred will improve sales figures, but companies also benefit politically. The issue of sporting sponsorship by cigarette companies illustrates this. In Australia, direct cigarette advertising on television is no longer permitted. When the advertisements were banned, televised sport became increasingly attractive to the companies. Over several years, they 'naturalised' their association with the most popular sports. In some Australian States the governments are claiming that the association between cigarettes and sport is both dishonest and unhealthy, and moves have been made to ban such sponsorships. The cigarette companies have been successful in defending their position because of the condensation that has occurred. To attack the cigarette company's right to advertise is perceived as an attack upon sport. The cigarette companies are perceived as the benevolent funders of major sports even though statistically it can be shown that a very minor percentage of sporting funds is derived from such sources. It is this combination of condensation of meaning created within a metonymic structure that has allowed the cigarette companies to convince most of the people about the merit of their industry. The community members are more easily convinced because they were active in the construction of meaning. This mental activity is internally interpreted as being responsible for the meaning. They have the feeling that they made up their own minds about the issue. This is far from the truth. To be able to forestall governments in this manner is to have a significant amount of political power.

Television news and current events programmes also develop meaning through a metonymic structure. Each evening on the news, specific news items are presented as being 'the news'. They become the known facts from which we shape our perceptions of the larger world. Within this metonymic news structure are numerous condensations. Several trains of thought, several issues are condensed into single representations. The simplicity of condensation is useful in television. Complex political issues can be condensed into the image of a political leader. The known image of the political leader is frequently featured in a news item, then from this item, a view of the greater world is created.

Exercise 13.E   Metonymy in news

News programmes are metonymic because a short verbal outline or a brief film clip is selected and then presented to the viewer as the whole event. The actual metonyms selected are very important because they determine the rest of the picture the viewer will construct. [*Special equipment (optional): Portapak*]

Gerald Stone, producer of the current affairs programme *60 Minutes* showed an understanding of the importance of metonymy when he stated: 'From the start *60 Minutes* determined that it would not try to deal in sweeping generalities but concentrate on very tangible and specific targets. That meant rather than offering a report on "What's Wrong With Our Education System" we would devote our research to finding one community or even one school to typify problems and issues'. (John Burney and John Hallowes, *60 Minutes, The Book*, Sydney: Angus and Robertson, 1983.)

1 You are going to plan the material for the segment Gerald Stone refers to above. Below are selections of possible visuals you could take for the programme and interviews you might collect. Circle the choices you think would best illustrate a report on 'What's Wrong with Our Education System'.

Selection 1
(Visuals)

School rose garden
School gymnasium
Rubbish in school yard
Brightly decorated classroom
Broken chair
Staffroom
Empty classroom
Canteen
Broken lockers
Lockers in good condition
Carpeted classroom
Uncarpeted classroom

Selection 2
(Interviews)

Principal
Unemployed school leaver
School graduate at university
Year 10 student
School prefect
President of P. and C.
Teacher
School gardener
Local police
Social worker
Guidance officer
Parent

2 Write a list of your chosen visuals and interviewees. Rearrange this list in the order you would present it for broadcasting.

3 Prepare a one-minute voice-over narration for your chosen visuals.
   Either shoot your chosen visuals on videotape or prepare some storyboard outlines with the appropriate narration.

4 As a class discuss:
   - the consistency of choices within the possible visuals.
   - other material you might have included in this programme.
   - selections you would make for a programme entitled 'Education is Looking Great'.

Exercise 13.F   Metonymy in dramas

Metonymy means a part stands for the whole. Family television shows employ metonymy because the family in the programme is meant to represent all families. Obviously the sort of family depicted will affect the message the viewers get about 'all families'.

1 Look at the still from a television series called *Father Dear Father*. Although it is difficult to judge from a still photo some generalisations can be made. Circle the words that you think best describe this family.
   - Poor
   - Rich
   - Working class
   - Middle class
   - Upper class
   - Happy
   - Unhappy
   - Close
   - Distant

From *Father Dear Father*

From *Leave it to Beaver*

2 Next to each word circled, list the symbols in the photograph that led you to this generalisation.
- What impression do you have of this family?
- How similar is it to your own family, or your best friend's family?

3 Look at the photo of another television family in the still from *Leave it to Beaver* which appeared nearly thirty years ago. Using the same procedure as above make some generalisations about this television family.

4 Compare your findings for the two photographs:

- What are the similarities?
- Are the differences caused by time or are they the result of different family images?
- One family is American and one is British. Is there any indication of a difference in nationality in the photos? Would you expect families to be different in the two countries?
- In Britain only one-third of households currently consist of man, woman and dependent children. Count up the number of 'television families' presently appearing on television. How many of them reflect the statistical reality above?

Symbolic codes: conclusion

In order to understand more about the ways in which the symbolic codes affect content's meaning, it is useful to understand the concepts of metaphor and metonymy. Metaphor informs about the unknown by a process of substitution. Metonymy informs through association, by touching or joining with other elements of information. The latter depends upon established patterns of association on the part of the perceiver whereas the metaphor can create meaning in more novel ways (though the known component must have cultural meaning). Metaphor, the more novel, more poetic device, is therefore very suitable for television advertisements and some aspects of television drama. Metonymy, as a cultural piecing together of information, is best suited to that which seems 'real' — news and current events. However the modes are not exclusive. There will be metaphors in news and metonyms in dramas, and it is also possible that one set of symbols is acting both metaphorically and metonymically (for example, the slum street scene).

When television language is used in a metaphoric manner, the psychological process of displacement is encouraged. Displacement is the process by which meaning is altered during its metaphoric transfer. Hence the Aboriginal camp might be used as a metaphor for the plight of the Aborigine in a white society, but through displacement, the magician's trick, the black man is perceived as deserving his lot because of the squalor in which he lives. With this displacement, the problem, the paradox, disappears. Displace-

Star image — Paul Hogan

ment is therefore a useful cultural or ideological tool because it shifts attention away from the central issue.

Similarly, condensation is the psychological process associated with metonymy. Condensation allows several images or ideas to be condensed into a single symbol or image. This can occur because the various elements of meaning are linked together to form a unified meaning. This is how the brand name so frequently featured in perimeter advertising telecasts gains its potency. Condensation is also observable in the way in which diverse elements in our culture are condensed into the image of one media star.

Important myths in our culture are the Aussie larrikin and the sincerity, the basic goodness, of the working man. Added to this is the more universal myth of the handsome prince. All of these are condensed into a star image, Paul Hogan.

These concepts of metaphor, metonymy, displacement and condensation are important in identifying the way in which symbol systems affect the social order, and vice versa.

Audio codes

Chapter 8 identified dialogue, music and sound effects as being the significant audio codes. These need to be reconsidered, recognising the distinctive forms of television.

One distinctive facet of television's development is that it was never vision without sound. From the inception, sound was a part of telecasting, not something used to embellish the images. This increased importance of sound is a direct inheritance from radio, the other broadcast medium.

It has already been indicated that television sets tend to be made with low quality speakers, consequently the possibility of communicating with extremely subtle sound tracks is lost. The move towards high fidelity video recorders, simulcasts and other innovations may affect this limitation.

The domestic nature of the television audience will also affect the way in which the audio codes are used. There may be a need to increase the amount of dialogue to overcome decreased attention to the screen, but again subtlety of music and sound effects may be lost on a partly attentive audience.

Television's demand for a great deal of product in order to fill the broadcast schedules also means that many of the ways in which the audio codes are used will be more formulaic.

It has also been illustrated that television is at its best when it is exploiting its broadcast potential; when there is a suggestion in the programme of a 'happening' or a sense of immediacy. Hence additional codes have been developed to enhance the sense of immediacy. Laugh and applause tracks and live microphones at sporting events are examples of such codes.

The human element rather than the spectacle has been identified as significant in television's form. Coupled with this is emphasis upon the close-up. It follows therefore that the 'talking head', in which the camera concentrates upon someone speaking, will gain significance in television. The popularity of 'chat' shows attests to this. Television drama will retain the filmic conventions of talking head in which the performer does not look towards the camera. In other television genres, such as news and current events, the authority figures address the cameras.

Given a knowledge of the ways in which the audio codes operate in film and an awareness of the implications that have just been outlined, it should be possible for the reader to identify the more specific functions of the audio codes. It is for this reason that this section is so brief, not because the audio codes are less important. Because the codes are so important, it may be worth the reader spending additional time on the exercises.

Written codes

In some television genres, written codes supplement the visual information. Sporting telecasts are examples of this. News and current events genres now tend to rework the longer 'talking head' statements into a written summary. When a translation from one set of codes to another occurs in this way, meaning must change. The changes are worth consideration.

Exercise 13.G   Metaphors in advertisements

Advertisements often employ metaphor because they use an image or an action as a metaphor for a product. Thus waterfalls, snow and clear mountain streams act as metaphors for menthol cigarettes in many advertisements. [*Special equipment: drawing materials*]

1 You are the advertising consultant for a new brand of Australian men's after-shave — 'Desert Gold'. You have hit on the bright idea of the Australian outback as an appropriate image for the after-shave. From the stills select those you would use in your advertising campaign as background settings.

2 Sketch the man and/or woman you would include in the visuals to promote your product. Use arrows and labels to identify such things as body build, facial expression, clothes, accessories, shoes etc.

3 Write the voice-over (to last no more than 20 seconds) that you would use in your advertisement. Indicate any music or sound effects (SFX) you would use.

4 Describe the editing style that you would use in a television commercial for your product. Fast cutting? Few cuts?
Discuss:
● On what basis did you choose the stills?
● What image were you looking for in your actor?
● What sorts of changes would you make if your product was a woman's perfume?

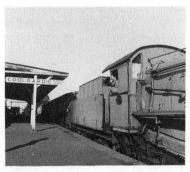

Exercise 13.H   Metaphor and cliché

Metaphors work by transposing meaning from a known (familiar thing) to an unknown (unfamiliar thing). Some metaphors are quite arbitrary and we recognise them without thinking about it; for example, a dissolve is a metaphor for memory, a wipe for location change. Other metaphors require us to use our imagination and our worldly knowledge.

1 Complete this chart of the film/television metaphors that are automatically recognised by the audience:

Metaphor	Meaning
Fade in and out	
Dissolve	Memory
Soft focus	
Wipe	Location change
Zip pan	
Sepia tone	
Violin music	
Thunder and lightning	
Black/white film	
Doors creaking	

3 Select one of the above metaphors and describe how the same meaning could be transferred without becoming a cliché. (For example, a red lampshade may subtly alter the light to imply danger. This is less of a cliché than a red filter.)

4 Discuss:
  • A symbol is something in our culture used to represent something else. How does this differ from a metaphor?
  • Is television more or less metaphoric than film?
  • How has an understanding of the metaphoric mode affected your understanding of the ways in which meaning is created in television?

2 Settings, scenes and costumes can also be metaphoric and can become a cliché. Complete this chart of metaphors which have become clichés — so that meaning is transferred from the well known scene to the plot line or performer.

Metaphor	Meaning
Sunset	
Slum scene	
	Anger
Black costumes	
Candle lit dining room	
	Love
Rocks and mountains	
Snakes	
	Nostalgia
Ripe fruit	
Red	Anger, aggression

Conclusion

There are sufficient similarities between the codes and conventions of film and television to allow the same convenient divisions of technical, symbolic, audio and written to be used. The differences in form mean some modification to the ways in which the codes create meaning. When the technical codes were examined, it became evident that close-ups were more common on television. These in turn affected the development of the montage but also had bearing upon the relationship between the human element and spectacle. Television's studio techniques have allowed producers to become quite proficient in generating a lot of programme in a comparatively short time. This is important for such a content-hungry medium. For similar reasons, the development of video technology has been important.

Instead of repeating information about the ways in which symbolic codes create meaning, a deeper analysis was made of the interplay between code and culture. Metaphor and metonymy were identified as two important ways of transmitting and transferring meaning. They are important concepts that have relevance to all codes, not just the symbolic.

Analysis of television's audio codes stressed that sound should not be regarded as the poor relation of television. Audio is an inherent part of television, not a set of codes used merely to enhance the meaning of the images. The most effective television sound is interactive rather than pleonastic. That is, the sporting commentary should add to what is being seen, not repeat it. The talking head visuals should add to what is being heard.

Attention to the written codes was deservedly brief, but it was suggested that the developing tendency to transfer some information from audio to written codes warranted some attention.

It is worth restating the earlier comment that codes do not act in isolation. They are complex patterns of associations through which meaning is generated. It is through the codes of television that we gain significant meanings about our society, our culture. Television is apparently the most transparent of all media and for this reason it is important to constantly remind oneself that through the codes we get a representation of reality, not a faithful 're-presentation' of the real.

Analysis and research

1 *60 Minutes* is Australia's most successful current events programme. Executive producer Gerald Stone claims that it is successful because it is the first public affairs programme actually made for television. He believes other public affairs programmes might just as well be on radio (*60 Minutes, The Book*).

Examine part of a *60 Minutes* programme. Give particular attention to the codes used, then make some comments about Gerald Stone's observations.

2 Select one company that, through sponsorship and perimeter advertising, has become closely associated with a particular sport. Analyse the metaphors that are used to develop meaning in their display advertisements. What is the image associated with the sport that the company sponsors? Are the two images consistent? How has this company generated meaning through its perimeter advertisements? What are the other known images that have been drawn upon to develop meaning in this metonymic fashion? Give as many examples as possible.

Library research

Chroma-key is widely used in television as a very effective means of creating special effects. It is used in drama, news, current events and sporting telecasts. Find out what chroma-key is, how it works and to what extent it has the capacity to change meaning.

Written response

1 a If you were a spectator at the Olympic Games, how would this experience be different from watching the games on television?

b One commentator at the Los Angeles Olympics claimed that the American telecasts had erred because they were biased towards American performers. Could they have been unbiased? To what extent does the point-of-view argument in film hold for live sporting telecasts?

2 *60 Minutes* records an average of 2 miles (3.5 kilometres) of film footage for every 500 feet (200 metres) (one story) that they put to air. Comment on this.

3 'On television, verbal statements are interconnected with visual images. One lives off the other.' (Zettl, *Television Aesthetics*) Comment upon this statement by giving examples from a television programme that you know well. Compare television's sound/image relationship with the ways in which these codes work in film.

4 If the metaphoric mode is most appropriate for poetry and television commercials are heavily dependent upon metaphor, to what extent are the commercials poetic?

Practical exercise

1 In the library find either a book of radio scripts, a tape recording of a radio play or an extract from a novel that is heavily dependent upon dialogue.

2 Convert this raw material into a video shooting script that will be shot almost exclusively in close-up. To do this it may be necessary to analyse 5 to 10 minutes of a midday television soap opera. They have some fairly standard methods to prevent the shots from becoming too static.

3 Allocate tasks to members of your group.

4 Shoot your soap opera in close-ups.

5 Review your results. What sorts of production short cuts were you able to take? To what extent would the professionals have adopted similar measures? How did the type of dialogue delivery compare with the soap opera that you viewed earlier? To what extent was this type of delivery conditioned by the extensive use of close-ups? What effect did the use of close-ups have upon the performers' facial expressions? How are these expressions interpreted in close-up?

References

Arthur Berger, 'Semiotics and TV' in *Understanding Television: Essays on Television as a Social and Cultural Force*, R. Adler (ed.) (New York: Praeger, 1981).

Umberto Eco, *A Theory of Semiotics*, (Bloomington: Indiana University Press, 1979).

John Fiske, *Introduction to Communication Studies* (London: Methuen, 1982).

James Monaco, *How to Read a Film* (New York: Oxford University Press, 1977).

Bill Nicholls, *Ideology and the Image: Social Representation in the Cinema and Other Media* (Bloomington: Indiana University Press, 1981).

Tim O'Sullivan et al, *Key Concepts in Communication* (London: Methuen, 1983).

Herb Zettl, 'Television Aesthetics' in *Understanding Television: Essays on Television as a Social and Cultural Force*, R. Adler (ed.) (New York: Praeger, 1981).

Chapter 14
Television Genre

A problem posed

The content of a day's television seems to be quite confusing. It seems to be a jumble of real programmes such as news and current events, of light entertainment like quiz programmes, comedies and very heavy dramas. From your study of ratings you know that quite often the same audience is tuned into this smorgasbord. Does this mean that we have a population of Jekyll and Hydes, who can change personality in an instant and demand a totally different form of entertainment? Does this mean the television producers can time to the minute the shifts in the split personalities? Or is there a simpler answer? Are there elements that all of the programme types have in common, allowing each programme type to provide novelty within this common pattern? If there is a common pattern, does this mean that a situation comedy is as real as the news?

Television communication is characterised by great diversity. At different times television serves the function of a newspaper, a theatre, a cinema, a sports arena, a classroom and a music hall. A brief glance at a weekly television guide or even a day's viewing agenda will demonstrate that through news, documentaries, dramas, situation comedies, live coverage and so on television manages to provide a huge range of material in a comparatively short amount of time. The purpose of this chapter is to select from that huge range of material and examine the particular characteristics of the genre and the nature of the mediation process operating within that genre.

Before specific types of programmes can be examined it is useful to remark upon some of the general characteristics of television content. One of the most apparent features of television is its overwhelming sense of reality. Television we know can bring real events happening thousands of miles away right into our lounge rooms. Television can show us Neil Armstrong stepping on to the moon, an athlete performing in another country, a ship floundering in the middle of the ocean and men at war in Iran. This sense of reality offered by television is not restricted to news events.

Sports coverage and even entertainment programmes such as quiz shows, dramas and situation comedies evoke a similar sense of reality; all of them portray real people behaving in a normal seeming manner. The programmes we know to be completely fictional are still heavily dependent on reality in their performance, sets, costumes and plots.

Television does not and cannot bring us reality. Television is a medium; it selects, orders and structures information for us. This mediation process means that television cannot offer us a transparent 'window on the world' through which we view reality but rather television constructs for its consumers a view of the world. Television processes reality for the viewer and offers it for consumption.

In order to examine this mediation process more closely and determine some of the characteristics of this constructed view of the world we will look at some of the highly popular genres of television: news, sport, quizzes and situation comedies. This examination must necessarily be brief and generalised which increases the chances of oversimplification. For this reason students are encouraged to undertake a more detailed analysis of one genre. Guidelines for such an analysis are given in the exercises in this chapter.

News

News appears to be the most real and most transparent of television genres. This apparent transparency is created because the news is presented by a 'neutral' observer, the news-reader, and is supported by visual information which seems to confirm the validity and truth of what the neutral observer says. But the news on television happens within a given time slot, has its own set of conventions and codes and is the end result of a continuous process of selection. These factors mean that the news is just as much a construction as any television drama and in common with other television entertainment the news must be sufficiently entertaining to attract an audience. News must rate.

To say that news is selective is to state the obvious. Not *all* news is or can ever be shown, but implied in any notion of selection are criteria in accordance with which choices are made. Repeated viewings of news programmes indicate the criteria upon which selections are made. One criterion would seem to be convention. There is always an overseas story, always a local story and usually a sport story. So regardless of supposed news-worthiness it seems that certain stories will always make the news because of their origins. Another criterion in operation is the availability of visuals. Television is a visual medium and material which best lends itself to presentation in the medium is that which can be shown in visual terms. Nearly every news story is accompanied by visuals and so those events that receive film coverage are more likely to be presented as news. If news is to rate then it must have some entertainment value and this is usually interpreted as drama. Some events have more dramatic potential than others and hence are more likely to be included in a news programme. The dramatic aspect of news can be seen in the amount of coverage given to conflicts and clashes: strikes, violence, accidents, disasters. Some groups such as blacks and unions are nearly always reported in terms of a conflict, not because they are continually in conflict but because this is more dramatically interesting than passivity. Finally, economic considerations will affect which events become news. The availability of equipment and personnel, budget limitations and sponsors means that news must be cost-effective. A news programme must attract the greatest number of viewers for the least possible outlay.

These are all general criteria for the selection of news. Within a community other considerations will be important from time to time, such as the perceived importance of a topic to the community or the relationship to special events occurring in the community such as natural disasters or elections. This means that the news programme in one city in Australia is quite likely to contain quite different stories to the news programmes in another city even to the extent that different communities will not perceive the importance of overseas events in the same way.

After the selection of news for presentation an order of priority must be established. Some news events are given higher priority in terms of the order of presentation and the length of time devoted to the item. News is not presented as being a series of items of equal interest and importance. The structure of the programme offers a hierarchy of importance of items and this hierarchy cannot be ignored or changed by the viewer.

For the viewer then, what view of the world does the evening half-hour of news (sometimes an hour which tells us something of the popularity of news) offer?

The news offers a hierarchically structured world. News coverage determines for the community those figures who are deemed to be newsworthy. Whether these people are newsworthy because they are on the news or appear on the news because they are news-worthy is a circular argument. The point is some people appear regularly and others

Television news tends to be people-centred. Certain figures are identified as newsworthy.

The friendly, authoritative newsreader reassures.

never appear. Television then, identifies for the viewer an élite group of people. It is interesting to note at this point how people-centred the news is. Events are reported in terms of who said what and who did what, never in terms of processes or community movements. Television news is really more about people than events.

The world constructed by the news is a world in a state of flux. The news items are presented as conflicts and threats to our stability. This feeling of a state of flux is heightened by the presentation format of news programmes. They consist of short segments about a specific event that offer little or no history or explanation of causes and processes. The television news does not attempt to trace relationships or make sense of the world but instead presents unrelated snippets of it for our consumption. At the same time as the news shows the world in a fluctuating rather chaotic state it also

reassures us. The reassurance comes from the structure of the programme not the content. The friendly authoritative newsreader looking directly at the viewer, the happy ending story, the cheerful weatherman and the rhetoric of reliability and expertise that runs throughout the show all serve to reassure us that the world is in capable hands. This last point regarding the rhetoric of expertise is a crucial one. The news uses experts to comment upon events, asks authority figures such as the police and the politicians for their opinions and guidance. This has the effect of reinforcing the authority of these groups and at the same time reassures us that we are in good hands. Our acceptance of and familiarity with the expert authority figures of our own community are made more obvious if you go overseas. As a stranger to a country the news sometimes seems uninteresting and rather confusing because we cannot identify with the authority figures of another community.

Exercise 14.A   News

Television news is visual. Nearly every story is accompanied by visuals. [*Special equipment*: *Portapak*]

1 Below is an excerpt from a police report. Your task is to create the appropriate visuals and commentary so that it is suitable for the evening news. The visuals must last between 80 and 100 seconds and consist of at least 10 shots. The news item will open with a newsreader talking head for 10 seconds and then cut to visuals. The commentary can be dubbed over the visuals.

Vandals attacked the Hope Street School at 3.10 a.m. today. Stolen were books, gym clothes and tennis rackets. One classroom was extensively damaged and material from students' lockers was burnt. Many students complained to officers of projects and assignments being ruined.

2 Script the news item, for example:

Visuals	Voice-over/Dialogue (remember that you may use interviews).

3 Assign crew positions: director, camera-person, sound, interviewer, newsreader.

4 Prepare locations for shooting. Shoot, and dub dialogue where necessary.

5 Review your work and solicit the comments of others. Discuss the criteria you used in creating and selecting the visuals.

Exercise 14.B   News and conflict

Because it must have dramatic impact, television news tends to concentrate on conflict. [*Special equipment*: *television monitor, television news tape*]

1 Watch either a commercial or non-commercial news broadcast. As you watch try to distinguish the types of conflict that are being depicted in the items. Put a tick in the appropriate box.
Conflict between
- two people ☐
- two groups of people ☐
- a person and his/her environment (for example, drowning) ☐
- nature and culture (earthquakes, fires etc.) ☐

2 Write down the words used by the newsreader to describe the conflict.

3 Replay one of the items dealing with conflict. Note carefully how the conflict is depicted: through the visuals, through dialogue, through voice-over. Is the conflict implied or overt? Is there a suggested villain in the conflict?

4 Using the same visuals write a new narration for the item analysed in question 3 that plays down the conflict.

5 Discuss your efforts with others.

Exercise 14.C   News conventions

Although the news tends to present a view of the world as rather chaotic, built into the structure of the programme is a degree of reassurance for the viewer. [*Special equipment*: *daily newspaper, Portapak*]

The codes and conventions of news presentation can be difficult to perceive because we take them for granted. Sometimes reversing or significantly changing a situation will reveal just how 'natural' the convention has become.

1 Here is a set of role cards. Make up similar cards and turn them face down. Work in a group of five. Choose a card each and reveal *only* your role position not what the card says.

2 The director will provide the daily paper to the newsreaders and weather person. From the paper the readers will cut out and edit items so that they can be read aloud as news items.

3 Rehearse the programme once. Shoot.

4 Replay the programme to the other class members. Discuss:
 - Which conventions of news presentation have been isolated?
 - Why did the changes appear ludicrous?
 - If the newsreader's personality remained the same but his/her looks were changed, for example, a front tooth missing, would the effect be the same?

5 Try the same experiment again but this time make up your own role cards that focus on different conventions. Consider station identifications, story order, sport, introduction, setting. There are many more factors.

Newsreader 1

You are aggressive and unfriendly in your reading of the news. You frequently comment on how 'bad' the news is tonight.

Camera person

You must set up the camera and shoot the newsreader's delivery of the news.

Director/floor manager

Responsible for set, provision of news from daily paper, timing, props etc.

Newsreader 2

You are very friendly and chatty. You make interested comments on the news items to the audience and openly criticise some people in the news.

Weather person

You are bored and lackadaisical. You do not find the weather interesting nor feel any loyalty to your viewing public.

Sport and quiz shows

Sporting programmes and quiz shows will be treated together here because although of different genres they share many commonalities in terms of the view of the world they offer. Similar to news programmes, both sport and quizzes seem real. Both depict real events, happening in real time with real people not actors. But we do not participate in sport or quizzes in any real sense — we are only spectators by proxy for it is the television that is the real spectator and it mediates the events for us. We, the audience, are the spectators of the television's portrayal of the event not spectators of the event itself.

As with the news both quizzes and sport present entertainment in the form of conflict. In the case of sport this conflict is usually between two players or two teams (although sometimes between a competitor and the elements as in skiing or canoeing but even

Quiz shows are becoming increasingly spectacular.

then it usually involves a race of some sort and hence conflict with another participant). In a quiz show the conflict lies in the competition between the players for the prizes and the compere performs the role of ringmaster, he/she orchestrates the pace and intensity of the conflict presented. But television does more than simply present the conflict, it signifies what constitutes achievement by clearly defining the winners and the losers. Winners are singled out for special attention and reward. They are interviewed after the event and asked to comment on their prowess and the lack of such in their opponents. The sporting commentators expound at length about previous achievements, possible achievements in the future and offer 'theories' to account for the achievement. In quizzes the winners are allowed to come out and talk to the compere, they are offered dazzling arrays of prizes (always consumer goods) and most important of all are given the chance to repeat the experience of being on television because they are invited to come back next week. The losers are never seen again.

The viewer is given a curious dual status in such programmes. The viewer is the superior observer, able to watch the conflict without the necessity of being an active participant with it. The viewer can identify with the expert commentator because he/she too can see and analyse the game from the outside. This position is superior to that of being a live spectator because the television viewer has the same access to the close-ups and the instant replays as the expert commentator. In a quiz show the viewer has the opportunity to identify with the quizmaster. The audience share with the compere the position of impartiality; the contestants are performing for their benefit and they, the viewers, run no risk if they do not know the answers. In some programmes the viewers' superior position is reinforced by printing the answers on the bottom of the screen so the viewer and the compere share a secret knowledge from which the participant is excluded. Similarly, split screen techniques are sometimes employed to let the viewer know what each competitor is doing at the same time, unknown to each other. This puts the viewer in an almost omniscient position. At the same time, however, the viewer is given the opportunity to share in the achievement of the winners. He/she is given, through the use of close-ups, interviews and exhortations, the chance to savour the achievement of the winner. Consider how in a quiz show at the end of the round the television audience is taken with the winners to view the array of prizes that might be won. The viewer is never left on the sidelines with the losers.

This dual status of both observer and achiever that is conferred on the audience ensures that the conflict presented is non-threatening. At any time we can never lose in a real sense because we are only ever observers but we can participate in the winning by identifying with that group.

What then is the message that comes from the structure and content of such programmes? In a way sporting programmes and quiz shows offer us a microcosm of the economic system in which we live. The emphasis on competition, the rewards for winners and risk-takers, the resultant chances of big success are both a reflection of the free enterprise system in which we live and a proof of its efficacy. The programmes prove that those who win are rewarded, usually in the form of money or consumer goods. Losers are not humiliated but simply ignored. Conflict is ritualised into competition and any overt or over-the-boundaries conflict is suppressed and negatively evaluated in terms of 'playing fair' and sportsmanship. These programmes also offer the viewers a definition of achievement. Achievement within the programme is interpreted simply as winning. Achievement in these programmes cannot include any considerations of hard work, commitment or economic need. It doesn't matter how much you need the new car you won't get it unless you can press the button faster than your competitor. Not only, then, do such programmes define the nature of achievement but they also provide the methods by which achievement should be judged. It is interesting to note that the evening replay of Victorian football is called *The Winners*. Similarly a popular quiz show is called *Family Feud*, another *Wheel of Fortune*.

The money showers down upon the winners.

The final aspect of these programmes to be considered is their attempt at depoliticisation. By using experts in the form of commentators, panels and judges the programmes are presented as operating outside any political or personal framework. The person who writes the questions and provides the correct answers on the quiz shows, the person who comments on the players' expertise after a football match is presented as an expert. He/she appears to have access to pure knowledge so questions of political belief (not party political but political in the sense of having a theory of society and government) are not evaluated or even considered as pertinent by the audience. No person, expert or otherwise, can function outside the framework of his/her society with all its beliefs, prejudices, concerns and yet the experts are presented as doing just that.

Exercise 14.D Quizzes

Both quiz programmes and sporting programmes present conflict in a ritualised form, define achievement and offer rewards in some form to winners. [*Special equipment: television monitor, Portapak (optional)*]

1 Watch a quiz programme. As you are watching, fill in the details below.

Number of participants _____
Nature of contest _____
Description of compere (looks and personality) _____
_____
Prizes offered _____

2 What do the prizes offered have in common? Are they necessities, luxury goods, for family or personal use? What is the compere's attitude to the prizes? At the conclusion of the show what happens to the winners? What happens to the losers?

3 Prepare a spoof of a well known quiz programme. (This will probably need to be done as a class group.) Assign the following roles:

Depending upon the type of show you intend to spoof you will need a number of contestants and perhaps a compere's assistant to introduce the prizes.

4 Perform your quiz show and if you have the capacity record it on video.

Discuss:
• The atmosphere of the programme.
• Techniques of personalisation. How did you make your audience interested in the contestants?
• Techniques used to create excitement.
• The 'spoofs' or exaggerations should reveal key elements of form. What are these?

Floor manager	**Producer**	**Compere**	**Adjudicator**
You must build up the enthusiasm and excitement of the live audience. How is this done on real shows?	Decide the prizes and the format of the programme.	You need an image — either copy that of another compere or make up your own.	You must make up the questions. Use a text book from one of your subject areas.

Situation comedies

While we know them to be fiction, situation comedies appear to a greater or lesser extent to reflect life to us. This appearance of being true to life comes from the high degree of surface realism operating in these shows. The performance, dialogue, sets, costumes and plots all look real and conform to our notion of what is real. The realism of the 'sit-coms' is enhanced by the use of content that is perceived by us to be the stuff of everyday life — love, sex, family, quarrels, work, friends, life, death. Situation comedies appear to deal with the everyday and not the great questions of life. Nevertheless any examination of situation comedies will show them to be highly constructed, coded views of reality.

Situation comedies tend to revolve around two basic situations, often insular but sometimes overlapping. Within these situations comedy is generated. The home and family is a common 'situation' employed by the 'sit-coms.' Think of some of the titles of situation comedies that you have seen over the years and the emphasis on home and family will be apparent — *Steptoe and Son, Man About the House, My Three Sons, Brothers-in-Law, The Brady Bunch, Family Affair*. The list could go on for pages. The family unit, whatever its form, is shown as stable and unchanging. Television families are no longer presented as mum, dad and the two children. Situation comedies have depicted single parents and melded families but within the show the family is shown as stable and unchanging.

Home and family, domestic in form and content — a scene from *Family Affair*

The family is the 'inside' group and other characters which usually develop the narrative are presented as outside. In this way characters can come and go from week to week without destroying or affecting the family situation which is the basis of the 'sitcom'. The 'family' is portrayed as a stable situation able to bear the onslaughts of the outside world because its strength comes from within. The family is portrayed as a strong, self-supporting unit.

The other common situation is work. The work situation provides stability of location and characters and again provides the opportunity for new characters to be introduced and to exit on a weekly basis. Think of titles again and the prevalence of the work situation will be seen — *On the Buses, M.A.S.H., Private Benjamin, The Rag Trade, Are You Being Served, Fawlty Towers*. The depiction of the work situation allows for the representation of class differences (often a source of the humour) through the grades, ranks or positions of the workers in the hierarchy. This stratification of the characters is a reinforcement of the realism of the programme — it's true to life to have bosses, colonels, superiors and they do often behave in an overbearing manner.

Authority figure in *Please Sir*

Class distinction in *Porridge*

When we realise just how limited the realism of these shows is we come to some understanding of the beliefs inherent in the construction of the programme. Even when the show purports to deal with some of the more pressing problems of our society such as poverty, war, urban living and such like, it is interesting how little we really learn about the problems. The shows tend to use the problems as a back drop, simply a setting, upon which the characters play out tightly constructed plots. The emphasis always remains on the characters and their motivations, emotions and interplay. The problem itself never receives our full attention. What did you learn of the history of the Korean War and the debate over the American role from *M.A.S.H*? Very little, because the emphasis was always on the characters, what fine, caring, feeling people they were and what fun they managed to have despite the conditions. When a social issue is raised in the programme — such as racism in *All in the Family* and *Till Death Us Do Part* or prison conditions as in *Porridge* — the very form of the show means that to some extent the issue must be trivialised. The format of a 'sit-com' depends upon finding something funny in any situation. To invoke laughter is to trivialise the problem and lessen its significance and potential threat.

Finally, situation comedies offer a consensual view of the world. Problems and difficulties are solved within the programme with humour and well within the bounds of the status quo. It is unthinkable in a 'sit-com' that one family member might choose to solve his problems with another by simply getting up and leaving. To do so would attack the very basis of the show — the family situation. Similarly, no worker ever punches his/her domineering boss in the nose in any of the work oriented situation comedies. Solutions to problems are always found within the basic structure of the programme and alternatives cannot be considered. This has a conservative effect since only limited codes of behaviour are presented as acceptable and desirable.

Exercise 14.E   The 'sit-com'

Situation comedies are highly formulaic. They consist of the same characters in the same situation every week. Novelty comes from the dilemmas faced by the characters.

1 Think of a situation comedy with which you are very familiar. Fill in the details below.

Situation	Sets used	Characters
e.g. home, office	e.g. lounge, kitchen	Major characters only

Referring to an episode of the above which you viewed recently outline the dilemma created in the programme.

2 Suggest a reason(s) why the same sets are used every week. Describe the resolution of the dilemma. What alternative resolutions might have been possible? Why do you think the writers favoured the one depicted?

Using your knowledge of situation comedies list the limitations the programmes operate within. Use these headings to help you clarify your thinking.
• budget limitations
• scripting requirements
• time slot/audience limitations.
Support your theories with examples from the shows.

Exercise 14.F   Content analysis

Some television researchers use a method called 'content analysis' to come to some generalisations about their area of investigation. The method's title is quite descriptive. Various aspects of the content are analysed in detail. The method has many limitations and pitfalls the most obvious being that the research results will be partly determined by the aspects the researcher has chosen to look at. [*Special equipment: television guide*]

Despite its limitations, it is useful to know of the technique of content analysis and it can help to give you an overall picture of the characteristics of some programmes.

1 Using a television guide to prompt your memory (see pp. 168-9), write a list of the situation comedies you are familiar with. Using your knowledge of these shows (ask others for help if you can't remember all the details), fill in the content analysis below:
  - Occupations of males in the programmes.
  - Occupations of females in the programme.
  - Activities/occupations of children and youth in the programme.
  - Number of old (over 60 years) people portrayed.
  - Number of middle aged (30–60 years).
  - Number of teenagers portrayed.
  - Number of children portrayed.
  - Number of non-white people portrayed.

2 Using the figures compiled above form some generalisations about ages, races and occupations portrayed in situation comedies.

3 What other aspects of the programmes could be looked at in a content analysis?

4 How could content analysis such as this lead you to some false conclusions?

5 Discuss your conclusions with others.

Conclusion

Television does not present a window on the world through either non-fiction or fictional programmes but instead offers a highly constructed view of the world. Television mediates reality; it softens and processes reality for the consumer.

Television news is a highly selective, constructed commodity which is sold to viewers as information but operates as entertainment. Television news presents a view of the world that is dramatic, chaotic and full of conflict but at the same time reassures the viewer of the basic stability of society. This reassurance is offered in the form of the programme, not in the content.

Sporting programmes and quiz shows similarly depict conflict but it is highly ritualised as competition. The values of sporting and quiz programmes both reflect our economic structures and reinforce their validity because within the programme, competition and risk-taking are presented as bringing great rewards. Such shows offer the viewer a very narrow and highly political definition of what is regarded as achievement in our society.

Situation comedies, whilst seemingly reflecting life, are tightly constructed fictions. Their apparent realism and use of humour tend to hide the values inherent in the programme. The value systems operating on situation comedies tend to be conservative and supportive of the status quo although it could be argued that some programmes go further than others towards questioning the structure and the values of the society in which we live.

Analysis and research

1 Do a detailed content analysis of one evening's news broadcast on a commercial station. You will need to write down the nature of the item, whether it was accompanied by film clips, its order within the broadcast and its length.

On the following evening do a similar content analysis of a non-commercial station's news broadcast.

Use the information gathered in your content analysis to answer the following questions.
a What criteria can you detect operating in the selection of news items for each station?
b What criteria do you believe were used to order the news items in each broadcast?
c How many items were presented in terms of a conflict on each station? How was this

conflict portrayed — through visuals, through interviews, through a newsreader?

    d Which people, if any, were interviewed as being authority figures? What codes were operating to establish them as authority figures?

2 Compare an American produced and a British produced situation comedy that use the family as the basic situation. Make your comparisons in terms of:
- family structures
- attitudes to problems/conflict
- family relationships
- sources of humour
- resolutions

Can you make any generalisations about the degree of surface realism in each, its response to social issues and the values of the programme?

3 Watch a television quiz show. What devices are used within the show to encourage the viewer to identify either with the compere or with one or other contestant? What is the attitude to consumerism within the programme?

Written response

1 Norman Lear at the 1979 Edinburgh International Television Festival said regarding the need to incorporate issues of the day into his comedy half-hour slot:

'For the first time we saw married couples in the same bed. Our stories dealt with death, infidelity, black family life, homosexuality, abortion, criticism of the economic and foreign policy, racial prejudice, problems of the elderly, alcoholism, drug abuse, menopause, the male mid-life crisis.'

From your experience to what extent and how successfully have situation comedies dealt with issues of the day?

2 Agree or disagree with this statement:
'Television news is bad news that is collected in order to see the good news — advertising.'

3 It has been suggested by some writers that quiz shows are simply half-hour long advertisements. If this is the case how do you account for their tremendous popularity? What do you think there is about quiz shows that attracts such a huge viewing audience?

Practical exercise

[*Special equipment: Portapak, video tape of 'sit-com'.*]

As a group watch the first 10 minutes of your favourite situation comedy. Turn off the television after about 10 minutes.
    Discuss:
- What the next scene will be about.
- How each character might be expected to behave.
- How the humour will be created.

You will now act out the next couple of scenes.
    Do not write a script but decide as a group roughly what will happen in the next two scenes. Choose actors to play the parts of the characters. Ad lib the lines copying the style of the programme as closely as you can. Act out the next two scenes.
    Discuss with your audience what changes need to be made to make it more like the television programme. When you are happy with the changes record the scenes on portapak. Watch the next two scenes on the video tape of the actual situation comedy. Compare them with your recorded scenes. Discuss:
- How close were you in guessing what the scenes would be about?
- Did you use any of the same techniques as the actual programme?
- How did the programme create humour?

References

Tony Bennett et al, *Popular Television and Film* (London: The Open University Press, 1981).

John Ellis, *Visible Fictions* (London: Routledge and Kegan Paul, 1982).

John Fiske and John Hartley, *Reading Television* (London: Methuen, 1978).

Len Masterman, *Teaching About Television* (London: Macmillan, 1980).

Roger Silverstone, *The Message of Television* (London: Heinemann Educational Books, 1981).

Raymond Williams, *Television, Technology and Cultural Form* (London: Fontana, 1974).

Chapter 15
Ideology

A problem posed

You have a friend who argues that whilst millions of people watch television, it is fairly mindless entertainment because even a 10 year old can understand all of the programmes. Your friend constantly uses expressions like 'chewing gum for the eyes' and 'idiot box'. Your friend argues that because it is such mindless entertainment, it is nothing more than that — entertainment. Your friend believes that there are more significant forms of entertainment, such as seeing films or reading novels. These are more significant because they affect the ways in which people live and think.

What arguments can you use to convince your friend that television is a most significant, perhaps the most significant language system in our society?

Construction of meaning

Chapter 10, 'Film Language', emphasised that beneath the narrative that attracts film patrons to the cinema is another language of deep meaning. It was illustrated that there is a shared set of cultural values allowing general recognition of the symbolic language that is used. That is, society creates a set of rules which determine the meaning of film and of other forms of communication. Because these meanings are usually taken for granted by members of the society (hence 'deep') they are often difficult to detect. For this reason, some suggestions were made about how to recognise 'deep meaning' in aspects of a film such as character, setting and plot. Recognition of 'oppositions' and preconceptions were two tools that were identified. Further attention will now be given to the ways in which these and the other issues that were raised in chapter 10 fit into the broader conceptual framework of ideology. Having done this, the function of television as an ideological instrument will be examined. That is, we will be asking the question 'How do we read television?' It is fitting that, as we draw towards the conclusion of the book, the emphasis is placed firmly upon the receivers of messages. 'Reading' television will be seen as an active

process because the receiver's perceptions of the world are used to draw meaning from the televised programmes.

An ideology is a mixture of theories, ideas, habits and activities that shapes the perceptions of those who are subject to them and, in the process, gives the people concerned a way of making sense of their world and their place in it. That is, meaning is being constructed by various social *practices*, not by an abstract set or list of things in our society. It follows that meaning is not something that is natural, having been inherited from our forefathers and their forefathers before them. Rather, as an active social practice, it is subject to change, to attack, to contradiction.

However, in spite of there being nothing natural about the creation of meaning, the ideas and social practices that have developed the ideology are so much a part of the lives of the people who share the ideology, that they are taken for granted; that is, they *appear* to be natural. This will become clearer through example.

In any society there will be an opposition between the importance of the individual and that of the larger group. The prevailing ideology in this opposition rests with the side that is foregrounded. For example, in our society, the individual is strongly emphasised, consequently meaning is constructed in terms of the individual. The school system is an example of the ways in which the individual is foregrounded in our society. Honour boards inform us about head boy and girl, school dux, champion athletes, those who have won, whilst the queues in front of the deputy's office inform us about those who have lost. The reporting system honours the achievements of the individual, as do the photographs, school magazines, comments from the principal. Meaning is constructed in terms of these ideas, structures and practices that pertain to individualism. A recent meaning that epitomises construction around individualism is the trend in some Australian education systems towards 'vocational and personal awareness'. Such course developments, even by title, worship at the shrine of individualism. Meaning has been constructed here through ideology for there is nothing 'natural' about such an educational emphasis. A different ideology could have produced an emphasis upon 'community contribution and community awareness' as it has in some other cultures. There were many theories, activities, ideas about the economy, religious beliefs and previous practices that contributed towards the establishment of vocational and personal awareness programmes. They were, and are, all so much a part of the lives of administrators, teachers, parents and students, that such a programme seems to be quite a natural development, not the consequence of an ideology. Once the programmes are operative, they then become ideological contributors that will in turn shape future meanings, for ideology is a dynamic process.

The pre-eminence of individualism in our school system is the outcome of a struggle between opposing values. There is the culturally held belief in the nobility of the individual, but this does not rest well with the culturally perceived need to retain authority over (and hence guidance of) the young. Evidence of this struggle can be seen in other aspects of school life. The personality of the individual student is subjugated through recourse to various instruments of anonymity. School uniforms, classroom seating, school 'spirit', school assemblies, are a few of the various habits, thoughts and practices that seek to homogenise the students. The outcome of this struggle is compromise that allows individuality to flourish, but only within the parameters prescribed by the authority-holding adults. Again the compromise seems to be a 'natural' situation, but it is really an ideological construct that is developed in order to retain the existing social order. 'Existing social order' suggests a strong element of conservatism in the notion of ideology, a suggestion that warrants further examination.

The ideas, theories, habits and activities that shape our perceptions are subject to change. As we have seen, there are conflicting positions that bring about compromise, but could also bring about change. For example, there is presently a move away from school uniforms, which suggests that there is a slight ideological shift towards greater individualism. If war broke out, it is likely that uniforms (particularly khaki) would again become popular. This would suggest an increased ideological emphasis upon the social group as a means of overcoming the threat. Threats to the community do not have to be as physical as a militaristic enemy. Within any society there are accumulations of power, respect and wealth. These have been developed within the framework of an ideology that, over time, has lost its social history and now appears to be natural. There are therefore many people with a vested interest in retaining the status quo who have as a powerful weapon ideology's veneer of naturalisation. Those who are advantaged are not necessarily plotting conspiratorially to keep things as they are, but the process itself works in their favour. The encapsulating cliché is 'a place for everything and everything in its place'. This conservatism ensures that those who have, retain.

The concept of a *dominant ideology* embodies this notion of a conservative ideology serving the interests of significant sub-groups. The expression is a recognition that, whilst there are many sub-groups in the society who compete to have their values and practices recognised, therefore challenging 'the way things are', there is also some consistency over a long period. This consistency allows meaning to be commonly interpreted when communication takes place. The specific elements of a dominant ideology cannot be pinpointed because they do not stand apart from the various struggles that occur in the ideological process. It is therefore quite a vague term and some would argue not a very useful one, but it does help explain continuity in the meanings that are generated. To use again the school example, there is a shared perception of teachers, students, report cards, school sports etc. that has been reasonably consistent over many decades. This is in spite of each being a 'site of struggle' for the ways in which each is perceived by various sub-groups. The children who hate school may have a different definition of teachers from the children who are academically successful, but in this struggle the status quo is likely to be retained, because those who have been successful previously have the greater power. That is, it is possible, even likely, that the amorphous dominant ideology is largely shaped by those who are most influential in society's various institutions. It is not a case of one person, one vote.

School spirit — an ideological construct

Exercise 15.A   Ideology

Ideology is a mixture of theories, ideas, habits and activities that shapes our perceptions of the world.

1 View the photograph and read the article about *Young Talent Time*.
  What ideologies are suggested? Consider:
  • The body language, clothing of the children
  • The appearance and role of the compere (described in the text)
  • The occasion, which is the 600th show of *Young Talent Time*.

2 If you know anything about this or similar shows, by using this knowledge, expand upon the outline you have made.

3 Discuss with your teacher the similarities and differences between this ideology and the ideologies that were earlier identified with school.

Good times, sad times...

JOHNNY Young, the host and executive producer of Young Talent Time, has some sad and fond memories of his past shows.

"I remember in the early days when our budget for each show was only $3000 and to make the money stretch we had to use cardboard cut-outs as sets," Johnny said.

"And I remember what an achievement it was to out-rate the football replay. There'd never been a show that could do that before.

"One of the funniest instances I can recall is when Denise Drysdale was guesting on the show. She was singing with a group of Catholic children, when all of a sudden she forgot her lines.

"She didn't know what to do, so she hummed and whistled along with the kids.

"There was another time when we had a wombat on the program and it urinated on my trousers. That was very embarrassing and I had to zip off the set and change my pants.

"I'm pretty strict with the kids because we're there to do a show, we can't muck around. But we've had a couple of cases where the kids have got a crush on another member. They're politely told to keep their mind on their work.

The sad moment on the show for Johnny is when one of his members has to leave.

"We have set an age limit of 16 for the show, so we can get new faces. But it's very sad when the kids leave, especially when they've been with the team for a long time," he said.

"Just recently everyone was howling when Tina Arena left because she had been with us for nearly eight years."

Maggie Burns, YTT choreographer and one of the original production people, said it was great watching the kids become successful.

Jacqui Johnson

SEPTEMBER 15, 1984—TV WEEK—Page 5

The perfect body...

A beauty from Sydney wins the TV WEEK-Kayser Perfects contest

BEAUTIFUL dark-haired Sydney girl Martine Bijoux has won the TV WEEK-Kayser Perfect Body competition — and a dream holiday for two on beautiful Toberua Island in the South Pacific.

The team of four judges, led by Perfect Match host Greg Evans, had a difficult job picking a winner from the six finalists from all states who flew to Melbourne for final judging of the contest.

As can be seen elsewhere on this page, girls from each state acquitted themselves well, and any one of them would have been a worthy winner.

Martine, one of a family of four children, has hopes of going on in the modelling world and her win might help her with that ambition.

Kayser general manager Hal Moss presented Martine with her prizes which included a holiday for two on the Fijian resort of Toberua Island plus $250 spending money, lingerie and cosmetics. The other finalists also received lingerie and cosmetics.

The state finalists were:

Victoria: Angela Andrews, from Melbourne. Tasmania: Judy Burr, from Launceston. Queensland: Suzanne Denton, from Coomera. South Australia: Jane McNamara, from Eastwood. Western Australia: Helen Goff, from Bunbury.

RIGHT: Chief judge Greg Evans with winner Martine Bijoux, of Sydney.
BELOW: Suzanne Denton, Queensland.
BELOW RIGHT: Jane McNamara, from Eastwood, South Australia.

LEFT: Tasmania's Judy Burr.
CENTRE: Helen Goff (Bunbury, Western Australia).
ABOVE: Angela Andrews (Victoria), from Melbourne.

Page 80—TV WEEK—SEPTEMBER 15, 1984

Exercise 15.B   Preferred readings

Ideological meaning is a result of active interaction between text and reader (or spectator). As such, there is the potential for different points of view about the meaning in a text. There is also the potential to oppose the preferred reading. If there is sufficient opposition, over time, the minority reading may become the dominant reading.

1 Read the article 'The Perfect Body'. What do you think the author perceives to be the dominant viewpoint about women?

2 What group/s in our society are likely to disagree with this viewpoint? How would they 'read' these images and text?

3 Discuss whether you see any evidence (outside of this text) to suggest that there is a shift in the ideological positioning of women in our culture.

Television and ideology

It is now necessary to examine the function of the mass media, and specifically television, in the context of this ideological framework.

We have seen through the example of the school, that ideology shapes meaning which in turn affects the sorts of experiences that you have. These experiences will then be part of the next shaping process, even though all of these processes may have been so internalised by those participating that it appears to be natural rather than culturally created. All of our experiences, all of our meanings are, to some degree, manifestations of the ideology. This book is in itself part of this ideological process. Language is a particularly important element of social practice and it is far from neutral or 'objective'. One example of ideology at work in the language in this chapter is an earlier reference to 'our forefathers and their forefathers before them'. This patriarchal expression reveals an ideological disposition towards a male dominated society. The fact that this expression was a deliberate plant so that it could now be referred to also reveals that the repetitive use of the male gender in our language is currently a site of ideological struggle. The previous dominant ideology has come under challenge by significant cultural sub-groups. On this

occasion the challenge has been successful, consequently the way in which we write and read and therefore perceive, is undergoing change. It is a very specific example of both the way in which ideology creates meaning and ideology being dependent upon cultural rather than natural forces.

By this stage of your investigations it should be clear that television is a most significant mass media language. It follows that television will be a significant institution in the determination of ideological practice. How the ideological process works may help to reveal some of the ideologies themselves. In their book, Berger and Luckmann (see references) have identified four stages in the process by which ideology becomes 'naturalised' or 'legitimised'. Television exhibits evidence of all four stages.

The first level is 'This is how things are done'. It is the equivalent to an answer to a little child's question of 'Why do I have to wash my hands' etc. A parent does not give a scientific answer, but generally implies that things are this way because they always have been. Built into television structures are several factors that encourage its messages to be considered in such a pre-theoretical way. The repetitive nature of programmes, genre and scheduling creates a patterned television experience that is so recognisable as to be 'normal'

— things have always been this way so they must be right. One famous American newsreader, Walter Cronkite (who incidentally was consistently ranked America's most believable person) always ended his programme with the same statement 'And that's the way it was'. Father-figure Cronkite's expression encapsulates the pre-theoretical answers that are given on television. We see it, there are those who anticipate questions and respond with more images and more symbols, not with developed arguments. Television news is particularly adept at this.

The second level of naturalisation is through culturally generated proverbs, maxims or wise sayings. These come to us in many forms. Consider again the ideology of individuality. A very popular song had the title and repeated the phrase *I did it my way*. This maxim is further evidence of the perceived separation of the individual from the rest of the social structures. Television abounds with examples, sometimes as succinct as this (as in television commercials), sometimes a little more protracted (as in the moral lesson at the conclusion of a family comedy).

The third phase of the naturalisation process occurs through projection of explicit theories about the ways that our society works. On television, these explicit theories are delivered by authority figures. The most obvious authority figures are the politicians who speak on news and current events programmes, but because their party political allegiances are so obvious, they are perhaps less effective than some of the other authority figures who address ideological theory via their pet subjects. For example, the science buffs who present us with the marvels of developing technology will be reworking an ideology that technology will be the salvation of our society. Because the presenter is an acknowledged authority on science he (how ideological is *he*?) carries that authority over to a legitimation of the associated ideology. Every television topic has its batch of authority figures. There are authorities on sport, news, nature, weather and a host of other subjects

in the non-fiction television field. Each, when delivering authoritative information, reworks an aspect of ideology, for we have hopefully made it clear that ideology and communication are inextricably interwoven. The stars who perform in both fiction and non-fiction television are also authority figures. They do not have to establish expertise in a particular subject in order to establish their authority because they are already an outcome of the cultural process. Their attributes have been deemed to be culturally desirable, so as cultural models, they become authorities on what is culturally appropriate. If this sounds circular, it is. We want to be recognised as part of the social order. We create stars who embody the social order then use them to recruit us into the same order. These authority figures then, are specialised personnel who transmit ideology in a fairly formal, if indirect manner.

The fourth level of naturalisation or legitimation of ideology occurs through the development of a symbolic universe. We have seen that film and television use codes that convey their meaning symbolically. Through the use of symbolic codes narratives are created. The created narratives in their turn act symbolically within the culture. To appreciate this, it is necessary to know about *myth*.

A myth is an explanation of some aspect of our culture. Unfortunately the term is a little confusing because in common language it also means something that is not true. Here, myth is being used as something that explains a culturally perceived reality, not as a term of derision. (However, because myths are no longer terms of derision, the reverse cannot be assumed. Myths are not necessarily 'good', nor are they 'real'. Good and real are value judgements.) Hence, the stereotypes that were discussed in earlier chapters are forms of myth. They are a culture's way of making some abstract concepts understandable. In our society there are commonly held concepts of policemen, Aborigines, teachers, parliament, fish and chip shops and so on. When we see a photograph of an Aborigine, we already have a cultural perception of what an Aborigine is and this is to some extent represented in the Aboriginal stereotype. The stereotype represents the dominant view, the dominant myth. In opposition to this are many who have a different conception of Aboriginality. Their counter-myth about Aborigines will be brought to any television programme that features Aborigines and consequently the meaning that they take from the programme will differ from the meaning generated by the dominant myth. However, in both cases, the myth exists before the programme and helps the groups to make meaning (though they differ) from the programme.

Stereotypes are not our only myths. We have myths about nuclear families, modes of production, other systems of government, the countryside, to example just a few.

The myths then are the preconceptions that were referred to at the beginning of this chapter. They are culturally not individually created preconceptions that are frequently represented and reworked in our society. This process is the least obvious of the naturalisations or legitimations, for the transfer of meaning is symbolic. Each time we see any television programme, our preconceptions are being cued by symbolic language contained within the programme. When we see a police car screaming through the streets, a large part of the sense of that scene is due to the mythology that surrounds the police. (There is a mythology of police, but police can be used symbolically to convey 'sub-meanings'. For example, there are slightly different meanings associated with a policeman in a police car, a policeman on the beat and a detective.)

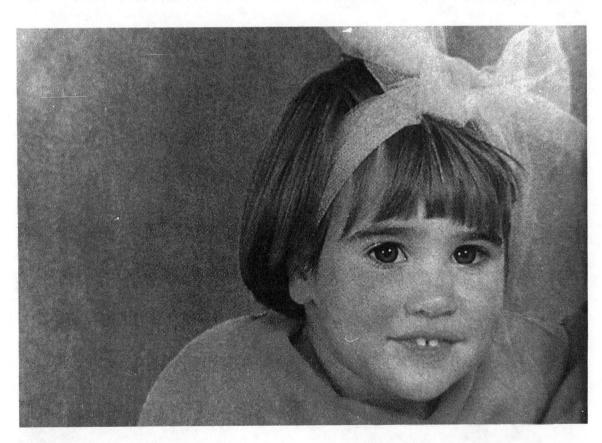

We have culturally determined preconceptions about children. Television reworks these beliefs.

Television, then, constantly re-creates our symbolic universe for us. It recognises to some degree the dominant mythology that rests in the culture, shapes programmes that are generally in accord with the dominant ideology, knowing that this is shared by a significant number of viewers.

Such accord between producer and viewer should lead to commercial success. However, dominant ideology created partly through dominant mythology is not monolithic. Sub-groups will and do interpret the symbolic constructions differently and if this occurs frequently enough with groups in a position to make that point of view significant, the mythology and the ideology will change. However, these changes will be a process of slow evolution, not revolution, for the symbolic universe that our culture has created is reassuring. It makes sense of the disparate elements and shows how we fit into that world. Radical shifts would therefore be most disturbing. Our myths, our symbolic universe and consequently our ideology are forces of conservatism.

Exercise 15.C   Myth

Myths are important in the development and perpetration of ideology. The myth is the understanding that we take to a television programme. There are both dominant and counter-myths.

Examine these images, each from a different television genre.

1 List the preconceptions that you can associate with each genre. Alongside each, indicate whether your preconceptions are likely to be widely held, or whether you feel that they form the basis for a counter-myth.

2 Expand upon the preconceptions that you think are widely held, for example, football: exciting, rugged, fast, vigorous winners, rewards, Australian. That is, develop the associations that you have.

3 Expand these associations into what you think may be some of the dominant myths associated with the genre.

4 Outline a few of the counter-myths that are likely to develop around the genre.

5 Explain the cases where your preconceptions run counter to the dominant view. What circumstances do you think have created your atypical view?
Discuss your findings with your group and with your teacher.

We have seen how ideology is the hidden hand that guides all of our lives and it has been illustrated how television is a significant instrument in the ideological process. It now remains, almost by way of summary, to indicate some of the specifics in the relationship between ideology and television. In doing this some aspects of television that have been discussed earlier will be raised again, but this time the emphasis will be upon the ideological perspective.

When consideration was given to television's form, important elements that were identified included the capitalist mode of production, the low definition image and sound, the domestic reception and the elements of repetition. Analysis was made of the ways in which these affected content. It is also worth exploring the ideological significance.

All television in our society, whether commercial or non-commercial, works within the capitalist framework. Some theorists believe that all ideology is attributable to economic factors, so in their terms, issues of ideology would begin and end with this fact. Even if the perspective is not adopted, it is still evident that the means of production will profoundly affect the production. It has been suggested that, in our society, television exists in order to sell eyeballs to the advertisers. It has also been indicated that even paternal television such as the A.B.C. must work within a ratings framework that is a consequence of the commercial perspective. Ratings measure the eyes that are watching a particular programme at any given time. Ratings determine what is programmed, what lasts and what is repeated. Like all ideological instruments, ratings appear to be quite a 'natural' way of indicating what should appear on the screen. In order to denaturalise ratings, consider alternative assessment structures that could be devised — structures that reflect the value that viewers gain from programmes, not value to advertisers. The sorts of questions that ratings surveys would then ask would find out which programmes provided most interest, excitement, information and perhaps even education. However to value these sorts of viewer preferences without considering the economic consequences is quite a different ideological stance.

Further evidence of the link between television and the capitalist ideology is found in the number of broadcast licences that are issued. Although it is technically possible to license many more channels for telecast, licences are restricted (in this country to four or less per captial city). The rationale is the economic viability of the commercial licence holders, not the issue of service to the viewers. Whenever there is speculation about an additional licence, resistance comes from the existing licence holders. Though it may seem ironic that these arguments are being mounted against increased competition in a society which boasts that competition increases efficiency, the existing licence holders generally win. As a result of the established capitalist ideological perspective, there are many naturalised assumptions about our television programmes. Some of these are addressed in the exercises.

Exercise 15.D   Naturalisation

The capitalist mode of production is so central to our culture that it is almost completely 'naturalised'. There are many often heard arguments that reflect the degree of naturalisation that has occurred. Many of the arguments become pseudo-scientific reasons for retaining the status quo.

Some of the arguments in favour of the present mode of television production are paraphrased below.

a 'We present these programmes because people will not watch anything different.'

b 'Commercial television relieves the taxpayer of the funding burden.'

c 'There is no room for another commercial television channel because none of the channels will make a profit.'

d 'There is no point in having a public access television channel because very few people would watch it.'

e 'Television commercials inform people, make the market bigger and therefore make goods cheaper. They provide a service to the community.'

Each of these arguments contains fallacies whose credibility depends upon naturalisation of the mode of production.

1 Examine the statements, but try to take each argument a step further (for example, **a**, Why won't they watch anything that is different?).

2 If the capitalist mode of production is not taken for granted, are the arguments as convincing? What alternatives could there be to the profit motive as a reason for television production?

The low definition image and sound of a television set are a technical limitation that has ideological significance. Coupled with the casual watching patterns of most viewers, the technical limitations provide an incentive to 'spell out' the significant attributes in detail. With characters, as we have seen, this results in a tendency towards stereotyping according to ideological representations. The limitations encourage use of a clear set of symbols in all aspects of television language. The symbols associated with the dominant myths are going to be those most clearly recognised by the large viewing audience. Therefore, though sub-cultural groups may interpret the messages differently, there will be a strong tendency to present the programmes in accordance with the norms of the dominant ideology. One writer (Ellis) has described this as a tendency towards consensus.

A great deal of emphasis has been placed upon television being a domestic medium and this too has its ideological consequences. It has been stated that the notion of domesticity goes further than the geography of the lounge room. It also embodies the concepts of the mythological nuclear family of mum, dad and two or three children. Mythological because, though such families obviously exist, the values that we associate with this representation are important cultural perceptions. The most obvious ideological outcome of programming with the mythological nuclear family in mind is in television censorship. Even with the little ones having been told by the channel's pet anthropomorphic creature to pop off to bed, the family pattern of entertainment is retained. The amount of violence and sex that is decreed to be permissible is culturally determined. That we choose to give censorial attention to sex and violence and not other dimensions of our society, is again culturally determined.

There are many occasions on television when the speaker directly addresses the domestic audience. Various authority figures (for example, newsreaders, sports commentators, quizmasters) speak directly to the camera. The spell of spectator as invisible voyeur, that was mentioned as being so powerful in cinema, is broken. The authority figure, by looking into camera, effectively becomes a member of the domestic group that is being addressed — a privileged member because the authority figure is the agenda setter. The ideological effect of this is to heighten the sense of a shared world. The authority figure is in your lounge room discussing world events with you. It is further evidence of Ellis' point that television is a medium that strengthens the sense of community consensus. It should be added however, that the consensus is not one arrived at with the help of direct audience participation. It is rather, consensus through the spectator perception that the television experience is one that is being shared at that moment by thousands of others. There is a real sense of television being a *mass* medium.

Finally, we should consider the ideological significance of the repetitive nature of television programming. Repetition is used here in two senses. First there are the repetitive programme styles or genres. These ensure that the values that become established in a format will get maximum exposure. The values are as much a part of a format as the costuming, setting or any part of the construction. Could you imagine for example, the doctor hero being an erratic drunk who alternates between saving and butchering the patients? The values that we associate with the doctor hero are so ingrained that they must be repeated in every series within the hospital genre. The repetition is another tendency towards ideological consensus.

The second form of repetition is through programme repeats. In many cases, children are watching the same programmes that their parents watched as children twenty years ago. *Gilligan's Island*, shot between 1964 and 1966, and still being programmed for children's time television, is but one example. In addition to the television series that are being repeated, there are cartoons dating back to the 1940s that are still being televised (obviously, the first audiences saw them in cinemas). Films too have many repeats and though the audience for an oft-repeated film will be comparatively small because it has been relegated to a midday matinee or school holiday slot, a large section of the audience will be the young children. The Tarzan films of the 1940s are examples of this recycling.

Along with product recycling must come some recycling of values. It has already been mentioned that there are many factors that make the community's ideologies quite conservative. Therefore, there will be similarities between the ideologies of the 1940s and those of the present — sufficient in fact to make the characters and actors quite believable. However, ideologies can and do undergo change. Different attitudes towards women in our society are evidence of this. Repetition of the old programmes tend to increase the conservative trend because the programmes continue to 'normalise' these past ideological behaviours.

In re-examining television's form, consideration has been given to the ideological consequences of the capitalist mode of production, the low definition television set, the domestic nature of the medium and the repetitive mode of programming. Some would argue that as generators of ideology all are merely sub-sets of the capitalist mode of production. This examination of television's form should emphasise that all aspects of the language, both form and content, have ideological significance.

Exercise 15.E Advertising and ideology

If television is a domestic medium, then this facet should reflect in the commercials. The television commercials should be strong bearers of the prevailing ideology about families. [*Special equipment: video or television monitor*]

1 Examine one segment of advertisements from any early evening programme.

2 Select the commercial that either directly or indirectly develops some perception of the viewing family.

3 Outline the perceived roles of the members of this hypothetical family. What does this reveal about family ideology in our society? To what extent is there a hierarchy in the family?

4 What does the advertisement say is good for the family? How is this translated into ideological terms?

5 Discuss your findings with your group or teacher.

Conclusion

Ideology is a mixture of theories, ideas and practices that pertain to a particular culture. The ideology of a culture underpins all of the language systems of that culture. Television is no exception, for television is a very rich and significant language system in modern cultures.

Although it is a social construct, ideology seems to be something that is quite natural. Consequently ideology is difficult to detect, even though it is actively and constantly shaping our meanings for us. Ideological preferences ensure that some aspects of our culture are foregrounded whilst others receive little attention.

Within any culture there are sub-groups which struggle to establish their meanings as the culturally acceptable meanings; therefore the ideology of a culture cannot be regarded as monolithic. However, a significant and generally held ideology is probably identifiable. Though this dominant ideology does enjoy some degree of community consensus, it is still multi-faceted. The dominant ideology in a community is quite conservative, but there are sub-groups that struggle to have other meanings accepted as the valid meanings. This ensures that change can occur.

The ways in which ideology is transmitted and reworked on television bears similarities with dissemination in pre-television cultures. Some transmission occurs in a pre-scientific manner. Through constant repetition, things are considered to be correct because they have always been that way. Wise sayings, maxims, are other ideological transmitters and they occur in all aspects of television, though they are most obvious in commercials.

Authority figures give ideology a more scientific, more theoretical veneer. All television genres have their authority figures. Finally, through its myth making capacity, television creates a shared symbolic universe.

Ideology underpins every aspect of a language system, meaning that both form and content have ideological significance. Chapter 10 gives attention to ideology and content. The capitalist mode of production, the domestic nature of the medium, low definition image and repetition have been identified as elements of television's form that have ideological significance.

Analysis and research

Choose a regular television publication (for example, *TV Week*). Examine in detail the ideology of the publication. Consider:
- The sorts of images that consistently appear on the front cover.
- The cover captions that invite you to buy and read.
- The types of advertisements
  — the group to whom they will appeal and
  — the basis of the appeal.
- The photographs in the magazine.
- The personalities who write in it.

What does your analysis reveal about the ideological stances regarding:
- men
- women
- children
- families
- winning/losing
- work

Library research

In television, ideology is transmitted through decrees, wise sayings, authority figures and cultural myths. All societies have transmitted their ideologies in a similar manner. Research the ancient Greek society and your society before the days of television. Identify how the four modes of ideological transmission worked in those societies. How did the transmissions occur if there was no television? How were the young informally educated about the ways of their culture? Who were the authority figures? What part did religion play in the transmission of ideology? What part does it still play?

Written response

1 'He who has the bigger stick has the better chance of imposing his definition of reality.' (Berger and Luckmann)

To what extent does this statement impose its own definition of reality, that is, how is it shaping meaning in a specific direction?

To what extent do you agree or disagree with the statement?

2 What is meant by dominant ideology? How useful is the term in explaining how meaning is created in television? Does the concept mean that there can be only one meaning created and interpreted? Who develops a dominant ideology?

Practical exercise

The British royal family is a family of a cultural significance. Because of its privileged place in society, the family has become a family of media superstars. The members therefore have ideological significance both as leaders within their culture and as media stars.

Bear in mind that ideology is a mixture of theories, ideas, habits and activities. Select one member of the royal family. Collect a portfolio of newspaper, magazine clippings and photographs about this person. Record also any radio and television references to that person. Develop your file over a period no longer than four weeks. Make sure that you record sources, context and any other pertinent details.

At the end of the collection period, examine your subject and make a list of the theories, ideas, habits and activities that the media have attributed to your subject. (Some deduction will be necessary on your part when photographs are being examined.)

On the basis of the evidence that you have gained, what are some of the ideologies associated with the royal family? Are the ideologies different from those generally held by the community? To what extent are the ideologies a product of the royal family themselves? Or are they produced by the group who reads the stories?

References

Peter Berger and Thomas Luckmann, *The Social Construction of Reality: A Treatise in the Sociology of Knowledge* (New York: Anchor, 1967).

Bill Bonney and Helen Wilson, *Australia's Commercial Media* (Melbourne: Macmillan, 1983).

John Ellis, *Visible Fictions: Cinema: Television: Video* (London: Routledge and Kegan Paul, 1982).

John Fiske, *Introduction to Communication Studies* (London: Methuen, 1982).

Bill Nichols, *Ideology and the Image: Social Representation in the Cinema and other Media* (Bloomington: Indiana University Press, 1981).

Tim O'Sullivan et al., *Key Concepts in Communication* (London: Methuen, 1983).

Chapter 16
Conclusion

If you have reached this point in the text then there is no doubt you will have acquired many valuable skills of analysis and greatly enhanced your understanding of film and television. A systematic approach to the material in this text should have provided you with an understanding of the following concepts. (You may like to use them as a checklist to help you identify areas that may need revision or further study.)

- The form of narrative.
- The major elements of narrative — setting, character, conflict and resolution.
- Montage.
- The codes of film — technical, symbolic, audio and written.
- The nature of film language.
- Ideology in film.
- The nature of broadcast television.
- The form of broadcast television.
- Televisual codes.
- Genre in television.
- The ideology of television.

Furthermore, attention to the development of the model of analysis of film should have provided you with a way of looking at cinema that takes you further than simply looking at plot. If you can get into the habit of mentally applying this model of analysis to films you enjoy you will gain both a greater understanding of the film and enhance your pleasure in it. Just as importantly however, you will be able to articulate your understanding and enjoyment because you have the tools of language to enable you to do this. Similarly your television watching will be made more pleasurable because of your understanding of the medium.

It is not sufficient to study the text and then relax under the assumption that you know it all. The true student of film and television will not only do a lot of viewing but will become an active consumer of the medium.

You must continually apply the skills you have acquired, seek out meaning and form your own opinions. Only then will you really understand the relationship between the cinema and television and your society.

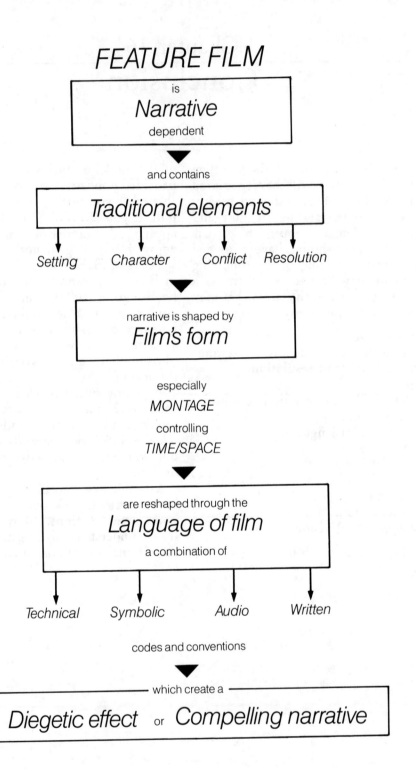

FEATURE FILM

is
Narrative
dependent

▼

and contains

Traditional elements

Setting   Character   Conflict   Resolution

▼

narrative is shaped by
Film's form

especially
MONTAGE
controlling
TIME/SPACE

▼

are reshaped through the
Language of film
a combination of

Technical   Symbolic   Audio   Written

codes and conventions

▼

which create a

Diegetic effect or *Compelling narrative*

TELEVISION

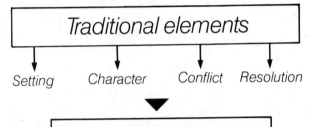

is

Narrative

dependent

▼

and contains

Traditional elements

Setting   Character   Conflict   Resolution

▼

narrative is shaped by

Television's *form*

especially

BROADCAST   MONTAGE   DOMESTIC   SEGMENTED

controlling

TIME/SPACE

▼

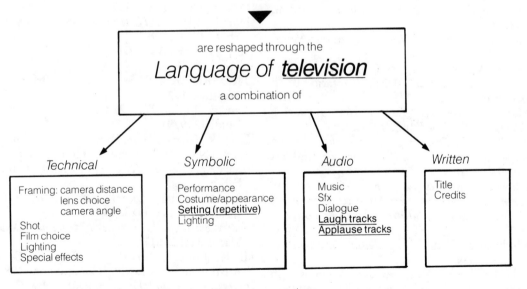

are reshaped through the

Language of *television*

a combination of

Technical	Symbolic	Audio	Written
Framing: camera distance 　　　　lens choice 　　　　camera angle Shot Film choice Lighting Special effects	Performance Costume/appearance __Setting (repetitive)__ Lighting	Music Sfx Dialogue __Laugh tracks__ __Applause tracks__	Title Credits

codes and conventions

Bibliography

References that are likely to be valuable to students are marked*.

Key teacher references are marked†.

Key research references have been marked at the end of each chapter.

General

Barthes, Roland, *Image — Music — Text* (Glasgow: Fontana/Collins, 1977).

Berger, Peter and Luckmann, Thomas, *The Social Construction of Reality: A Treatise in the Sociology of Knowledge* (New York: Anchor, 1967).

Bonney, Bill and Wilson, Helen, *Australia's Commercial Media* (Melbourne: Macmillan, 1983).

Eco, Umberto, *A Theory of Semiotics* (Bloomington: Indiana University Press, 1979).

Fiske, John, *Introduction to Communication Studies* (London: Methuen, 1983).

Hall, Stuart, 'Rediscovery of "Ideology": Return of the repressed in media studies' in *Culture, Society and the Media* (Methuen: London, 1982).

Jung, Carl, *Man and his Symbols* (London: Aldus, 1964).

McLuhan, Marshall, *City as Classroom: Understanding Language and Media* (Ontario: Book Society of Canada, 1977).

McMahon, Barrie and Quin, Robyn, *Exploring Images* (Perth: Bookland, 1984).

Metz, Christian, *The Imaginary Signifier: Psychoanalysis and the Cinema* (Bloomington: Indiana University Press, 1977).

O'Sullivan, Tim et al., *Key Concepts in Communication* (London: Methuen, 1983).

Williams, Raymond, *Culture* (Glasgow: Fontana, 1981).

Windschuttle, Keith, *The Media* (Melbourne: Penguin, 1984).

Woollacott, Janet, 'Messages and Meanings' in *Culture, Society and the Media* (Methuen: London, 1982).

Film

Armes, Roy, *Film and Reality* (London: Penguin, 1974).

Bare, Richard, *The Film Director: A Practical Guide to Motion Picture and Television Techniques* (New York: Macmillan, 1971).

Bazin, Andre, *What is Cinema?* Volume 1, (Berkeley: University of California Press, 1967).

Bazin, Andre, *What is Cinema?* Vol 11 (Berkeley: University of California Press, 1971).

Burch, Noel, 'Narrative/Diegesis — Thresholds, Limits' in *Screen* 23 No 2 July/August 1982.

Casty, Alan, *Development of The Film: An Interpretive History* (New York: Harcourt Brace Jovanovich, 1973).

Cohen, Keith, *Film and Fiction: The Dynamics of Exchange* (New Haven: Yale University Press, 1979).

Cook, David, *A History of Narrative Film* (New York: Norton and Co., 1981).

*Chaneles, Sol, *Collecting Movie Memorabilia* (New York: Arco, 1977).

*Dolan, Edward, *History of the Movies* (New York: Bison, 1983).

Durgnat, Raymond, *Durgnat on Film* (London: Faber, 1976).

Dyer, Richard, *Stars* (London: British Film Institute, 1979).

*Eames, John, *The M.G.M. Story* (London: Sundial, 1979).

†Eidsvik, Charles, *Cineliteracy: Film Among the Arts* (New York: Random House, 1978).

Eisenstein, Sergei, *The Film Sense* (London: Faber, 1968).

Giannetti, Louis, *Understanding Movies* (New Jersey: Prentice Hall, 1972).

Heath, Stephen, *Questions of Cinema* (London: Macmillan, 1981).

Hinde, John, *Other People's Pictures* (Sydney: Australian Broadcasting Commission, 1981).

Jowett, C., *Film the Democratic Art* (Boston: Little Brown, 1976).

*Hall, Ken, *Australian Film. The Inside Story* (Sydney: Summit, 1977).

*Jay, Michael (ed.), *Great Movie Posters* (New York: Galahad, 1982).

*Keylin, Aiken and Bent, Christine (eds), *The New York Times at the Movies* (New York: Arno, 1979).

Kracauer, Siegfried, *Theory of Film: The Redemption of Physical Reality* (London: Oxford University Press, 1960).

La Biennale, *The Cinema in the Eighties: Proceedings of the Meeting, Venice 1979* (Torino: Eri Edizionirai, 1980).

Lindgren, Ernest, *The Art of Film* (London: George Allen and Unwin, 1970).

Lotman, Jurij, *Semiotics of Cinema* (Michigan: Ann Arbor, 1976).

*Malone, Michael, *Heroes of Eros: Male Sexuality in the Movies* (New York: Dutton, 1979).

Mast, Gerald, *The Comic Mind. Comedy and the Movies* (Indianapolis: Bobbs-Merrill, 1973).

Mast, Gerald and Cohen, Marshall, *Film Theory and Criticism: Introductory Readings* 2nd edn, (New York: Oxford University Press, 1979).

Mast, Gerald, *A Short History of the Movies* (New York: Pegasus, 1971).

May, Larry, *Screening out the Past: The Birth of Mass Culture in the Motion Picture Industry* (New York: Oxford University Press, 1980).

*Mathews, Sue, *35 mm Dreams* (Melbourne: Penguin, 1984).

Metz, Christian, 'Current Problems of Film Theory' in *Screen* 14, No. 2 Spring/Summer 1973.

Metz, Christian, *Film Language: A Semiotics of the Cinema* (New York: Oxford University Press, 1974).

Metz, Christian, *Language and Cinema* (The Hague: Mouton, 1974).

†Monaco, James, *How to Read a Film: The Art Technology Language, History and Theory of Film and Media* (New York: Oxford University Press, 1977).

*Murray, Scott, *The New Australian Cinema* (Australia: Cinema Papers, 1980).

Nichols, Bill, *Ideology and the Image: Social Representation in the Cinema and other Media* (Bloomington: Indiana University Press, 1981).

Parks, Rita, *The Western Hero in Film and Television* (Michigan: Ann Arbor, 1982).

Perkins, V.F., *Film as Film: Understanding and Judging Movies* (London: Penguin, 1972).

Reader, Keith, *The Cinema: A History* (New York: Hodder and Stoughton, 1979).

Reader, Keith, *Cultures on Celluloid* (London: Quartet, 1981).

Robinson, W.R., *Man and the Movies* (Baltimore: Penguin, 1967).

*Saturday Evening Post, *The Saturday Evening Post Movie Book* (Indianapolis: Curtis, 1977).

Shale, Richard, *Donald Duck Joins Up* (Michigan: Ann Arbor, 1982).

Sklar, Robert, *Movies Made America: How Movies Changed American Life* (New York: Random, 1975).

Soloman, Stanley J., *The Film Idea* (New York: Harcourt Brace Jovanovich, 1972).

Stephenson, Ralph, and Debrix, Joan R., *The Cinema as Art* (London: Penguin, 1978).

Thomson, David, *America in the Dark: The Impact of Hollywood Films on American Culture* (New York: William Morrow, 1977).

Tulloch, John, *Australian Cinema: Industry, Narrative and Meaning* (London: Allen and Unwin, 1982).

*Umphlett, Wiley Lee, *Mythmakers of the American Dream* (New York: Bucknell University Press, 1983).

*Vance, Malcolm, *The Movie Ad Book* (Minneapolis: Control Data Publishing, 1981).

*Whitaker, Rod, *The Language of Film* (New Jersey: Prentice Hall, 1970).

*White, David, *Australian Movies to the World* (Melbourne: Fontana, 1984).

Wolf, William, *Landmark Films: The Cinema of our Century* (New York: Paddington, 1979).

Wollen, Peter, *Signs and Meaning in the Cinema* (Bloomington: Indiana University Press, 1972).

Television

Adler, Richard (ed.) *Understanding Television: Essays on Television as a Social and Cultural Force* (New York: Praeger, 1981).

Barnouw, Erik, *Tube of Plenty: The Evolution of American Television* (London: Oxford University Press, 1981).

Bennett, Tony (ed.) *Popular Television and Film* (London: British Film Institute, 1981).

Brunsdon, Charlotte and Morley, David, *Everyday Television: Nationwide* (London: British Film Institute, 1978).

*Burney, John and Hallowes, John, *60 Minutes: The Book* (Sydney: Angus and Robertson, 1983).

Conrad, Peter, *Television: The Medium and its Manners* (Boston: Routledge and Kegan Paul, 1982).

*Davies, Brian, *Those Fabulous TV Years* (Sydney: Cassell, 1981).

Dyer, Richard, et al., *Coronation Street* (London: British Film Institute, 1981).

†Ellis, John, *Visible Fictions: Cinema: Television: Video* (London: Routledge and Kegan Paul, 1982).

Fiske, John and Hartley, John, *Reading Television* (London: Methuen, 1978).

*Groves, Seli, *SOAPS: A Pictorial History of America's Daytime Dramas* (Chicago: Contemporary Books, 1983).

*Halliwell, Leslie, *Halliwell's Television Companion* (London: Granada, 1982).

Hunt, Albert, *The Language of Television: Uses and Abuses* (London: Eyre Methuen, 1981).

†Masterman, Len, *Teaching About Television* (London: Macmillan, 1980).

McArthur, Colin, *Television and History* (London: British Film Institute, 1978).

Millerson, Gerald, *Basic TV Staging* (London: Focal, 1974).

Newcomb, Horace (ed.), *Television, The Critical View* (New York: Oxford University Press, 1979).

Newcomb, Horace, *TV. The Most Popular Art* (New York: Anchor, 1974).

*Price, Jonathon, *The Best Thing on TV — Commercials* (New York: Penguin, 1978).

Silverstone, Roger, *The Message of Television* (London: Heinemann Educational Books, 1981).

*Self, David (ed.), *Situation Comedy* (London: Hutchinson, 1982).

Walker, R.R. *Soft Soap Hard Sell: Adland in Australia* (Melbourne: Hutchinson, 1979).

Williams, Raymond, *Television Technology and Cultural Form* (London: Fontana, 1974).

Zettl, Herb, 'Television Aesthetics' in *Understanding Television: Essays on Television as a Social and Cultural Force* (New York: Praeger, 1981).

Index

223–5; *see also* culture, values

narrative image, 11, 13, 20–3, 26, 126, 129, 152
naturalisation, 221–2, 226
news, 155, 157, 159, 163, 167, 172, 183, 189, 195, 197, 198, 204–7, 214
Notorious, 76
novelty, 170, 173; *see also* aesthetics, innovation

October, 45
On the Buses, 212
Once Upon a Time in America, 87
open-endedness, 171, 173, 178
oppositions, 141

pace, 49, 73, 188
pan, 56, 73, 75
parallel cutting, 51
paternal television, 157
performance, 30, 91–6, 192, 211
performers, 12, 91–6
Phar Lap, 2, 23, 26, 30–5, 111
place, 175
plot, 4, 12, 38, 129, 137, 167, 173, 176, 177, 178, 203, 211, 216, 231; *see also* conflict, resolution
point of view, 142–4, 145
Porridge, 213
preconceptions, 144–5
predictability, 147
preferred readings, 221
Pride and Prejudice, 31
Private Benjamin, 212
Professionals, The, 175
publicity, 13, 16, 22, 23, 152; *see also* advertising, marketing
Pudovkin, Vsevolod, 177

Quincy, 175
quiz programmes, 162, 165, 167, 203, 207–10, 214

radio, 161, 164, 165, 186, 198
Rag Trade, The, 212
Raging Bull, 2, 82

Raiders of the Lost Ark, 2, 38, 129, 158
ratings, 154, 155, 159, 160, 161, 163, 165, 204, 225
realism, 82, 97, 98, 211, 212, 214
    illusion of reality, 10, 85
    reality, 39, 40, 43, 54, 61, 64, 69, 86, 114, 120, 126, 144, 160, 179, 203
repetition, 167–70, 171, 173, 174, 178, 227, 228
resolution, 30, 36, 37–9, 40, 41, 96, 136, 137, 171, 231
Return of the Jedi, 19, 37
reviews, 16
Reynolds, Burt, 92
Right Stuff, The, 20
Robin and Marian, 111–12
Romancing the Stone, 32

Safety Last, 79
Scacchi, Greta, 14–15
scheduling, 157–8
Schepsi, Fred, 26
Scorcese, Martin, 82
segmentation, 155–6, 157, 164, 165
selection, 204
serials, 159, 171
series, 159
set design, 89
sets, 153, 174, 203, 211
setting, 27–9, 39, 41, 51, 96–8, 136, 137, 174, 175, 176, 178, 184, 192, 216, 231
Seven Beauties, 132
shot duration, 67, 81, 86, 183, 187–8, 190
silent film, 120
Silent Movie, 129
Silkwood, 2, 130, 140–2
situation comedy, 162, 163, 173, 176, 177, 183, 203, 211–13
60 Minutes, 195, 201
slow motion, 52, 85
soap operas, 159, 163, 165, 173, 177, 183, 184
sound, *see* audio
sound effects, 106, 107–10, 114, 162, 198

Sound of Music, The, 28
sound tracks, 110
space, 52–6, 57, 58, 67, 73
special effects, 67, 85–6, 183, 189, 190
Special Squad, 192
spectacle, 201
spectator, 153–4, 155, 161, 162, 184, 185, 207, 208, 227; *see also* audience, viewer
Spielberg, Steven, 129
split screen, 58, 68, 85, 189, 209
sport, 155, 160, 187, 194, 198, 203, 207–10, 214
stability, 173
Star Wars, 2, 7, 19, 33, 35, 37
stars, 11, 13, 17, 19, 91–6, 222
Starsky and Hutch, 175, 181
Steptoe and Son, 211
stereotype, 38, 93, 138, 139, 164, 222–3, 226
Streep, Meryl, 92
Streets of San Francisco, The, 175
sub-titles, 121
Sunday Too Far Away, 121
Superman, 19, 33, 35, 36, 38, 121
Sweeney, The, 175
symbol, 133, 134, 142, 145
symbolic codes, 34, 89–100, 125, 191, 197, 222

Tarzan's Rescue, 145
technical codes, 67–86, 100, 125, 183
technology, 190
telemovies, 160
telephoto, 70, 73
television drama, 155, 156, 167
Till Death Us Do Part, 213
time, 43, 48–52, 55–7, 58, 73, 81, 175, 188
tracking shot, 56, 73, 75
Turner, Kathleen, 32
2001: A Space Odyssey, 107
typage, 47, 92
    typed characters, 175, 177

Uncivilized, 26
unpredictability, 129, 130, 131

Acknowledgments

The authors wish to thank:

John Fiske for his guidance and criticism.

Other staff of the English Department of the Western Australian Institute of Technology.

Jan McMahon for her assistance in collecting the appropriate photographs.

Betty Thomas for her diligent and underpaid manuscript work.

Additional photography by Robyn Quin, Jan McMahon, Barrie McMahon

We are grateful to the following for permission to reproduce copyright material:

The author and Arco Publishing for the photographs on pp. 6 (left), 11, 12 (top left and right), 69 (top), 145 and 146 from *Collecting Movie Memorabilia* by Sol Chaneles (from the author's private collection); Sundial Publications for the collage of headlines on p. 12 (top centre) from *The MGM Story* by John Eames; the Herald & Weekly Times Ltd for the article on p. 14 from the *West Australian*; the Independent Group of Newspapers for the articles on pp. 15 and 16; Time, Inc. for the 'People' page on p.17 from *Time*; John Fairfax Ltd for 'New York, New York' by Frank Crook on p. 18 from *Woman's Day*, and the article and photograph on pp. 102–3 from *Cosmopolitan*; Consolidated Press for the photograph on p. 32 from *The Australian Women's Weekly*; Yaffa Darlington Licensing for the comic strip on p. 33 from *Giant Superman Album* no. 21; the producers and William Collins Pty Ltd for the photographs on pp. 35, 44, 45, 48–50, 74 and 81 from *Phar Lap*; the Australian Film and Television School for the photograph on p. 56 (left) from their 1983 handbook; Film-Video Equipment Service Co., Denver, Colorado, for the photograph on p. 56 (right); Granada Publishing Limited for the photograph on p. 61 (top) from *Halliwell's Television Companion*; Snowy River Productions and Angus & Robertson Publishers for the photograph on p. 61 (bottom); the Museum of Modern Art/Film for the stills from *Paper Moon* on p. 72 and from *Blow-Up* on p. 132; Macmillan Publishing Co., Inc. New York, for four photographs on p. 74 from *The Film Director* by Richard Bare; Prentice-Hall, Inc. for the photographs on p. 83 (right) and p. 84 (top) from *The Language of Film* by Rod Whitaker, and the photographs on p. 189 from *Understanding Television Production* by Frank Iezzi; Longman Group Ltd for the extract on p. 104 from *Rumble Fish* by S. E. Hinton; News Ltd for the photograph on p. 153 (top) from the *Sunday Times*; the *Western Mail* for the photograph on p. 153 (bottom) and the TV programmes on pp. 158, 168 and 169; Herald-Sun TV Pty Ltd for the advertisement on p. 160; *Look and Listen* magazine for the photographs on p. 170; Southdown Press for the articles and photographs on pp. 179–80, 193, 219, 220, 223 and 224 (right) from *TV Week*; the author for the photographs on pp. 205 (left) and 209 from *Those Fabulous TV Years* by Brian Davies (Melbourne: Cassell 1981); and the ABC for the photograph on p. 225 (right) from *Rock and Roll Royalty* magazine.

Films

Buena Vista International, Inc. for the photograph on p. 71 from *Splash*; Columbia Pictures for the photographs on pp. 87 and 132 from *Easy Rider*, on p. 78 from *The Big Chill*, on p. 53 from *Taxi Driver* and on p. 94 from *Tootsie*; Dino De Laurentiis Entertainment Group for the photograph on p. 71 from *The Bounty*; Effie Holdings Pty Ltd for the photographs on p. 97 from *The Gay Divorcee* and on p. 108 from *Top Hat*; Margaret Fink Films Pty Ltd for the photograph on p. 90 from *My Brilliant Career*; Forest Hume Films Pty Ltd for the photograph on p. 135 from *The Irishman*; Fox Columbia Film Distributors Pty Limited for the photographs on p. 22 from *Nine to Five*, on p. 82 from *Butch Cassidy and the Sundance Kid*, on pp. 40 and 143 from *Das Boat* and on p. 85 from *Alice's Adventures in Wonderland*; Lucasfilms Ltd for the photographs on pp. 78 and 83 from *Indiana Jones and the Temple of Doom*, on p. 37 from *Return of the Jedi* and on pp. 34 and 122 from *Star Wars*; Manson International for the photograph on p. 71 from *The Terry Fox Story*; Paramount Pictures (Australia) Pty Limited for the photographs on p. 72 from *Chinatown* and on p. 88 from *Startrek III*; Quality Films for the photographs on p. 46 from *Battleship Potemkin*; Roadshow International Pty Ltd for the photographs on p. 132 from *Bonnie and Clyde*, on p. 36 from *Flash Gordon*, on pp. 68 and 71 from *Face to Face*, on p. 91 from *The Getaway*, on p. 117 from *Greystoke, The Legend of Tarzan*, on p. 127 from *High Road to China*, on p. 7 from *It's Alive*, on pp. 53 and 87 from *Once Upon a Time in America*, on p. 98 from *The Outlaw Josey Wales*, on p. 135 from *Rio Bravo*, on p. 141 from *Silkwood*, on pp. 71 and 109 from *Breaker Morant*, on p. 76 from *The Devil's Playground*, on pp. 109 and 111 from *Sunday Too Far Away*, on p. 38 from *Superman*, on p. 7 from *The Towering Inferno*, on pp. 76 and 79 from *Voyage of the Damned*, on p. 110 from *Zelig* and on p. 94

from *Midnight Cowboy*; John Sexton Production for the photographs on pp. 35, 44, 45, 48–50, 74 and 81 from *Phar Lap*; Thorn EMI Screen Entertainment Ltd for the photograph on p. 54 from *Cross Creek*; United Artists for the photographs on p. 132 from *Blow Up*, on p. 28 from *Cannery Row* and on p. 9 from *Gone With the Wind*; and Vega Film Productions Pty Ltd for the photograph on p. 112 from *Winter of Our Dreams*.

Television
ABV Channel 2 for the photograph on p. 163 from *Countdown*; BBC Enterprises Ltd for the photograph on p. 212 from *Porridge*; GTV Channel 9 for the photographs on pp. 186 and 224 from *Days of Our Lives*, on p. 208 from *Sale of the Century* and on p. 209 from *Family Feud*; HSV Channel 7 for the photographs on p. 159 from *Falcon Crest*, on p. 162 from *Jeopardy*, on p. 172 from *Marcus Welby MD*, on p. 184 from *Against the Wind*, on p. 196 from *Father Dear Father* and *Leave it to Beaver*, on p. 211 from *Family Affair*, on p. 212 from *Please Sir* and on p. 225 from *The Man from UNCLE*; and SAS Channel 10 (Adelaide) for the photograph of Fat Cat on p. 224.

While every care has been taken to trace and acknowledge copyright, the publishers tender their apologies for any accidental infringement where they have been unable to trace copyright. They would be pleased to come to a suitable arrangement with the rightful owner in each case.